the giant panda

the giant panda

Ramona and Desmond Morris

Revised by
Jonathan Barzdo

PENGUIN BOOKS

Penguin Books Ltd, Harmondsworth,
Middlesex, England
Penguin Books, 625 Madison Avenue,
New York, New York 10022, U.S.A.
Penguin Books Australia Ltd, Ringwood,
Victoria, Australia
Penguin Books Canada Limited, 2801 John Street,
Markham, Ontario, Canada L3R 1B4
Penguin Books (N.Z.) Ltd, 182–190 Wairau Road,
Auckland 10, New Zealand

First published in Great Britain under the title
Men and Pandas by Hutchinson Publishing Group Ltd 1966
First published in the United States of America under the title
Men and Pandas by McGraw-Hill Book Co. 1967
This revised edition first published in Great Britain
under the title *The Giant Panda* by Kogan Page Ltd 1981
This revised edition first published in the United States of America
in Penguin Books 1982

LIBRARY OF CONGRESS CATALOGING IN PUBLICATION DATA
Morris, Ramona.
    The giant panda.
    Rev. ed. of: Men and pandas. 1967, c1966.
    Bibliography: p.
    Includes index.
    1. Giant panda.   I. Morris, Desmond.   II. Barzdo,
Jonathan.   III. Title.
QL737.C27M68   1981   599.74'43   81-15421
ISBN 0 14 00.6132 0   AACR2

Printed in the United States of America by
Offset Paperback Mfrs., Inc., Dallas, Pennsylvania
Set in Times Roman

contents

acknowledgements

The authors are grateful to the many people who have assisted in the preparation of this book. To the Zoological Society of London for providing access to their files and documents; to Granada TV for supplying valuable photographic material on Chi-Chi; to the World Wildlife Fund for useful conservation documents; to the Peking Zoo for photographs of Ming-Ming and Lin-Lin; to the British Museum for checking ancient records; and to the Librarians of the London Zoo for their repeated helpfulness. In particular we would like to thank Tony Dale, P.R.O. at the London Zoo, for valuable discussions; Professor D. B. Fry of London University for his help in preparing sound spectrograms of giant panda calls; Oliver Graham-Jones for details of Chi-Chi's hospital treatment; Dr L. Harrison-Matthews for reading parts of the manuscript and for lending us a packet of Chinese cigarettes; Mrs Mary Haynes and Miss Caroline Jarvis for providing us with much needed information from China; Dr Rainer Lorenz for ascertaining details of Happy's tour of Germany in 1939; The Hon. Ivor Montagu for indispensable information and photographs from Peking; Head Keeper Sam Morton for permission to publish details from his giant panda record-book; George B. Rabb of Chicago Zoo for access to unique panda documents from the 1930s; Richard J. Reynolds for lengthy and painstaking correspondence on many aspects of recent panda history; W. G. Vanderson for devoting much time and patience to obtain special panda photographs for us; and to Dr Geoffrey Vevers for casting his mind back over a quarter of a century with great precision, and also for lending us valuable and otherwise unobtainable books.

We would like to express our gratitude to Graham Nicol and Elizabeth Stockwell of Hutchinson's for their continual encouragement and assistance throughout the production of the original version of the book, and to Jonathan Barzdo and Katy Carter for their help in revising and updating it to create this new edition. For the revision of this volume several people kindly helped by providing written information, access to their files, or valuable time to chat about breeding pandas, notably: Brian Bertram, David Jones and Colin G. C. Rawlins at the Zoological Society of London, Michael Brambell (of Chester Zoo), keeper of the giant panda studbook, Shigeharu Asakura of Ueno Zoo, Devra Kleiman of the U.S. National Zoo, Jean F. Schoch of Chapultepec Zoo, Mexico City, Pat Ellis of *International Zoo Yearbook* which has also allowed us to reproduce its graphs, Janet Barber of World Wildlife Fund, Paula Summerhayes (secretary to Sir Peter Scott) and the Zoological Society of London for permission to reproduce illustrations.

introduction

At first sight the giant panda is an enigma. Discovered in China just over a century ago, it is as much loved as it is little known. The details of its life in the wild remain largely unrecorded, and no more than thirty-two live specimens have been seen outside the Orient. Fifty years ago the western world had encountered nothing more than stuffed specimens in a few museums. Then, in a series of dramatic moves, the giant pandas arrived. They came to America and Europe. The public saw them and were conquered. The chubby, clumsy, black-and-white form quickly became a national and then an international image. Still essentially a mystery beast, this fascinating animal swiftly rose to the top of the animal popularity charts, and it has remained there ever since.

What exactly do we know about this strange creature? What is the secret of its success? This is the challenge we set ourselves when we started work on our 'panda project'. Had we been writing a book about any other large, popular mammal the primary task would have been one of selection and co-ordination of information from the mass of facts available. With pandas, the problem was, by contrast, to seek out every tiny scrap of evidence from the scanty supply that existed, tucked away for the most part in obscure journals and yellowing press cuttings. The search proved to be an exciting one, providing us with a story with some unexpected twists and several unsolved mysteries.

We first published this book in 1966 under the title *Men and Pandas*. That book is now both out of print and out of date. In 1966, London's Chi-Chi and Moscow's An'-An' were the only giant pandas in the West. They both died in 1972, but that year the People's Republic of China presented pandas to both Washington D.C. and Tokyo zoos, and five other capitals have since received pairs. Over the past fifteen years, co-operative breeding attempts between zoos have intensified, but the one western birth so far did not survive. It now seems that only about one thousand pandas exist in the wild, and they are endangered by the death of vast areas of their staple diet, bamboo. In the attempt to save the panda, major research and conservation projects are now under way in China, and at least ten special reserves have been established. Meanwhile, the (abortive) mating attempts between Washington's Ling-Ling and London's Chia-Chia have once again made pandas headline news.

The text of the original edition of this book has been carefully revised and updated by Jonathan Barzdo, taking account of all these developments, to produce the present volume. The illustrations have also been restyled, with some of the old pictures omitted and more recent ones added. We hope you enjoy reading the panda story as much as we enjoyed our detective work when assembling it.

RM. DM. Oxford, 1981

the beautiful red panda

In June 1825, Frédéric, son of the famous French zoologist Georges Cuvier dated, with a flourish no doubt, the first published account of an animal new to science. The popular name for this exciting discovery from the Himalayan Mountains was 'the panda'. In scientific circles it was known as *Ailurus fulgens*, a 'fire-coloured cat' or 'shining cat'. Later generations thought that the choice of this particular name was unfortunate and misleading, but to Frédéric Cuvier it seemed appropriate enough. He wrote, 'I propose for the generic name of this panda that of *Ailurus*, on account of its exterior resemblance to the cat and for its specific name that of *Fulgens*, because of its brilliant colours.' He added that in his opinion this rare creature was quite the most handsome mammal in existence.

We see from the coloured plate accompanying Cuvier's description that the panda was an attractive medium-sized, basically rust-red animal with a bushy tail and a rather foxy white face, quite different in general appearance from the animal popularly known as the panda today. At the present time, the small red panda is usually called the lesser panda to distinguish it from its more spectacular relative the black-and-white giant panda. But, for half a century, Cuvier's *Ailurus fulgens* was the *only* panda known in the West and proved itself to be a highly interesting and unusual animal in its own right.

For many years the lesser panda remained an enigma and not a single living specimen reached European shores. When preparing his description of the animal Cuvier was obliged to work from a few remains and a general outline of its shape provided by his son-in-law, Alfred Du Vaucel. Even so, with only a skin, paws and incomplete jaw bones and teeth at his disposal, the French zoologist realized that the panda was unique, there being no evidence of any other mammal of the same type among the relics stowed away in the Paris Natural History Museum.

Despite Cuvier's efforts, it is usually recognized that the real discoverer of the lesser panda was in fact an Englishman in Indian Service, Major-

General Thomas Hardwicke, who explored the country where he was stationed in the early decades of the nineteenth century, with a keen eye for animal rarities. On 6th November 1821, he read a paper before the Linnean Society of London, entitled 'Description of a New Genus of the Class Mammalia, from the Himalaya Chain of Hills between Nepaul and the Snowy Mountains.' The creature in question was none other than the red panda for he gave considerable detail about the external appearance of the animal and pointed out that it must rank as a new genus owing to its striking and prominent peculiarities. Of its habits the general wrote: 'Its haunts are about rivers and mountain-torrents. It lives much in trees, and feeds on birds and the smaller quadrupeds. It is frequently discovered by its loud cry or call, resembling the word Wha, often repeating the same: hence is derived one of the local names by which it is known. It is also called Chitwa.' Six years passed before Hardwicke's paper finally appeared in print, in 1827, and so he not only lost publication priority to Frédéric Cuvier but also the honour of naming the animal.

As far as the official printed word was concerned British zoology had been indisputedly pipped at the post by its enterprising French counterpart, but it is possible that neither country should take the credit for the actual discovery of the red panda. In 1820, a Danish botanist, Nathaniel Wallich, was appointed director of the East India Company's Botanical Gardens at Calcutta. Naturally plants were his primary interest and he made a number of collecting trips to the northern mountain regions of Nepal in this connection. At the same time he also brought back animals from this particular region for both General Hardwicke and Cuvier's son-in-law, Alfred Du Vaucel, and it so happens that the area that he visited is the heart of lesser panda territory. The facts are unrecorded but this co-incidence leaves us with the interesting speculation that the obliging Dane may have provided either the Englishman or the Frenchman, or both, with their red pandas.

Some twenty years passed before another European naturalist contributed to western zoology's knowledge of the Himalayan 'fiery fox', or 'raccoon', as the panda was popularly called. He was Brian Houghton Hodgson, who in 1845, after a stormy career in the Indian Civil Service, retired to a modest bungalow situated in a remote beauty spot in the high mountains of Sikkim. Here, for thirteen years, he led the life of a hermit and acquired the nick-name 'the Darjiling recluse'. Cut off from the world though he was, he none the less took the opportunity to indulge in one of his primary interests, natural history. In 1847 all his frustration and pent-up emotion about the appalling way in which Britain had neglected the study of Indian animals was unleashed in the *Journal of the Asiatic Society of Bengal*, reaching a pitch of outraged patriotism on the

Brian Houghton Hodgson

subject of the lesser panda.

Cuvier, insisted the English eccentric, knew little about *Ailurus*. Even the popular name 'panda' bequeathed to it by the Frenchman was outlandish. In Hodgson's view, it was scandalous that in the mid-nineteenth century the French still held a monopoly in contemporary knowledge of the Wah, as he preferred to call the red panda. He declared that Cuvier 'defined or rather indicated the Genera late in his career from imperfect specimens transmitted immediately after their arrival in the East by Vaucel and Diard, gentlemen whom the Jardin des Plantes sent out to glean the harvest which English perverseness could not or would not take any sensible or intelligible steps to glean . . . I myself assisted Du Vaucel's researches with alacrity. But at the same time I stated to the leaders of this science in England what a pity it was that want of ordinary measures on their part to secure the co-operation of their countrymen in the East should thus continue to prevent England's reaping the zoological harvest of her own domains; and I pointed to my own drawings, specimens and description of the structure and habits of *Ailurus* lying unused in their hands whilst their Journal (the *Zoological Journal*) was putting forth the mere crumbs gathered from Cuvier's table . . . and whilst his active son-in-law was then preparing under my very eye and with my own aid to com-

plete the supercession of what ought to have been from the first, and
might even yet be in part, English researches. How and why my appeal
failed I know not. They order these things better in France...'

Behind Hodgson's outburst lay a very specific and personal com-
plaint. As we have seen, he refers to his own important information about
the lesser panda being neglected and completely overlooked by the
Zoological Society of London. In 1833, when he was acting as Resident in
Nepal, as a Corresponding Member of the newly formed society,
Hodgson had sent it 'a full and careful description of the habits and of the
hard and soft anatomy of *Ailurus*'. This, presumably, he felt should have
superseded Cuvier's description, for he was apparently unaware of
General Hardwicke's paper of 1827. But, he continues, 'What became of
that paper I know not, and have now to regret that the original M.S. was
lost with many others of great value at the period of my hurried departure
for Europe.' The result was that nothing of any great significance
appeared on the subject of the red panda between 1825 and 1847. Hodgson
therefore decided to publish what remained of his notes compiled some
fifteen years previously.

Whatever its shortcomings, his article represented the sum total of
information available on the lesser panda for more than two decades.
Indeed, since no one has really studied the habits of the animal in the wild
to this day and virtually nothing is known of its behaviour, except from

The red panda from the Hodgson folio

captive specimens, he still remains an authority on the subject.

Solitary, self-taught and embittered naturalist that he was, Hodgson was none the less a keen observer of animal life. Most of his information about the red panda was obviously based on the behaviour of several live specimens which he had kept in Nepal. His sketches of the animal's sleeping postures have the realistic quality of drawings from life. Many pandas were brought to him for they were easily caught, having 'little speed, cunning or ferocity to protect them'. Since their flesh was never eaten and their only economic value lay in the manufacture of fur caps, this lack of self-defence against man the predator was, apparently, no serious handicap. Hodgson was obviously very fond of his pandas for he wrote: 'The amenity of their ordinary disposition is finely portrayed in their gentle countenances, and, as they are free from all offensive odour, they would make nice pets for ladies, particularly when young. They drink by lapping with the tongue and moderately. They hiss and spit like cats when angered, and, if extremely so, utter a short deep grunt like that of a young Bear; but ordinarily they are quite silent.'

As to the panda's habits in the wild, Hodgson wrote: 'They are alivorous climbers, frequenting trees much, but breeding and feeding chiefly on the ground, and having their retreat in the natural resiliences of rocks.' The adults he believed to be monogamous, living in pairs or small families until the next brood was about to appear at which point the mother would drive the grown young away. He observed that two offspring at a time was normal, born in spring or early summer. The animal slept a good deal during the day and had a strong aversion to bright light, but was not nocturnal in its feeding habits. It ate tuberous roots, acorns, beech mast, eggs and bamboo sprouts. 'In general the wahs eschew flesh, fish, insects, reptiles, absolutely. But they love milk and ghee, and constantly make their way furtively into remote dairies and cowherd's cottages to possess themselves of these luxuries.'

For many years Europe eagerly awaited the arrival of the first living panda, the animal that Cuvier had hailed as the most beautiful creature known to man. Under the circumstances it was with considerable satisfaction that the Secretary of the Zoological Society of London announced at a meeting of the Fellows on 13th May 1869, that he had received a letter from Dr J. Anderson of the Indian Museum, Calcutta. It contained the news that the three lesser pandas to be presented to the zoo by Dr H. Simpson had already arrived in Calcutta, although whether they would reach English shores alive seemed doubtful. Anderson wrote: 'I have taken them under my charge, and am doing all I can to mitigate their sufferings from the heat, which has been very great during the last few days, reaching as high as 95° on the cool shaded side of the house. I have a man attending to them all day; and when the sun goes down I have them carried out into a cool breezy spot. I have had a new and comfortable airy cage constructed, as the one they were in was filthy in the extreme. The original specimen, which I found at Darjeeling, and which now belongs to Dr Simpson, is in capital condition, and may live through the heat of the Red Sea; but I doubt much if the others will.'

Two of the red pandas did, in fact, die on the voyage and the third reached the London Zoo on 22nd May clinging to life by a thread. The pitiful creature was taken under the wing of the Zoo's superintendent, Abraham Dee Bartlett, or 'Papa' Bartlett as he was affectionately known to the Press. At the time, the British were becoming animal conscious and Bartlett was one of the first great animal popularizers, providing the public with entertaining and instructive stories about his charges. He was a

Portrait of first living panda at London Zoo

splendid figure of a man, invariably dressed in a top hat and long frock coat whether wielding a scalpel or a stable broom.

The wretched object that arrived at the Zoo was anything but lovely. This is how Bartlett described the panda: 'I found the animal in a very exhausted condition, not able to stand, and so weak that it could with difficulty crawl from one end of its long cage to the other. It was suffering from frequent discharges of frothy, slimy faecal matter. This filth had so completely covered and matted its fur, that its appearance and smell were most offensive.'

With the panda came feeding instructions to the effect that it should be given a quart of milk, with a little rice and grass each day. Bartlett felt that this diet was obviously inadequate and set about changing it at once. Although the exhausted animal refused chicken, it readily accepted sweetened beef-tea and arrow-root or oatmeal porridge mixed with yolks of eggs. Soon it was strong enough to be let loose in the superintendent's garden and supplemented its diet with leaves, rose shoots and unripe apples. Above all it relished the yellow berries of *Pyrus vesita*. The panda, says Bartlett, 'would grasp the branch with his paw, holding it tightly and bite off these berries one by one; so delighted with his food was he, that all other food was left as long as these berries lasted'. Appropriately, the panda was commemorated in its official portrait using its forepaw to clutch its favourite food. The animal's manual dexterity aroused a great deal of interest, since, curiously enough, Brian Hodgson had never reported his captive specimens using their hands in this way.

At first the red panda had hardly lived up to its reputation for beauty, but as it became stronger it shed its old matted and ragged coat. Then a vividly coloured, lustrous new fur began to grow and its real glamour emerged at last. To hasten this process of transformation, Bartlett encouraged the animal to groom itself by spraying it every morning with a garden syringe. As far as the panda's temperament was concerned the improvement in its health brought about no change. Far from being sweet-natured and docile, as the world had been led to expect by Hodgson, it was bad-tempered, even ferocious at times, and refused to allow itself to be caressed. Bartlett wrote: 'When offended, it would rush at me and strike with both feet, not like a cat, sideways or downwards, but forward, and the body raised like a bear, the claws projecting but not hooked or brought down like the claws of a cat; for although the claws are partly retractile, the animal cannot use them in that manner. At the moment of making the attack, it would utter a sharp spitting hiss . . . ' No doubt this is why the lesser panda became popularly known as the 'cat-bear' at the time.

Unusual and attractive though it was, the first 'panda' to reach Europe did not produce any great impact on the animal-loving public at large. There were undoubtedly many reasons for this. It was not sufficiently dissimilar from a red fox or a raccoon and did not show itself to real advantage, being semi-nocturnal. But perhaps the most important factor was that its story ended abruptly and sadly, for it died suddenly during the night of 12th December 1869, without ever having had a real chance to capture a devoted human following. Its body was sent to the Royal College of Surgeons the next morning and there it came under the expert scalpel of William Henry Flower, Conservator of the Museum, who was delighted to have the opportunity to dissect such an interesting

A baby red panda, with parents

specimen. In 1870, Flower published a detailed paper about his findings
that helped correct a number of inaccurate statements that had previously
been made about the animal.

Zoologists were still puzzled, however, by the problem of exactly
where the red panda should be placed in the classification of animal life.
William Flower, and others, felt that it had sufficient peculiarities to
merit being put in a distinct family. But how, exactly, should this family
with its sole representative, the panda, be related to the other families of
carnivores such as the raccoon group? In other words, which animals
were the panda's closest relatives? Cautiously, Flower concluded, 'This is
a point which may still be left open for discussion. Some light will probably be thrown upon it when details are published of the structure of a
remarkable new mammal lately obtained in Eastern Tibet by M. L'Abbé
David . . .'

This remark proved to be prophetic. Unwittingly, since he believed
that he had found a new kind of bear, the famous French priest and missionary, Père David, had, in fact, discovered another kind of panda, the
giant panda as we know it today. In a sense, this is where our story really
begins, for the beautiful and rare small red panda, which had held the
stage for half a century, was about to be overshadowed by its more
impressive black-and-white cousin from China. Nowadays, hardly anyone cares about the lesser panda, but there is hardly an infant alive who
does not know and love the giant panda.

the giant panda discovered

Today the giant panda holds a secure position amongst the 'Top Ten' animal favourites. We tend to take this climb to fame for granted, but in some respects it is rather unusual. One of the strangest aspects of the panda's success is that it lacks the traditional background of ancient mythology and legend so typical of the other great animal stars. For centuries, history and folk-lore have been enlivened by tales of fabulous elephants, winged horses, sacred monkeys and regal lions, but it is difficult to unearth more than a mere handful of references to the giant panda before Père David arrived on the scene in the nineteenth century.

Most people who write about the giant panda seem to feel obliged to provide something in the way of an historical background for it, no matter how second hand. They obviously feel that it is inconceivable that such a strange and striking creature should not have produced some reaction in a culture as civilized as that of China. To state blandly that the giant panda has been known to the Chinese since time immemorial may be the easiest way to dismiss the problem. It is undoubtedly true in a sense, but how well was the animal known and at what point was the interaction between men and pandas first recorded?

The earliest instance we have discovered is given by J. H. Edgar, who mentions that this animal was included in the tribute of Yu from Liangchow, Szechuan, over 4000 years ago. If this claim is justified then the suggestion is that before 2000 B.C. the panda, or, at least, its luxurious black-and-white pelt, was a sought-after commodity of great value. Since Liangchow lies in the giant panda's range, the statement certainly makes sense in geographical terms. On the question of antiquity, however, there is room for doubt. The orthodox list of Chinese rulers starts at the equivalent of 2852 B.C. If we accept this system of dating then the Emperor Yu is supposed to have reigned from 2205 to 2198 B.C. This also fits well, but unfortunately modern scholars are sceptical about the possibility of dating events accurately in this remote period of Chinese history when fact and legend were still confused.

The giant panda then fades from the scene until the seventh century A.D. when the bei-shung, or white bear, makes a more convincing historical debut. Willy Ley says that 'Mention of this bei-shung is said to occur in Chinese chronicles as far back as our year 650 A.D.', while Ruth Harkness gives a slightly earlier date. In conversation with Arthur de Carle Sowerby, who was then Curator of the Shanghai Museum and an authority on pandas, she discovered that 'The Chinese have known since the T'ang dynasty which began about A.D. 621, that this rare animal . . . lived in the mountains of far-western Szechuan, on the Tibetan border.' Bernard Heuvelmans makes a similar claim: 'As far as we know, the first mention of the bei-shung is in a manuscript dating from A.D. 621, during the reign of the first of the T'ang emperors.' All this is rather vague, but a more elaborate account of seventh-century pandas is given by Herbert Wendt, who says: 'A white bear from the mountainous bamboo forests of Yunnan province is already mentioned in a chronicle written in 621, during the reign of the first T'ang emperor. Then the Japanese imperial annals describe how, on October 22, 685 the Emperor of China sent the Tenno of Japan a gift of two living white bears and seventy white-bear skins. Thenceforth the pei-hsiung appears repeatedly in tax rolls, history and children's books.'

Under the rule of the powerful T'ang emperors, whose dynasty spanned the period 618-907, China was the arbiter of the whole of Oriental Asia and combined political influence with intensive commercial activity. Trade flowed along the arteries of the 'Silk Route' system, which linked the countries of Europe to central Asia and China, and one of these well-worn trails passed through panda country. Caravans carrying luxury merchandise over this particular route may well have acquired skins and even live specimens of the white bear, so enabling the emperor to make his lavish gesture. As these panda trophies were considered suitable gifts for a neighbouring ruler they must certainly have been highly prized. But the most astonishing feature of this story is the delivery of the two living animals to Japan. The transportation of pandas has proved a headache even in modern times. Given the difficulties of long distance travel in the seventh century it must have taken a major feat of animal husbandry to ensure that the Tenno's white bears reached their destination safely. What is more, this appears to be the first recorded occasion on which live giant pandas were exported from their native land.

This was a most notable event in panda history, providing the animals in question really were giant pandas. One intriguing suggestion which has been put forward is that the white bears were not giant pandas at all but were, in fact, polar bears, the snowy white giants of the Arctic, brought back from the North by Chinese hunters. In favour of this theory it can be

Polar bears

argued that the polar bear is more common than the giant panda, so that seventy skins could be more easily assembled. Also, the polar bear is mentioned by Marco Polo in his travels, so that in the thirteenth century, at least, the Mongols must have known of it. If the Mongols had encountered it, then why not the ancient Chinese?

However, against the theory must be placed the fact that giant pandas live on Chinese soil, while polar bears are natives of the far north, thousands of miles away over inhospitable terrain. It is true that occasional sitings of the great Arctic bear have been made around the eastern coast of Siberia, and a few have actually penetrated south towards Japan, but these appear to be freak cases. They could hardly account for seventy skins.

In what quantities, or with what degree of regularity, white-bear skins found their way from the remote regions of the Tibetan borderland to the centre of Chinese civilization is uncertain. We must make a leap of a thousand years to find further mention of the bei-shung. David Crockett Graham, who spent many years working at the West China Union

University in Chengtu, suggests that the Chinese certainly knew of the 'white bear' in the seventeenth century. 'During the Manchu dynasty skins of this animal were sent as tribute to the government of China by the aborigines of western Szechuan and eastern Tibet.'

Assuming that the bei-shung skins mentioned in the early oriental records really came from giant pandas, why were they valued? They seem to have served two main purposes. Firstly the pelts made good sleeping mats. The fur on the giant panda's back is thick and woolly but, at the same time, wiry, so providing a dense yet springy surface when used as a mattress. Secondly, the bold, sharply defined black and white markings of the animal are very decorative, so panda skins were also used as ornamental rugs. Although it looks attractive, the fur is very coarse to the touch and was seldom, if ever, employed in the making of garments. This limits its uses considerably. For the experienced hunter, panda country is a paradise containing a number of animals whose skins have far more attractive qualities from the furrier's point of view.

Whatever its limitations, the pelt was the only part of the giant panda that seems to have had any economic importance at all. This could have been very little, given the difficulties of trapping the creature in its remote and impenetrable bamboo forests. In other respects, it was almost totally ignored. No mention of the bei-shung appears to have been made in the great Chinese *Materia Medica, Pen Ts'ao Kang Mu*, for instance. This work, written by Li Shih-chen, in 1597, contains a compilation of drugs made from animal materials. The author spent twenty-six years painstakingly cataloguing the whole traditional knowledge of drugs from China's remote past up to the sixteenth century. The omission of the bei-shung is surely significant, since the Chinese had a passion for using every conceivable animal ingredient for medicinal purposes.

There are several reasons why the giant panda may not have been included in the list. The obvious one is that the animal was not sufficiently well known or available as a potential therapeutic aid. Another possibility is that it was protected by religious sentiment. As a third alternative, it may have been too common to be considered worthy of attention. The evidence suggests that the giant panda was hardly sacred, since it was slaughtered by hunters. Moreover, any animal believed to have religious significance would surely have played some role in Chinese folk-lore and art. This would be equally expected if the giant panda was a very familiar creature, since common animals are invariably celebrated in this way. Yet the giant panda apparently made little, if any, impact either on oriental artists, or story-tellers. After a singularly unsuccessful search for early giant panda pictures and legends, we consulted an expert from the Oriental Department of the British Museum, but he was unable to help us. He replied that 'although an occasional skin may have reached Peking as tribute from the aboriginal tribes of Szechuan, this species was never sufficiently well-known to play any part in Chinese folk-lore. I have never seen any representation of it in Chinese painting or in bronzes or jades.'

We can only conclude from this that in the more civilized regions of China, at least, the giant panda was virtually unknown in the past. The explanation appears to be largely connected with the fact that, as we have mentioned earlier, the geographical range of the species is restricted to remote and inhospitable areas of western China where the local inhabitants were no doubt by-passed by the mainstream of Chinese culture. Further east, giant pandas were virtually never seen in the flesh. They only appeared occasionally as sleeping mats, or rugs, acquired through trade or as tribute to the Chinese government, and in this disembodied form they were scarcely sufficiently stimulating to produce a crop of portraits or legends.

There is also another important point which must be taken into consideration when assessing why the Chinese neglected the giant panda, namely that, as far as they were concerned, the panda was just another kind of bear. Therefore, even if the giant panda was, in fact, better known than we have suggested, and Herbert Wendt really has good grounds for saying that it was a familiar character in oriental children's books from the seventh century onwards, it would simply have been amalgamated with the general bear image. In its homeland, the giant panda is known by several names, but they usually include the term for bear plus some descriptive word. Amongst its Chinese names are hsiung-maou (cat-bear), pei-hsiung or bei-shung (white bear), hua-hsiung (speckled bear) and ho shien (monk among bears). Superficially, bears and giant pandas are strikingly similar in appearance so it is easy to understand how the confusion arose. It is true that the giant panda has very characteristic markings, but certain bears, including the Himalayan bear, which is comparable in size and whose range overlaps with that of the giant panda, have similar coloration. The main difference is that, whereas the Himalayan bear is basically black with a large off-white crescent on its chest, the giant panda has rather more white than black in its fur. But at what point is a black animal with white markings clearly distinguishable to the unscientific eye from a white animal with black markings? There is also the added complication that in the Himalayas bordering on panda country there is a pale local race of the brown bear which almost qualifies as being white, since its coat is silvery-white with a creamy under-fur.

Judging by twentieth-century reports, we can be reasonably certain that in the past even people who inhabited panda territory itself often lived and died without ever setting eyes on the elusive creature. Many of them were probably unaware that the animal existed. Others may have heard about it, but had no clear idea of what the giant panda looked like, and confused it with bears in general. Only the local hunters who made a living from the quarry which fell to their primitive fire-arms, or blundered into their spear-traps would have had any clear notion of the bei-shung. But to these men, struggling to survive in difficult and hostile country, the giant panda no doubt represented just another pelt in the bag. There is no evidence that they made a special point of hunting this animal. The traditional spear-trap was a device for taking not only giant pandas but any kind of large game. It consisted of a spear with an iron head wedged horizontally in the ground between two upright sticks, the tip of the weapon being set at an appropriate height to pierce the heart region of a large ungulate or bear. The device worked automatically, for a sapling was attached to the shaft of the spear and sprung by a trigger. From this a cord was run over the game's trail, so that when it was tampered with by a potential quarry, the spear, guided by the upright sticks, was driven forward with tremendous impetus and plunged into the animal's body. The giant panda skins recorded in tax rolls in ancient times were presumably part of the random haul gathered by these effective, but non-selective traps. Given the inferior quality of giant panda fur, it is even possible that their pelts were not over-enthusiastically received by the Chinese government, except in so much as they were considered unusual and rare.

If this then was the situation in China, small wonder that the white bear aroused little interest in the West before its official discovery in 1869. Few people knew that the creature existed and among scholarly circles it was either dismissed as a fanciful legend, or thought to be just another type of bear. The most popular theory, as we have already noted, was that the Chinese bei-shung, being reputedly white, must be a polar bear, the only well-known white species. This suggests that westerners were unfamiliar with skins of the animal, since the black patches in its coat are too striking to be over-looked. However, melanistic polar bears, not to mention partial albino black bears, are not beyond the bounds of biological possibility. If the odd giant panda pelt had reached Europe through trade, or missionaries, it could have been explained as an unusual bear mutation. Or the pelt may have been thought to belong to some ordinary domestic animal since, due to selective breeding by man, black and white markings are very characteristic of many domestic species. Superficially, there is nothing remarkable about the actual quality of a giant panda's fur that would have distinguished it from either the zoologist's or the furrier's point of view.

There is a fascinating rumour that a living bei-shung actually reached Paris during the eighteenth century. Unfortunately, the author who reports that this is said to have happened was unable to recall the source of his information. We, too, have been unable to locate it. If a giant panda had reached Europe in those days, it also may have passed for a freak bear, so disappearing from the pages of history leaving scarcely a trace. Yet the story seems highly improbable. The eighteenth century was a golden era for the study of animal anatomy and one imagines the French zoologists hovering like vultures around any strange specimen, competing anxiously to pounce on its corpse and carry it off to their dissecting tables.

As late as the middle of the nineteenth century, the rich plant and animal life of China was still largely unexplored. About this time military pressure from the European nations forced the Celestial Empire to open up to foreign penetration. The position of missionaries and traders became rather more secure and both expanded their spheres of activity. Now Europeans were given their first glimpse of the wonderful flora and fauna of such remote areas as Mongolia and Szechuan through the efforts of French Catholic missionary priests and, notably, the pioneer work of Abbé Armand David.

This remarkable man combined intense religious devotion with a passionate interest in natural history. He wrote on one occasion, 'I passionately love the beauties of nature; the marvels of the hand of God transport me with such admiration that in comparison the finest work of man seems only trivial.' Even as a young boy he showed a keen enthusiasm for his favourite subject. Guided and encouraged by his father, Fructueux Dominique, a doctor and eminent citizen of the little town of Espelette in the Basses-Pyrénées, David browsed through scholarly books on natural history and collected butterflies and insects in the mountains around his home. But his main ambition was to become a priest and, in 1850, he took his vows in the order of St. Vincent de Paul whose missionaries were known as Lazarists. As early as 1852, while teaching at a college on the Italian Riviera he wrote to his superior that he dreamed of Chinese missions and it was for this reason that he had become a priest in the Lazarist order. Ten years passed, however, before he was ordained a missionary and set sail for China. Before he left, he had been commissioned by the authorities of the Museum of Natural History in Paris to collect botanical and zoological material. This he proceeded to do soon after his arrival in Peking and so impressed the Museum's director, Henri Milne-Edwards, with the excellence of his specimens that it was arranged for Abbé David to undertake special scientific work, sponsored by the French government.

Père David, as he is usually known in scientific literature, was stationed in China from 1862 to 1874 and during this period undertook three import-

Père David

ant journeys for the Museum of Natural History. The scientific discoveries that he made ensured his undying fame as a naturalist and
explorer. The earnest, black-haired, keen-eyed missionary, who had gone
to China 'pursued with the thought of dying while working at the saving
of infidels', returned home convinced that, at the current rate of progress, it would be forty or fifty thousand years before the Celestial Empire
would be wholly Christian. He himself, however, was not destined to
become a martyr in that cause and survived not only religious persecu-
tion, but bandits, the severe hardships of travel, inadequate food and
severe illness. The last twenty-six years of his life were spent mostly in
Paris as a celebrity honoured throughout the scientific world. By then a
handsome white-haired old man he entertained his friends with vivid
accounts of his adventures and the marvels he had seen. Although
modest, he had a sense of humour and a flair for dramatic effects. Just
before his death in 1900, at the age of seventy-four, he made a point of
carrying around with him a huge pet spider which he is said to have
trained to run back to him on the word of command.

   Père David's fame was well deserved for, during his stay in China, he
had sent back to Europe a vast collection of plants and introduced many
lovely new species now familiar in our gardens. He discovered fifty-eight

birds new to science, about a hundred new insects and many mammals. The latter included the extraordinary snub-nosed Roxellana monkey and the milou, now known as Père David's deer, a curious creature, extinct in the wild, before it was discovered in the Imperial Park at Peking. Many plants and animals were named after the French priest, yet ironically his most important discovery of all does not bear his name. This animal was, of course, the giant panda.

The discovery was made during his second journey which took him to Szechuan and the independent principalities of western China and lasted from 26th May 1868 to 25th July 1870. On each of his three major collecting trips, Père David kept a diary which he filled with copious notes recording his impressions and scientific data that would help him later in writing up his collections. These field journals were all published, apparently with little editing or revision, and their lively on-the-spot flavour is retained in print. The diary of the second journey, so momentous in giant panda history, appeared under the title *Journal d'un Voyage dans le centre de la Chine et dans le Tibet Oriental*, in the form of Bulletins appended to the Nouvelles Archives du Muséum d'Histoire Naturelle de Paris, in 1872, 1873 and 1874.

Unfortunately, it is impossible to tell from his diary whether Père David deliberately set out to look for the Chinese bei-shung, or whether he stumbled upon it almost by accident. We know that he was encouraged to go to the western frontiers of China by reports from fellow missionaries who assured him that there were many interesting animals to be found in the high mountains which had escaped the deforestation that invariably accompanied Chinese agricultural expansion. On 16th June 1868, he met, in Shanghai, a Chinese who was formerly a pupil of the missionary college in Moupin. The director of this institution, M. Arnal, was already engaged in preparing many interesting new birds and mammals to be sent to France, but the task was a huge one. Père David wrote, 'This young man tells me that, although M. Arnal's researches have lasted two years, his hunters have not succeeded in procuring all the animals living in the woods of Muping. So there will still be some gleanings for me, at least among less remarkable species.'

Had David been told of the white bear before setting off on the long and uncomfortable boat trip up the Yangtze River, past the dangerous rapids to Chungking, on 13th October 1868? Or did he learn of the creature from missionaries in Chungking itself when he arrived there, more than six weeks later, weary and travel-worn? From Chungking he pressed on to Chengtu, the ancient walled city which for years had been an outpost of the caravan trade where, again, he gleaned as much information as possible about the zoological treasures to be found in the nearby mountains. On the eve of departure from Chengtu he obviously felt gloomy and rather sceptical and wrote in his diary, 'I am busy preparing my numerous pieces of baggage to leave tomorrow and, if it please God, spend a year in Muping, the promised land where everyone has said there are marvels. I admit, however, that I am not enthusiastic, knowing how often I have been misled by Chinese promises.'

By 1st March he had reached Moupin and was comfortably installed in the Catholic college there. This teaching establishment had been founded fifty or sixty years before, when persecutions in China had obliged the missionaries to seek refuge in the independent kingdom of the prince of the Man-tzu. Père David noted that the people living in the inaccessible mountains of this tiny barbarian state made a meagre living from gathering medicinal herbs, hunting, and making potash. In type and language they differed considerably from the Chinese, for whom he had little admiration and seldom a good word. He was therefore saddened to observe that, even in Moupin, 'the industrious, increasing population of the Celestial Empire is penetrating quickly and taking possession of the land under one pretext or another, and will end by having its customs, language, costume, and also its faults adopted. A few years ago no Chinese had access to Muping. Now they are to be found throughout the principality'. But Père David did not spend long pondering on this unhappy state of affairs, since he had important work to do. He hastily set about collecting specimens and made arrangements with local hunters to bring him some large mammals. Acquiring material through these contacts proved to be expensive and he noted resentfully that the hunters demanded five or six times the normal prices. Certain bans were imposed on hunting by the prince of the district, superficially, at least, on religious grounds. These the poverty-striken inhabitants were willing to flout, but they expected to be well rewarded for their pains.

The very first mention of the giant panda is made in Père David's diary entry for 11th March 1869. It was a beautiful sunny day and the priest, accompanied by a student, had gone on an expedition into the lower valleys of Hong-chan-tin in quest of specimens. 'On returning from our excursion we are invited to rest at the home of a certain Li, the principal landowner in the valley, who entertains us with tea and sweet-meats. At this pagan's I see a fine skin of the famous white and black bear (du fameux ours blanc et noir), which appears to be fairly large. It is a very remarkable species and I rejoice when I hear my hunters say that I shall certainly obtain the animal within a short time. They tell me that they will go out as early as tomorrow to kill this carnivore which it seems must constitute an interesting novelty for science.'

From the way that Père David describes this incident we can only infer that he already knew of the famous black-and-white bear. But we know from his diary that he had already met a hunter called Li who was presumably his host on 11th March. The interesting question is whether David recognized the pelt at once or whether he learnt what it was from the landowner. He invariably questioned people he met about the animals of the district, and it was possibly as a result of this, that Li produced his handsome skin and explained to the foreigner that it belonged to the famous bei-shung which lived in the Hsifan Mountains. Whether Père David had heard it mentioned before or not, he would have found out as much as he could about the creature and made every effort to obtain a specimen to send back to Paris. He did not realize that the animal was quite unique or call it a giant panda but, even as a remarkable species of bear, it was sufficiently interesting to the zoological world.

On 23rd March, he wrote, 'My Christian hunters return today after a ten-day absence. They bring me a young white bear, which they took alive but unfortunately killed so it could be carried more easily.' Since he regarded himself as a follower of St Francis, David deplored the unnecessary taking of animal life and always regretted having to kill animals in order to prepare specimens. Yet, dead or alive, the young animal fascinated him as a naturalist. He continues, 'The young white bear, which they sell to me very dearly, is all white except the four limbs, ears, and around the eyes, which are deep black. The colours are the same as those of the adult's skin which I examined the other day at the home of Li, the hunter. This must, therefore, be a new species of *Ursus*, which is very remarkable not only for its colour, but also because of its paws which are hairy underneath, and for other characters.' Père David's conviction that the animal must be a new species of bear was further confirmed when on 1st April, 'They bring me a white bear which they tell me is fully adult. Its colours are exactly the same as those of the young one that I have already, only the black is less pure and the white more soiled. The animal's head is very big and the muzzle round and short instead of being pointed as in the Pekin bear.'

Père David did not delay in informing his friends in Paris of his discovery. A description of the animal, which he named *Ursus melanoleucus* (black-and-white bear), was sent to Professor Alphonse Milne-Edwards, son, and later successor, of the director of the Paris Natural History Museum. In a letter from Moupin, dated 21st March 1869, David explained that he was forwarding a collection of specimens but, knowing that the shipment would not arrive in France for a long time, requested that the description of the new bear should be published immediately. It did, in fact, appear in the Museum's Bulletin of the same year and read as follows: '*Ursus melanoleucus* A.D. Very large according to my hunters.

Ears short. Tail very short. Hair fairly short; beneath the four feet very hairy. Colours: white, with the ears, the surroundings of the eyes, the tip of the tail and the four legs brownish black. The black on the forelegs is joined over the back in a straight band. I have just received a young bear of this kind and I have seen the mutilated skins of adult specimens. The colours are always the same and equally distributed. I have not seen this species, which is easily the prettiest kind of animal I know, in the museums of Europe. Is it possible that it is new to science? For the past twenty days I have employed more than ten hunters to capture some old specimens of this remarkable bear.' A postscript is then added to this brief description. 'April 4 – An adult female of the black-and-white bear has just come into my possession. The coat is yellowish and the black is darker and shinier than in the young specimen.'

When Père David's specimens reached Paris, Alphonse Milne-Edwards naturally paid particular attention to the remarkable Chinese bear. But after a detailed examination of skins and skeletons he realized that his friend David had been wrong in identifying the creature as a bear, although he felt that at first sight any naturalist might have mistaken it for one. In an article entitled, 'Sur quelques Mammifères du Tibet Oriental', published in 1870, Milne-Edwards wrote: 'In its external form, indeed, it very much resembles a Bear, but the osteological characters and the dental system clearly distinguish it from the Bears and come nearer to the Pandas and Raccoons. It must constitute a new genus which I have called *Ailuropoda*.'

Later when he found that the scientific name *Ailuropoda* had already been used in a different context, the French zoologist modified it to *Ailuropus*. The name was originally selected to recall the resemblance between the feet of the newly discovered carnivore and those of *Ailurus*, the lesser panda, the only animal known as a panda in those days. So, during the nineteenth century, the full scientific title of the animal, which we know today as the giant panda, was *Ailuropus melanoleucus*, or the 'panda-like black-and-white animal'. Later taxonomists changed the name back again to Milne-Edward's original suggestion and the giant panda is known today as *Ailuropoda melanoleuca* meaning, literally, 'black-and-white panda-foot'.

On the many occasions when Père David referred to 'the most important zoological discovery I have been given to make', he was repeatedly obliged to mention that his name *Ursus melanoleucus* had been dropped because it was misleading. Yet, unlike certain other scientists, he accepted Milne-Edward's new name for his greatest discovery. Perhaps he sometimes felt annoyed with himself for failing to spot the relationship between his 'bear' and the lesser panda, particularly as he had obtained specimens of both within a short space of time and had noticed that there were similarities between their heads and feet. With a flash of genius his good friend Milne-Edwards had pin-pointed the connection, but this the unassuming priest accepted with considerable good grace.

While Alphonse Milne-Edwards was busily writing up his anatomical evidence to substantiate his classification, Père David, in December 1871, gave a report to his sponsors, the scientific administrators of the Natural History Museum. It was published the next year and included the first description of the habits of the giant panda in the wild. Brief as it was, his information is well worth mention. He wrote: 'This animal which the hunters call Paé-shioung (white bear) is very much rarer than the black Tibetan bear, which inhabits the same forests; it stays much higher and appears to have a vegetable diet. But, nevertheless, it does not refuse flesh when the occasion presents itself; and I even think that this is its principal food in winter, a season in which it is not inclined to remain asleep.' It is interesting that Père David did not record the giant panda as an exclusive bamboo-eater. As we shall see, later authors frequently did so. We know now that Père David was right and they were wrong, although he went too far when he suggested that in winter the animal was predominantly carnivorous.

The first detailed account of the anatomy of the giant panda, together with an attractive portrait and six other plates showing the bony structure, appeared in 1874. It was part of Alphonse Milne-Edward's contribution to the monumental work on the natural history of mammals which he published in conjunction with his father, Henri, between 1868 and 1874, under the title *Recherches pour servir a l'histoire naturelle des Mammifères*. Bone by bone and tooth by tooth, the younger Milne-Edwards analysed minutely the ways in which the 'Ailurope', as he called the giant panda, resembled or differed from other carnivores. The giant panda's penultimate molar caused him grave concern because of its similarities with the equivalent tooth in certain fossil pachyderms, but he concluded that, 'nevertheless, it is between the Bears and the Pandas that the Ailurope must take its place in our methodical classification'. One quite unique feature of the giant panda, the 'sixth claw', which we know today assists the animal in grasping bamboo stems with its front paws, did not escape Milne-Edwards' thorough eye, although he makes no suggestion about its possible function. He mentions that, whereas the back feet of *Ailuropus* have 'a row of five little fleshy pin-cushions' at the base of the toes, on the front feet there is an extra 'fleshy pin-cushion, without hairs, near the heel'. On the basis of all the anatomical evidence at his disposal the French zoologist believed that *Ailuropus* constituted a separate genus more valid than many of the other genera in the Order Carnivora.

Yet, although the giant panda was now officially 'known to science', for many years to come it still remained very much a creature of mystery. It came to be popularly known as the 'clawed bear', or the 'bamboo bear' and some scientists thought that 'harlequin bear' would be a suitable common name. In other words, the giant panda was still widely regarded as a bear. At the turn of the century a specimen at the British Museum was still being exhibited as a 'parti-coloured bear'.

About the same time the German zoologist Max Weber undertook a general re-classification of the mammals and pronounced that the *bambushbär* (bamboo bear), far from being related to the lesser panda and the raccoon, as Milne-Edwards had suggested, was in fact a living fossil, the last remaining ally of *Hyaenarctos*, a hyaena-sized Miocene carnivore. Weber believed *Hyaenarctos* to be a primeval vegetarian bear and therefore decided that *Ailuropoda melanoleuca* must be an ancestral bear which, by some fluke, had survived into modern times.

Even today, controversy over the exact classification of the giant panda still rages, although the animal is much better known than it was barely a century ago. Then, the whole of zoological knowledge about this particular species rested on just a few specimens in the museums of Europe. There were four examples in the Natural History Museum of Paris, obtained through Père David, and one other in the museum of Stuttgart, in Germany, which was acquired some time later. This fifth specimen was apparently purchased from a hunter in panda country by a Chinese merchant who then traded it to a German.

A scant handful of mounted specimens could hardly be expected to advance knowledge of the giant panda to any degree, but one unsolved historical riddle remains. Is it possible that several live giant pandas actually reached Europe in the nineteenth century? Several authors have claimed that they did. Helen Fox, for instance, who translated Père David's diaries into English under the auspices of Harvard University and published the results as *Père David's Diary* in 1949, implies that there were live giant pandas in Paris in the nineteenth century. In the introduction to the book she writes: 'Among the animals discovered by Abbé David, the giant panda, *Ailuropoda melanoleuca*, created the greatest interest. It can be imagined what a stir was caused when the panda arrived at the Jardin d'Acclimatation. For a while it was the only example in Europe; but the first to come did not long survive its transference from the mountains of Szechuan.'

Could this have been the adult female that the local hunters brought Père David on 1st April 1869? In his diary he does not mention whether the animal was alive or dead. True, it seems unlikely that the hunters would take the trouble to bring back a live adult from the mountains when a young one had provided them with such a transport problem that they killed it. But the possibility remains that the priest gave them sufficient financial reward for the young specimen to encourage them to try and trap a live giant panda for him.

In 1951, Jessie Dobson, Curator of the Hunterian Museum at the Royal College of Surgeons in London, published a paper in the Proceedings of the Zoological Society of London which also suggests that Père David was instrumental in obtaining live giant pandas for the Paris Zoo. Her main subject was the discovery of Père David's deer, but she also refers briefly to the French priest's interest in the 'white bear' that was

The skull of the giant panda. (From *Milne-Edwards*)

said to live in the mountains of western China. After describing how local hunters obtained a young giant panda for Père David, she adds, 'For convenience of transport, this specimen had to be killed, but later several others were obtained alive and sent to Paris. (In 1888 the Jardin des Plantes had four Giant Pandas, the only examples outside China.)' Miss Dobson's story has been elaborated by later authors so that the implication is that the few living specimens of the giant panda which Père David organized to send home were on display in the Paris Zoo for a number of years.

The authorities at the Jardin des Plantes and Natural History Museum in Paris have not, unhappily, been able to give us any further information about this fascinating story. Moreover, Miss Dobson is unable to trace her notes which, apparently, contained a great deal of information from original sources. She is convinced that her claim is based on sound evidence, if only it could be located. The contributions of Père David himself throw no further light on the subject. In a paper presented in 1888 on *La Faune Chinoise*, which was published a year later, he simply states that only four museum examples of *Ailuropus* existed at that time and all of these he had brought back from Moupin. It seems rather strange that he did not mention the fact that some of these animals were still breathing, if, in fact, there were living examples in Paris at the time. Also, would these not have been housed in the Zoo rather than in the Paris Museum which was devoted to dead specimens? We cannot eliminate the intriguing possibility that living giant pandas set foot on European soil before the twentieth century, even if the stress of the journey and lack of knowledge of their needs cut their stay to a very short one. Unless new evidence comes to light, however, we feel obliged to adhere to the traditional story that all Père David's specimens were dead on arrival in France, and that many years were to pass after his original discovery before scientists, or the public, had a chance to study the extraordinary animal in the flesh.

We feel that perhaps there has been some confusion between the arrival of giant pandas and lesser pandas in Europe in the late nineteenth century. The small red panda, *Ailurus fulgens*, then itself a rare and sensational animal, was known as *the* panda ever since Frédéric Cuvier gave it that popular name in 1825, whereas its big cousin, the giant panda, despite Milne-Edwards' efforts, was still generally known as a bear.

The giant panda was so little known that, in the 1890s, the English zoologist E. Ray Lankester, was thrilled when his friend, Professor Alphonse Milne-Edwards, sent him a cast of the skull 'of the remarkable bear-like animal brought home from Tibet by Père David'. On being appointed Director of the Natural History Department of the British Museum in 1898, Lankester looked up the material 'relating to *Aeluropus* in the Collection, and was much pleased to find that, in addition to a fine skull and mounted skin, the Museum possessed certain of the limb-bones and incomplete feet of *Aeluropus*, obtained in 1896'. These odd bones, discovered tucked away in one of the countless cupboards of his new domain, excited Lankester much more than the spectacular skin. (We know that in the 1890s the British Museum was enriched by the remains of two pandas. One of these specimens was secured by the Russian explorers Berezovski and Potanin and the other, a male, was captured by the local hunters employed by F. W. Styan in Yangliupa in north-western Szechuan. Probably it was the former specimen which Lankester unearthed so unexpectedly.)

The new Director of the Natural History Department of the British Museum had already decided, after studying his panda skull cast at Oxford, that, despite the claims of certain other eminent zoologists, it differed greatly from the skull of any bear and in certain respects came close to that of the lesser panda. The foot and leg bones which he discovered at the British Museum only confirmed his opinion 'that in very important and distinctive points *Aeluropus* agrees with *Aelurus*, and *Procyon* (more closely with the former) and differs widely from *Ursus*'. In other words, Lankester, like his colleague Milne-Edwards, felt that the giant panda was much more closely related to the red panda, and to a lesser degree the raccoon, than to the bears. One of the principal opponents of this theory was Richard Lydekker, whom Lankester consulted before taking action on his decision. In a paper addressed to the Linnean Society on 21st February 1901, the then Director of the British Museum describes what followed. 'Having satisfied myself on these points, I requested Mr Lydekker, who had not previously examined the limbbones of *Aeluropus*, to go over the specimens and give me the result of his observations. He entirely accepted my conclusion that *Aeluropus* must be removed from association with the Bears, and associated with *Aelurus* and *Procyon*. It has accordingly been removed to that position in the exhibition gallery of the Museum, and is no longer to be spoken of as "the parti-coloured bear", but as "the great panda".'

For the first time, the giant panda was exhibited under a name very similar to the one by which it is known throughout the English-speaking world today. It was described as the great and later as the giant panda in order to differentiate it from its smaller relative, now known as the lesser or red panda. The new popular name caught on rapidly and no doubt inspired the western zoologists and trophy-hunters who went to China in quest of the rare and beautiful animal. Soon the peace of the giant panda's mountainous bamboo-forest retreat was to be shattered by intrepid Europeans and Americans eager to be put on record as the first westerners to shoot the mysterious and retiring 'giant', and to glorify their local museum with a stuffed exhibit of the elusive prize.

the panda killers

For many decades the giant panda remained one of the rarest animals known to man, despite the invasions of panda country that followed its discovery. A few specimens, trapped by local hunters and purchased by western explorers or missionaries, found their way into museums outside China, but for a long time the animal eluded all the foreigners who tried to shoot it. As a result, it became the most challenging animal trophy on earth.

True, most of the expeditions that went to the wilds of Szechuan were by no means designed exclusively as panda hunts. The cost of such specialized ventures would have been far too high and the chances of success too remote. Finances were available, however, for expeditions of a more comprehensive type. For instance, thirty years or so after Père David discovered the giant panda, Britain and America sent new explorers to China, whose task was to repeat David's scientific work under more favourable conditions. Amongst these botanists and zoologists were Ernest H. Wilson and Walter Zappey. When in west-central Szechuan they saw very definite signs of the giant panda and noticed that it had beaten tracks through the thickets, 'frequenting the same haunts for long periods, as is evident from the large heaps of its dung which are often met with in the Bamboo jungle.' Wilson recorded various pieces of information which he gleaned from the local inhabitants and noted that the animals fed exclusively on bamboo shoots. He wrote: 'The young shoots which continue to spring up from June to the end of September, according to the altitude and species, are white within and excellent eating. The Giant Panda shows good taste in confining his diet to this excellent vegetable!' Yet, while combing the animal's homeland for plant and animal treasure, neither Wilson, nor any of his fellow scientists, caught so much as a glimpse of the panda itself.

So powerful was the allure of the mysterious panda that it sometimes proved fatal. One unfortunate explorer, Lieutenant J. W. Brooke, was murdered in 1910 by the Lolos, the strange and often inhospitable people who inhabited remote areas where giant pandas were to be found. Later, his widow presented to the British Museum a giant panda skin that her husband had purchased while in Szechuan.

There is some controversy as to who could claim to be the first westerner actually to see a living panda in the wild. One contender for this particular honour was Brigadier-General G. E. Pereira, an Englishman who made many contributions to zoological knowledge by way of new animal discoveries. He longed to kill a panda and kept a sharp watch for it while on his various expeditions through Western China and Eastern Tibet. His ambition was never fulfilled and he even failed to find so much as a trace of the animal in local tales. Then, one magical day, for a brief moment he saw a furry white animal perched in a distant tree which may just possibly have been a giant panda. In 1916, J. H. Edgar had a similar experience. While travelling in wild country near Kinsha he spotted a large white animal curled up in the fork of an oak tree. Being unarmed at the time he did not dare approach any nearer than a hundred yards, so we shall never know for certain whether the sleeping giant was a panda or not.

At last, after nearly fifty years of frustration for panda-seekers, another naturalist, like Père David, held a giant panda in his arms. But there was a difference – this young animal was alive. The lucky zoologist was a German called Hugo Weigold, a member of the Stoetzner expedition to West China and Eastern Tibet that took place during World War I. His personal attempts at panda hunting yielded nothing, although being an athletic person he took part in a number of strenuous native hunts. The technique used was to put dogs on to a fresh trail and then follow their lead at top speed, hoping to catch up with the animal and shoot it. The nearest Weigold came to seeing his quarry was a flurry of waving branches as the animal fled from its pursuers. None the less, he was given an opportunity to study a giant panda in the flesh in its homeland.

While in the province of Wassu, east of the Min River, in 1916, he bought a giant panda from the local inhabitants. Unfortunately, it was a baby 'bamboo bear', as the panda was popularly known in Germany, and despite Weigold's loving attempts to hand rear it, died after a very short time for lack of the right kind of food. This is the official story anyway, although there are rumours that the animal was killed shortly after it was brought in by Chinese hunters. In any case, this particular episode in the panda story was not generally known in America or Britain, no doubt on account of the war. Nor was the fact that the expedition secured no less than five other specimens, the skins of three adult males and one female together with their complete or incomplete skulls, and a skin minus any bones. These specimens were eventually sent to the Berlin Museum,

The mountainous countryside of Szechuan. (WWF/Kay Schaller)

although the infant panda, at least, appears to have been first displayed at Dresden where Weigold held an academic post during this period.

The Stoetzner expedition proved conclusively that the giant panda was by no means extinct, as certain scientists were beginning to fear. It still survived in the remote Hsifan Mountains, if nowhere else. For the big game hunters, in particular, it remained a supreme challenge, for as yet no westerner had experienced the thrill of personally shooting one. All past experiences had shown that this rare and beautiful Chinese prey was incredibly difficult to locate in the flesh, but soon the chase was on again.

Undaunted by the problems involved, brothers Colonel Theodore and Kermit Roosevelt, sons of the famous American President and ardent big game hunter Teddy Roosevelt, laid a daring plan. They would undertake a hunting expedition to Indo-China and West China proper with the killing of a giant panda as their main goal. Indeed, they swore that they would not return home until they had shot a panda. Since it was led by two such prominent Americans, the Roosevelt Expedition was naturally widely publicized and the world waited with eager anticipation to see whether they would fulfil their boast.

Before setting off for the East in 1928, the Roosevelts consulted experts and gleaned every scrap of information available about the special characteristics and likely whereabouts of the giant panda. In so far as possible, nothing was left to chance. The expedition had sound backing, for it was sponsored by the Chicago Field Museum of Natural History and financed by William V. Kelly, one of the Museum's patrons. The members of the party were selected with great care and included Suydam Cutting, the Tibetan explorer, and Jack Young, a New York born Chinese big game hunter, who we shall meet again later in our story. Only one real problem remained. What was to be done if only one giant panda presented itself as a target? This the Roosevelts solved by agreeing in advance that if one of them sighted the beast both brothers would fire simultaneously so that they might share the unique honour of being the first white man to kill a giant panda.

When the expedition arrived at its destination, the rugged mountains of the lonely borderland between China and Tibet, it found the provinces of Yunnan and Szechuan devastated by bandits and terrorized in particular by an outlaw leader named Chang Chi Pa, the 'stutterer'. This ex-muleteer had a sinister reputation for cruelty and had recently tortured a lama by suspending him from a tree by his thumbs and weighting his feet with rocks. Apart from such perils, the country itself presented other hazards from the hunter's point of view. Kermit Roosevelt wrote later: 'The parts of Yunnan and Szechuan through which we passed can by no stretch of the imagination be termed a big game paradise. It is no country for the inexperienced hunter nor for one who wishes to secure a large bag without undue expenditure of time and effort.'

The giant panda was, of course, the first prize which this wild terrain had to offer, if only it were possible to find one. One obvious way to go about this was to question the local inhabitants, but as Kermit Roosevelt lamented: 'Native information required careful checking, for even after a detailed description of the animal, accompanied by a showing of a plate depicting it, we could not rely on a native's word as to its presence in a district. Sometimes this was due to very hazy notions of coloration and the assumption that the white crescent on the black bear's chest entitled it to be called a bei-shung. At other times misinformation was wilful, whether with the common impulse to give pleasant and agreeable news or because the native counted on earning some money as guide before his deception would be discovered.'

Given this situation, the members of the American expedition came to mistrust all local information and to rely on more concrete evidence for guidance in their search. Secretive though it might be, the giant panda invariably left behind obvious clues in the shape of copious droppings that could easily be identified owing to the animal's unusual diet of bamboo shoots and stalks. Using such signs, the party first came across indubitable evidence of its quarry in Moupin country in Szechuan. It was now March and the mountains were covered with deep snow so that the animal's tracks also betrayed its former presence. The Roosevelts were convinced that given a good pack of bear hounds, of the type available in the United States, the coveted giant panda would be within their grasp. Unfortunately all they managed to muster in the way of canine support was a group of small wiry local dogs each accompanied by its master. These dogs proved a distinct disappointment for 'their sense of smell was quite evidently only fair, and we felt that their value lay in perhaps startling an animal, and driving him up a tree'. The odds against their being able to shoot a giant panda under these conditions seemed too great and so the Roosevelts decided to try their luck elsewhere.

Despite warnings of danger from the Chinese authorities and Western missions, the intrepid hunters ventured into Lololand, still an almost legendary district in those days. But instead of being murdered or enslaved by these intriguing people, after an initial period of coolness and veiled suspicion, they received hospitality and help. The Lolos said that they knew of the giant panda but it was extremely rare. They themselves only killed the animal to protect their beehives, which it raided occasionally, but in general regarded it as a semi-divinity.

Slender as its chances seemed, the party did not give up hope and soon its optimism was rewarded. The Roosevelts described the ultimate triumph in their book *Trailing the Giant Panda*, which was published in New York in 1929. 'On the morning of the 13th April we came upon giant panda tracks in the snow near Yehli, south of Tchienlu in the Hsifan Mountains. The animal had evidently passed a goodish while before the snow ceased falling, but some sign that one of the Lolos found proved to be recent enough to thoroughly arouse all four natives ... We had been following the trail for two-and-a-half hours when we came to a more open jungle. Unexpectedly close I heard a clicking chirp. One of the Lolo hunters darted forward. He had not gone forty yards before he turned back to eagerly motion to us to hurry. As I gained his side he pointed to a giant spruce thirty yards away. The bole was hollowed, and from it emerged the head and forequarters of a bei-shung. He looked sleepily from side to side as he sauntered forth and walked slowly away into the bamboos. As soon as Ted came up we fired simultaneously at the outline of the disappearing panda. Both shots took effect. He was a splendid old male, the first that the Lolos had any record of as being killed in this Yehli region. Our great good fortune could only with much effort be credited. After holding aloof, the Hunting Gods had turned about and brewed the unusual chain of circumstances that alone could enable us to shoot a giant panda, trailing him without dogs and with the crowning bit of luck that permitted us to fire jointly.'

News of the death of this inoffensive panda, so rudely interrupted at his siesta, flashed around the world. At the time the killing was regarded as a splendid feather in the sporting Roosevelts' cap, although Kermit Roosevelt himself admitted that the animal had put up no resistance. In a scientific article published a year after his book and illustrated by a plate showing a remarkably sombre and surly looking beast, he says that: 'The giant panda, from all we could learn is not a savage animal. After the shooting, our Kashmir shikarries remarked that he was a sahib, a gentleman, for when hit he had remained silent, and had not called out as does a bear.' Equally he had no qualms about acknowledging that the animal was extremely rare and, strange as it may seem to us today with our great preoccupation with the problem of animal conservation, he felt that this only added to the expedition's achievement.

When the success of the Kelly-Roosevelt expedition was announced everyone was delighted, including the zoologists, who felt that this was a definite contribution to scientific knowledge. They were still worried about how the giant panda should be classified taxonomically. For instance, when one of the Roosevelt brothers had sought the advice of Royal Pocock, a former superintendent of the London Zoo, before setting off for China, the Englishman had begged him to try and obtain a certain anatomical structure, if he did shoot one, 'to settle finally the point at issue in its classification'. Pocock was anxious to show that the giant panda was definitely related to the lesser panda and not to the bear or the raccoon family. The vital piece of evidence which interested him so much was apparently the giant panda's genitals, although he is rather coy on this subject. Roosevelt did not disappoint him for, as Pocock explained some time later, 'On his return to London, he told me how he had shot a specimen, skinned it, took such parts as were wanted for mounting for the Chicago Museum, and made his way back to camp, his attendants carrying the spoils, but forgot all about my request. Just however, as he was settling down for the night, the recollection of it flashed across his mind; and, fearing lest jungle scavengers should destroy what was left of the carcass before daylight, he roused a couple of his men and, tired as he was, retraced his steps to the spot by lantern light and recovered the "missing link".'

The skin of the Roosevelts' fully grown male panda was sent back to the United States with another specimen which the expedition obtained from local hunters, to be stuffed and displayed with pride in the Field Museum. Chicago's panda exhibit aroused the envy of other American museums and produced a rash of explorers all anxious to emulate the Roosevelts' example. The Philadelphia Academy of Natural Sciences, determined that the second giant panda to be killed by westerners should end up in its own exhibition halls, prepared a full-scale expedition to Western Szechuan organized and led by the young American, Brooke Dolan. Ironically it was a foreign member of this expedition, Ernst Schaefer, a young German naturalist, who accounted for the next giant panda. He shot a young female that was little more than a baby on the 13th May 1931 at Shen-wei in Wassuland. In addition Brooke Dolan and his companions acquired three adult specimens from the local inhabitants. One of these was donated to the Metropolitan Museum of Natural History at Nanking, while the other two, together with Schaefer's infant giant panda were mounted in a fine family group set in naturalistic surroundings in the Free Natural History Museum at Philadelphia.

So far three westerners had killed one adult and one juvenile giant panda. Not every expedition that went to China to search for the animal, however, was rewarded with a personal success in this way. For instance, Floyd Tangier Smith, a colourful character who was later to play a major role in the pursuit of the live giant panda, apparently failed to qualify as the fourth panda slayer. He led the Marshall Field Zoological Expedition to South-east Asia from 1930 to 1932, at the same time that the Brooke Dolan expedition was in action but, as far as we know, Tangier Smith had to be content with providing his sponsors in Chicago with two more specimens secured through Chinese hunters to enhance the Roosevelt group already displayed there. As an official collector for this particular museum Tangier Smith became entrenched as a familiar landmark of panda country which few subsequent expeditions failed to miss. Meanwhile Jack Young, who, as we have already mentioned, played a supporting role in the Roosevelt expedition of 1928, shortly afterwards organized his own quest to the same regions and returned with two skins complete with skulls. One of these was donated to the Shanghai Museum and the other went to the American Museum of Natural History in New York. Claims have been made that both Floyd Tangier Smith and Jack Young actually shot giant pandas themselves, but there seems to be no conclusive evidence of this.

The great American natural history institutions vied with one another to obtain giant pandas and, once the ice had been broken with respect to panda-shooting priorities, the manner in which their specimens were obtained seemed less important than the numbers involved. The United States National Museum in Washington had found a reliable panda purveyor in Dr David Crockett Graham, a missionary at the West China Union University. Although he apparently never spilled a drop of panda blood in his life, he took full advantage of his favourable on-the-spot position to purchase specimens from local hunters. Between the years

1929 and 1942 he provided Washington with no less than fifteen skins and skeletons.

Yet there was a certain prestige attached to a museum sponsoring its own collecting trip, and one expedition after another departed hastily for China, each with its sights set upon the giant panda. As a result, these hunting parties began to overlap with increasing frequency. In 1934, it was reported that Brooke Dolan and Ernst Schaefer were off once again, convinced that they now knew the vital secret of successful panda shooting. It was their belief that, rather than look for the animal on the ground, where it was virtually invisible in the jungle of bamboo and rhododendron, the hunter should concentrate on scanning the trees. When asleep, or sunbathing in the fork of a tree, the giant panda was a comparatively conspicuous target. These underhand tactics do not seem to have stood them in good stead and their expedition faded into oblivion as far as the story of the panda killers is concerned.

It was yet another American expedition that chalked up the third giant panda to fall to western guns. In 1934 Dean Sage, accompanied by his wife Anne, T. Donald Carter and William G. Sheldon, departed for the highlands of Szechuan province in search of unusual game. The wild blue sheep or bharal was one of their goals and they managed to shoot four of

Dean Sage (left), Anne Sage and William Sheldon

these before the fogs of October defeated them. But as Sage wrote later:
'There were other and more exciting game to wet our appetites, namely
the giant panda . . . This rare and little known animal inhabits the dense
bamboo jungles . . . To the best of our knowledge, only two giant pandas
have ever been shot by white men. The spectacular appearance of this
creature, his scarcity, and the extreme difficulty of hunting him on the
rugged and treacherous bamboo-covered slopes; all these factors made
him a prize for which we aspired with the keenest enthusiasm.'

The party, therefore, made its way northward to panda territory and
came to the valley of Cheng Wai, where it was rewarded with the first
definite reports of the presence of the animal in the shape of two bei-
shung skins discovered in a farmer's house. The quest was really on. Dean
Sage described the dramatic events that followed: 'Day after day we
climbed the bamboo ridge of Cheng Wai and Mao Mo Gou, in the first of
our optimism confident of success, and as time went on less confident but
ever hopeful.' The months passed, and although the expedition amassed
a formidable collection of bird and mammal skins for the American
Museum of Natural History, by December 1934, they had still failed to
achieve their main objective. As Donald Carter expressed it, this was 'to
secure the animals and necessary accessories for a proposed giant panda
group'. It sounded prosaic enough when put in this way. Panda signs in
the shape of chewed ends of bamboo and droppings were plentiful and
the Americans even managed to buy a skin from a Chinese hunter, but
their own endeavours yielded absolutely nothing. Yet the effort required
was enormous. Dean Sage wrote: 'It was hard work climbing the
mountains, thrashing through snow and creeping over ice-covered ledges.
We set spear traps; we searched acres and acres of bamboo-covered slopes
with our field glasses, looking for a tell-tale white spot. We hunted with
dogs. Unreliable curs that would run anything from a deer to a pheasant,
they were a sore trial to our patience.'

By early December the quest was virtually over. Mrs Sage was lame in
her game knee and Donald Carter had gone on to Tsaopo, the first step of
their homeward journey, to pack skins left there. Only one day's hunting
remained, and Dean Sage and William Sheldon decided to make the most
of it. They had in the meantime acquired a vicious dog which was
reputedly ready to tackle anything and, it was hoped, fierce enough to
hold and worry a giant panda. Encouraged by this and a panda trail discovered the previous day, they determined to make one final all-out
effort. So the two Americans accompanied by four Chinese hunters and
their dogs, including the new savage one, set out early on the morning of
8th December.

They combed the vertical planes of bamboo jungle and found a panda track that at first appeared to be only two to three days old. But by one o'clock the party was dispirited. The dogs showed little interest in the trail and it looked as though this their last excursion would be as fruitless as all the previous attempts. Since there seemed to be nothing to lose, the dogs were unleashed to range about for a while in the hope that they might pick up the scent. The rest of the hunters disappeared ahead of Dean Sage and his gun-bearer Wong. Sage climbed laboriously up on to a ledge and was resting disconsolately against a spruce tree when he noticed William Sheldon 50 yards above him. Suddenly the dogs gave tongue and he heard the unmistakable sound of crashing bamboo. Wong said the single word 'Beishung!'

How did the leader of the expedition feel now that the moment of truth was imminent? This is the way Dean Sage recorded his emotions in his diary: 'Up the ravine came the dogs, their barking growing steadily louder, and the bamboos crackling at a great rate. Suddenly, I heard the deep angry growl of a large animal, and I began to get really excited. And then – as if in a dream – I saw a giant panda coming through the bamboos about sixty yards away from me. He was heading straight up the ravine with the dogs at his heels. I fired but missed. The panda made a right angle turn and came straight for the ledge I was standing on. I fired again.

'He came right on, not running – walking rapidly is the only way to describe it. His head hung low and swayed from side to side. His tongue was out, and he was panting. He appeared to be looking at the ground and apparently did not see me at all. I frantically worked the bolt of my rifle and snapped the hammer on an empty chamber. In a daze thoughts flashed through my mind: "No more bullets; what'll I do? He's only twenty feet away, now fifteen, he's coming straight at me. Can I kill him with the butt of my rifle?" I felt a cartridge thrust into my hand. Wong had seen my predicament . . . I jammed it into my gun and fired it into the bei-shung's fur. He was less than ten feet from me! At the same moment Bill shot from above, and the animal, struck by our bullets, rolled over and over down the slope and came to stop against a tree fifty yards below.

'We had killed a giant panda.'

Once again, as in the case of the Roosevelt brothers, two American hunters had killed a giant panda between them. Their jubilation after the event is also recorded in Dean Sage's diary: 'It was, of course, absolutely fantastic and utterly incredible that I had seen and shot a Giant Panda, that almost fabulous animal. But I am forgetting the rest of the story. Bill came flying down the mountain in a frenzy. I had forgotten him completely! I found he had been shooting at the panda from above! We both practically had hysterics on the spot, and so did the men. We fired all the rest of our bullets in the air, jumped around like loons and screamed ourselves hoarse. It appeared now that Wong had fired two barrels of ball from my shotgun and so believed he had taken part in the killing, but we never found any evidence to confirm this. However, every one was delighted, so it did not matter much.'

Before beginning the triumphal procession back to camp, the Americans examined the 'most coveted trophy' that China had to offer the zoological world. The slaughtered panda, just under 5 feet in length and weighing about 225 pounds, proved to be an old female who looked as if she were a nursing mother. Within an hour-and-a-half the body had been skinned and her skeleton and viscera removed. Such as remained of her carcass was then abandoned. The vital portions of the animal's anatomy were taken back to the American Museum of Natural History and the expedition gloried in the fact that their mission was completed successfully. Not only had two members of the party achieved the honour of becoming joint third on the official list of western panda-slayers but, for the first time, scientists were provided with the opportunity to study the internal anatomy of the animal.

As we have seen, by the end of 1934 one European and four Americans had personally participated in the shooting of three giant pandas. Theodore and Kermit Roosevelt had accounted for one adult male, Ernst Schaefer, the German zoologist, for a baby, and Dean Sage and William Sheldon for an elderly nursing female. Then, in 1935, Britain entered the panda-killing race when Captain H. C. Brocklehurst shot one or, according to some authorities, two. He was a former game warden in the Sudan who undertook a solitary expedition to Wassuland and while there shot a fully grown adult male, so officially becoming the sixth Westerner to kill a giant panda. His specimen was duly mounted and caused a considerable sensation when displayed at the Big Game Exhibition held in Berlin in 1937.

Given the very great efforts involved, the total bag of giant pandas seems remarkably low. In fact, compared with the wholesale destruction of orang-utans and other rare animals that has occurred once the West began to take an interest in them, it seems almost insignificant. Even when we take into consideration the encouragement given to local Chinese hunters by the demands from panda-hungry museums, the black-and-white giant seems to have eluded its pursuers with remarkable success. Such giant panda victims as were claimed during the course of all this feverish activity did benefit zoology to some extent, for thanks to the expeditions of the late twenties and early thirties a little more was now known about the animal's distribution, habits and anatomy. But even though it could now be viewed in a state of suspended animation in many of the world's larger museums, the giant panda still remained an oriental enigma and perhaps the most tantalizing challenge presented to man by the whole of the animal kingdom.

CHAPTER 4

the panda pursued

While the trophy-hunters and explorers, apparently quite uninhibited by the rarity of the giant panda or the discomfort and difficulties of hunting in panda country, attempted to satisfy the clamorous demand for dead specimens from the museums of America and, to a lesser extent, Europe, more far-seeing and ambitious hunters nursed their dreams of capturing the coveted prize alive. Such a quest would be a gamble, a shot in the dark, but the impact that a real live black-and-white teddy bear would produce on the now panda-conscious West seemed, to two men at least, to justify the financial risk. Both were Americans, and their story and its sequel appear to spring straight from the pages of a Hollywood script.

The first of the two men we have already mentioned. He was the animal collector with the colourful name of Floyd Tangier Smith who had led the Marshall Field Expedition in 1930-2. Around about 1934 he was reported to be making urgent attempts to be the first to succeed with a live capture. A Shanghai resident, he had been a banker in the Orient, had then turned to big game hunting, and finally to collecting. By 1934 he was already in his early fifties and had acquired considerable knowledge of panda country. He knew the local inhabitants well and had organized them to assist him in his exploits. Despite this, he had so far failed.

While Tangier Smith's native hunters were combing the remote bamboo mountain forests, another American was laying plans in New York. In the summer of 1934, William Harvest Harkness, Jnr, was making preparations to provide the Bronx Zoo with a living panda. He had already caused a great stir by catching several live Komodo dragons for them – spectacular giant monitor lizards from small islands in the middle of the then Dutch East Indies – and delivering them safely in May of that year. In the early autumn, accompanied by four strapping young men in whose company, it was said, he resembled a terrier amongst a bevy of Great Danes, he set sail for the East again on an even more exciting quest.

We know comparatively little about William Harkness except that he had some zoological qualifications and a long-standing yen for travel and

Tangier Smith (left)
with Donald Carter

adventure in faraway places. For over ten years he had swopped explorers' books, stories and schemes with a striking, dark-haired, New York dress designer who, in a frantic last-minute ceremony, became Mrs Ruth Harkness just two short weeks before he departed on the panda trail. In order to avoid embarrassing incidents in an otherwise all-male expedition, the bride was left behind in America, consoled only by the thought that perhaps one day she would be able to accompany her husband on a future trip. As it happened, she was destined to be disappointed.

After a series of lively and much-reported misadventures in the Celebes Sea and Borneo, the William Harkness expedition reached Shanghai late in January 1935. By this time, only two of the original party remained and, when his last companion was then recalled to New York, Harkness was left completely alone. During the months that followed, everything went wrong. Frustrations, delays and disasters mounted up until, in February 1936, Harkness lay dead in Shanghai, apparently never having set eyes on the elusive panda.

From various sources Ruth Harkness later pieced together as best she could the course of events during her husband's thirteen-month stay in China. It seems that he began by teaming up with a young Englishman who, like himself, had an urge to travel into remote corners of the world, and another man that she describes only by his nickname of 'Zoology Jones'. 'Zoology', according to her, was an unsuccessful soldier-of-fortune in his fifties, who had hunted in panda country for nearly twenty years, and who had acquired several panda skins from native hunters, but had never encountered the living animal. Although Mrs Harkness never once mentions the older man's real name, it is almost certain that 'Zoology Jones' is none other than Tangier Smith. Not only was he the right age, with the right background, but, as the Shanghai expert on pandas, he was the obvious person for the stranded Harkness to contact. Furthermore, the authors Willy Ley and Herbert Wendt both refer to an association between William Harkness and Tangier Smith at the time.

Before departing on the long boat journey up the Yangtze River, Harkness attempted to obtain formal authorization for the expedition from the Academia Sinica in Nanking, the branch of the Chinese Government that controlled all educational and scientific activities and from which foreign scientists had to acquire permits. This proved to be a lengthy procedure and eventually, impatient to be on their way, the three men set off without official blessing.

They reached Szechuan Province, on the very threshold of panda country, only to be turned back at Kiating by the Chinese authorities, who refused to allow foreigners to enter what was, at that time, 'politically unstable' territory. As a result, they were forced to spend an uncomfortable summer in the intense heat of the bustling river-port of Chungking. With the arrival of autumn the three disappointed men decided to return to Shanghai to make yet another approach to the Chinese Government for official backing. Eventually, after still more delays, the long-awaited permission was forthcoming in the January of 1936. But, ironically, it came too late. William Harkness was by now a sick man and he died of some mysterious illness late in February, back in the city where he had begun his unhappy quest.

'Zoology Jones', alias Tangier Smith, had in the meantime, it seems, returned once again to panda country, and did not witness Harkness' death. Ruth Harkness writes: '"Zoology" had been up-country expecting Bill to join him at the time that Bill died. He continued the expedition half-heartedly for a time, and then finally left the funds that Bill had sent him with missionaries to pay his hunters to continue collecting.' In the spring of 1936, he must have gone again to Shanghai, for it was there, in July, that he came face to face with his late partner's widow.

On recovering from the shock of her husband's death, Ruth Harkness, much to the surprise of her sophisticated friends, had left the United States in April to 'inherit' the expedition. It was her avowed intention to complete his task and fulfil their dream of bringing home a live giant panda. She had no practical experience of animal collecting and one of her first acts on reaching Shanghai was to contact 'Zoology Jones'. He did not exactly welcome her with open arms and was as discouraging about her ideas as possible. 'No foreign woman could travel alone in that country. There were bandits; there were petty officials to stop you on one pretext or another . . . dysentry . . . The sensible thing to do, apparently, was to join forces with Zoology, who planned to go up in the autumn on a collecting trip.' For some reason, she resisted this offer, determined to go all out for just the panda, rather than become involved in gathering up a general collection of mammals and birds.

It is almost certain that this was not their only point of disagreement. A more serious rift appears to have developed between them. Probably it was the classic case of the experienced but disillusioned professional versus the enthusiastic novice; perhaps, too, there were financial complications. In her book *The Lady and the Panda*, written two years later, Ruth Harkness has little more to add about either 'Zoology' or his projected expedition. As we shall see later, this omission was undoubtedly far from accidental.

Towards the end of August, after making little progress with her own plans, she was considerably heartened by a phone call from the famous American-born Chinese hunter, Jack Young. He was well known for his part in many scientific expeditions into Tibet and Western China, and had accompanied the Roosevelt brothers on their epic trip in 1928. Not only did he offer to help her in any way he could, but introduced her to his younger brother, Quentin, who was to become her invaluable right-hand man in the weeks that followed.

Scarcely twenty years old, Quentin Young, a shy, tall, loose-limbed boy, was a crack-shot whose great goal in life was to shoot a giant panda for the Nanking Museum. He not only spoke good English, but also knew the Szechuanese dialect. Above all, he was not particularly concerned about financial rewards. Together Ruth Harkness and the Youngs quickly laid their plans and assembled the necessary equipment. Somewhere in Shanghai, tucked away in a garage, they unearthed some of her husband's original stores, including a collection of outsize male clothing. Woollen underwear, trousers, an old tweed jacket and even a pair of gigantic masculine boots were miraculously whittled down by ingenious Chinese tailors and shoemakers to fit Mrs Harkness' 5-foot 4-inch frame. All unwanted stores, including seven army saddles complete with blankets, halters and spurs, were auctioned to raise funds.

The American Embassy had advised her to apply to the Academia Sinica in Nanking for the usual permit, but after the delays and frustrations that her husband had encountered on a similar quest, she decided that she 'did not propose to cool her heels waiting for government red tape to be unwound'. On 26th September she and Quentin Young departed for the interior. After the tedium of the usual 1500 mile Yangtze boat trip, they reached the disembarkation port of Chungking, there to be greeted by the news that a rival expedition for live pandas had passed through ahead of them nearly three weeks before. In her book, Ruth Harkness makes no mention of the members of this other expedition, although she must surely have known who they were. Reading between the lines, it seems highly likely that the rival group was led by 'Zoology Jones', alias Tangier Smith. He had learned of her successful negotiations just over three weeks before her actual date of departure from Shanghai. He was already preparing for an autumn trip and was no doubt in a position to move rapidly, once his mind was made up. The thought that she, despised novice, might get to panda country first and beat him to the post as the first westerner to bring a live panda out of the interior, was probably too much for him. The fact that his native hunters had been out searching for some time meant that a valuable quarry might already have been located and was simply sitting waiting to be picked up. Worse still, the hunters had been paid by the local missionaries with funds left there by him, but belonging originally to William Harkness. The situation required immediate action.

With the two rival groups converging hopefully on panda country, it was a toss-up as to who was going to win the prize. For Ruth Harkness, the overland journey of more than 300 miles was a colourful and eventful one, involving absconding, opium-addicted, Chinese porters, and an unwelcome bodyguard of sixteen tenacious soldiers. At one point, following the loss of chair-coolies, they were forced to proceed with as much dignity as possible in wheelbarrows, but this was a luxury compared with the later stages of the trek, when they had to move on foot through the bamboo thickets in the mountains.

At Wenchuan, the last outpost before the panda wilds, Quentin Young tried with little success to obtain the assistance of local hunters and porters for the last gruelling lap of the expedition. 'A certain Wang of the town came to him and offered his services. Wang, it seemed, was Zoology's hunter, and lived very nicely in the town without bothering himself much about going out to hunt. He informed Quentin that he knew that he was still being paid each month from money that had been sent to Zoology by the foreign devil's husband before he died, but that made no difference – for still more he would work for us . . . we decided that as long as we had secured porters we would continue the next morning and trust to luck to find honest and efficient hunters up in the mountains.'

However, just before they departed from Wenchuan, their breakfast in the Buddhist Ghost Temple was interrupted by an ancient, leather-faced, toothless and squint-eyed little man accompanied by two mongrel dogs be-decked with tinkling bells. His name was Lao Tsang and he claimed to be a great hunter and an influential headsman of his district. As he insisted that he knew where pandas could be found and that he could lead the party there, they hired him on the spot and, with two porters, moved off westwards. After a few days of rough climbing, Mrs Harkness was beginning to lose heart. 'Nearing the top of the ridge in the late afternoon, when I was tired enough to have burst into tears, we suddenly came on Panda sign. Pure gold couldn't have been more exciting. Carefully Yang stowed away the droppings and on we went.' But this first clue proved to be disappointing. When examined by Quentin, it was pronounced to be too old to indicate the definite presence of a giant panda.

They broke camp the following morning and made for the village of Tsaopo, in the ancient Kingdom of Wassu. There Quentin interviewed native hunters who came to offer their services and the following morning he went off exploring for three days, leaving Ruth Harkness behind. He returned with encouraging reports about the neighbouring country and by 4th November the expedition's first panda camp was established, one day's march from the village. In anticipation of the ferocious quarry they were about to encounter, Quentin Young had sent back for extra wire and ropes for the traps, a collar and chain, a big pair of iron tongs to hold the panda down with, and a fine red cock to sacrifice to the god of the mountain to ensure good hunting.

Mrs Harkness stayed at the base camp and prepared to settle down for a month or six weeks, while Quentin established a camp for himself higher in the mountains and a third scout camp. Within a few days Quentin was back, firing his gun in high spirits. Everything was going splendidly and Mrs Harkness was to join him at his camp the next day. Climbing through the moist landscape, past bamboo thickets, patches of snow, and giant rhododendrons 30 to 40 feet tall, she reached Camp Two soaked to the skin on the evening of 8th November. The following day she was to make history.

In the morning they set off – Mrs Harkness, Quentin Young, old Lao Tsang and the local hunters – to inspect the traps. At the first one she saw 'A bent sapling with a wire noose in a tiny pitfall just big enough for an animal's foot. The leafy covering would give way under the weight, releasing a cleverly placed peg that held the noose; the sapling would spring up – and right then and there I had visions of an unwary Panda at our mercy.' But the going was tough and the bamboo thickets were dripping wet and slimy. After a while Mrs Harkness was 'proceeding mostly on hands and knees, and only Yang remained behind to give me an occasional lift by the seat of my pants. Without warning, a shout went up from the jungle ahead of us. I heard Lao Tsang yell, the report of his blunderbuss musket, and then Quentin's voice raised in rapid and imperious Chinese. Falling, stumbling, or being dragged by Yang, we

*The route taken by the
Ruth Harkness expedition*

crashed through the bamboo.'

Lao Tsang, it seemed, had seen a fully grown panda and shot at it. He and the other hunters had then rushed off after it. This made Ruth Harkness angry, as she had given strict instructions that there was to be no panda-killing while she was there (although she knew that Quentin Young was going to stay on and hunt them after she had left). On this occasion, Quentin did not join the chase, but stayed behind with Mrs Harkness. 'We listened for a moment, and went on a few yards farther where the bamboo thinned slightly, giving way to a few big trees. Quentin stopped so short that I almost fell over him. He listened intently for a split second, and then went ploughing on so rapidly I couldn't keep up with him. Dimly through the waving wet branches I saw him near a huge rotting tree. I stumbled on blindly, brushing the water from my face and eyes. Then I too stopped, frozen in my tracks. From the old dead tree came a baby's whimper. I must have been momentarily paralysed, for I didn't move until Quentin came toward me and held out his arms. There in the palms of his two hands was a squirming baby *Bei-shung*.'

This tiny creature, with its eyes still closed, was destined to become the first giant panda ever seen alive by the western world. In a few short months it was to become the most famous animal of the twentieth century. As Mrs Harkness held it in her arms for the first time, she records simply that, 'That little black-and-white ball nuzzled my jacket, and suddenly, with the sureness of age-old instinct, went straight to my breast'.

There then began a frantic dash back to the base camp, where milk and nursing bottles were packed away. Quentin carried the baby panda tucked in between his inner and outer shirt as they slithered down the steep mountain slopes. At the camp all went well and they celebrated while the baby fed from its bottle. The animal weighed less than 3 pounds and was thought to be no more than ten days old. Ruth Harkness named it after Jack Young's wife, Su-Lin, whose name was best translated as 'a little bit of something very cute'. (Although it was found, on postmortem, to be a male, throughout its short life the animal was thought to be a female.)

Great care was taken to supply the young panda with a snug cradle, their shirts, sweaters and towels being torn up to provide the necessary bedding. During these parental duties, porters arrived, bedraggled and weary, carrying heavy tongs, a stout collar, chains and padlocks, and a large red, sacrificial cock. Their comments on seeing the exact size of the captive panda are not recorded. Out of courtesy, a sacrificial ceremony was arranged and, by the light of flares, the unfortunate cockerel was stabbed through the neck three times, paper money was burned, wine poured on the earth, and fire-crackers let off. As an impromptu embellishment to the ceremony, Mrs Harkness fired a revolver three times in the air.

She was now faced with the problem of getting Su-Lin back to the United States. Quentin accompanied her back to Chengtu and then returned to his promised reward of panda hunting in the hills. (In fact he not only killed one for the Nanking Museum, but a second one as well.) Su-Lin was proving an exhausting infant in more ways than one. Not only was there the problem of round-the-clock feeding, but also the perpetual bombardment of queries from the curious and fascinated Chinese. At Chengtu special arrangements were made for the panda to travel to Shanghai by air. After the overland journey from the mountains this was a great luxury and Mrs Harkness could at last relax, if only momentarily. As she flew east to the coast, taking 'a little bit of something very cute' with her, she was leaving behind her, under the gnarled roots of a great rhododendron tree in the mountains, the high price she had paid for it: a small sealed cardboard box containing her husband's ashes, that she had carried with her all the way in a steel cash-box to the panda country that he never saw.

At Shanghai airport the little woven bamboo basket containing Su-Lin was rushed to a waiting car to avoid the crowd of newspaper photographers and reporters, alerted by their agents in Chengtu. There followed days of chaos and confusion during which attempts were made to obtain permission to export the panda to America. The earliest boat was the *Empress of Russia* sailing on 27th November. Passages were booked and all went well until the very last minute. Then, after boarding the tender to go out to the ship, she was stopped by customs officials and brought back. She had obtained no export permit and had paid no export tax. While the *Empress of Russia* sailed, she slept with Su-Lin on a bench in the Shanghai customs sheds. The following day was a nightmare of officialdom and panda husbandry mixed together, and the classic panda pun was printed in a newspaper for the first of many times: 'Panda-monium in Shanghai Customs House'.

Garbled newspaper reports of the situation began to appear, including wild guesses at the value of the panda. One report estimated the figure at 25,000 dollars, which did nothing to ease the export situation. Influential Americans in Shanghai rallied round, however, and on 2nd December the now voiceless Ruth Harkness and the baby panda sailed at last for the United States on the *President McKinley*, complete with an export tax receipt, an export permit and an animal passage voucher reading 'One Dog, $20.00'. The panda epoch was about to begin.

During her five crowded months in China, Ruth Harkness had not only achieved her goal and completed the work her husband began, but she had also pipped at the post the professional animal collector 'Zoology Jones', alias Tangier Smith. In her book *The Lady and the Panda*, she makes no mention of his activities or movements after she has acquired her panda. All we hear is that one of his native hunters (Wang) at Wenchuan tried to incite the soldiers in the town to prevent her from leaving with Su-Lin. Beyond this, nothing.

How is one to interpret this? What exactly was going on in the rival camp? Was the other expedition hot on the panda trail, or did Smith-Jones simply fade from the picture, as Mrs Harkness would have us believe? There are some scattered clues that throw a strange, if somewhat multi-coloured light on the affair. They differ in certain vital respects, but nearly all agree on one intriguing point, namely that Mrs Harkness was not, after all, the only successful panda captor in 1936. According to several reports, she was not even the first, that honour belonging in fact to Floyd Tangier Smith.

The only way to assess the validity of these statements is to examine them in turn. Taking the wildest one first, Herbert Wendt in *Out of Noah's Ark* claims that, far from being a dismal failure, the original William Harkness-Tangier Smith expedition succeeded in catching a young giant panda in 1936. They are supposed to have ear-marked it for the London Zoo, but 'It breathed its last in Singapore. And William Harkness died about the same time in Shanghai.' This seems highly improbable, as Harkness died in February and the expedition had, reportedly, more or less petered out towards the end of 1935.

In *Dragons in Amber*, Willy Ley makes a similar statement, but gives all the credit for the first panda capture to Tangier Smith: 'Floyd T. Smith seemed to be the first to succeed. In 1936 he captured a giant panda which was destined for the London Zoological Garden. But the specimen died in Singapore.' With no mention of William Harkness, this report could refer to any point in 1936 and could easily relate to a later expedition made by Tangier Smith alone. It could, in fact, relate to the mysterious 'rival expedition' that was three weeks ahead of Ruth Harkness at Chengtu, on the way to the mountains. If Tangier Smith had been successful on that trip and hustled a living panda hurriedly back to the coast, he might well have done so with some degree of secrecy, if only because his hunters were still being financed with William Harkness' funds, thus giving Ruth some claim to the spoils. This could also have been the reason for the animal being sent off to London, rather than New York, his original zoo contact in the West.

The plot thickens with a newspaper report from Singapore in which secrecy features again. S. H. Benson, writing in the *Scottish Field* in 1942 recalls that 'about 1936' a friend in Singapore sent him a cutting from a Singapore paper in which banner headlines declared that two pandas had been caught for the London Zoo by Tangier Smith. The article reads: 'Asia's rarest animal, a giant panda, on its way to London Zoo, died between Hong Kong and Shanghai on the French Liner *Andre Lebon*. Only the third animal of its type to be caught alive, it joined the vessel at Shanghai. The heavier of the two caught, which weighed 200 lb., died, but the other weighing about 100 lb., and carefully dyed to appear like a brown bear in order not to attract attention, was safely taken to Shanghai . . .'

If we are to believe this report, the unhappy Tangier Smith must have made a desperate attempt to beat Ruth Harkness to it by the ingenious method of disguising his animal as a young bear and thus getting it through the customs without official delays. If the date, 1936, is accepted, then he must almost certainly have won the race, as regards being the first person to take a living panda out of China, as she did not finally get away until December. (Weigold was, of course, the first occidental to hold a living giant panda, but his short-lived encounter seems to have been over-looked in all accounts of 'who was first'.) The situation in Shanghai, with the two successful panda-hunters both jealously guarding their prizes and frantically trying to board ship for the West, must have been bizarre enough, but the ultimate confusion that would have arisen if Tangier Smith's brown-stained protégé had survived the voyage to England is even more intriguing to contemplate. Presumably both the New York and the London Zoo would have been offered the 'very first' giant panda ever to leave the Orient. If only this had happened, a great deal would undoubtedly have been forced into the open and we would now be able to tell the whole story in much more detail.

An interesting point in the Singapore statement is that the dyed panda was the third to have been taken alive. As the original Weigold panda was so little known, this indicates that Su-Lin, as well as Tangier Smith's bigger one, had already been caught and implies that Ruth Harkness was at least first with the capture itself. If we believe a report in the *China Journal* by Arthur Sowerby she was also first to export a panda, despite the rumours of Tangier Smith's 1936 success. He states that 'Mr Smith . . . with the help of his native hunters, succeeded in the spring of 1937 in securing two adult giant pandas, one a fully adult male weighing, it was said, about 400 lbs., the other, an adult female, weighing about 200 lbs. Of these the male died at Chungking on the Upper Yangtze from blood-poisoning through an injury to its foot when it was trapped. The other died on the voyage from Shanghai to London before it reached Singapore, presumably from the excessive heat of the Tropics.'

This report tallies in most ways with the previous one, except for the date and the weight of the animals. If Sowerby is correct, then Mrs Harkness was already safely in America some months before Tangier Smith reaped his short-lived reward. Unfortunately Sowerby's writings show considerable bias in Ruth Harkness' favour and, like her book, reduce to a minimum any mention of Tangier Smith's activities, so that they are not entirely above suspicion.

Whatever the exact dates were, it seems certain that Tangier Smith did capture two pandas at some point before the summer of 1937. Or was it three? Let him speak for himself. Later in 1937 he came to England and broadcast on the B.B.C. on this topic. His comments were as follows:

'It has been my great good fortune to have been the active agent in effecting the capture of the only three giant pandas that have ever been taken alive. That has been possible only after some several years of careful study of the animal's habits and the systematic organization of the inhabitants in a certain area. My central collecting headquarters are at a village called Chaopo . . . The first specimen thus secured – the baby panda recently sold to Chicago – it was not my privilege to take home myself. It had been brought into Chaopo at a time when I was absent some several days before a party of travellers pitched their camp about fifteen miles up the valley from Chaopo, and it was sold to them for a tempting cash price. There were more than forty other animals and birds collected in the camp at the same time, but nothing but the panda was purchased by the visitors, and I brought most of the others with me on this trip to England . . . I have not yet finished with the business of capturing pandas. I expect to return to China in the very near future, and when I do it will be to go all out for bigger and better pandas.'

Alongside this statement, the other discrepancies fade into insignificance. We are now dealing with a major falsification. But whose? Was Ruth Harkness lying when she wrote her account of the dramatic capture of Su-Lin? Had she, in reality, bought it knowingly from Tangier Smith's collecting centre and then fled for the coast? Or was Tangier Smith lying, trying to distort the whole situation to save his professional face?

Most certainly, the baby panda that Tangier Smith refers to was Su-Lin, Chicago being that animal's ultimate destination as we shall see in the next chapter. Also Ruth Harkness' village of Tsaopo was without doubt Tangier Smith's village of Chaopo (the difference being merely one of spelling, not pronunciation). The mystery, therefore, surrounds the action that took place at that spot in the autumn of 1936. Re-reading the Harkness account, there are several strange features that make one wonder. When so many experts had trailed the panda without success, it was very odd that, within days, a complete novice could find a young one. Tangier Smith, on the other hand, had had hunters out working for months, if not years, and if anyone was likely to have located one, it was he. According to another report altogether, Tangier Smith had 'had his eye on Su-Lin for a long time and had just waited for her to grow a little older'. As the animal's eyes were still shut and it only weighed 2 or 3 pounds, the 'long time' he had been watching it could not have been so very long.

What can one possibly conclude from all this? Was Ruth Harkness a courageous, dedicated widow desperately completing her late husband's unfinished business, or an imaginative, scheming liar? Was Tangier Smith an honest, victimized professional, or was he a neurotic, embittered man, deliberately falsifying the evidence to save his pride? Perhaps there is yet another answer. Perhaps they were both innocent, but were thrown into conflict by the dishonesty of certain of their companions. Quentin Young and his hunters, for example, had ample opportunity to buy the information concerning Su-Lin's whereabouts from Tangier Smith's hired men. They could even have bought the animal itself and 'planted' it in the old dead tree. Alternatively Tangier Smith's Wenchuan hunter, Wang, could have lied to his employer, inventing the story of Su-Lin's sale to cover his shame at allowing newcomers to find the panda so near to his supposedly well-watched territory.

Unless some new evidence comes to light, we shall never know the true story. All we can be sure of is that a baby panda was brought out of the Orient just before Christmas 1936 and that it caught the imagination of the whole western world. But the cost was high. Already it had claimed the life of William Harkness, turned two remarkable explorers against one another, and forced someone into uttering deliberate and serious falsehoods. But these problems and quarrels must now be allowed to fade into the mists of the cold mountain forests of Szechuan, for aboard the *President McKinley* a Very Important Panda was rapidly approaching America. Su-Lin was about to arrive at San Francisco.

CHAPTER 5

pandas in america

On 18th December 1936, the western world encountered for the very first time a living giant panda. For Ruth Harkness the experience was even more exhausting and chaotic than the departure from China; 'The final consensus of the press was that not since Bernard Shaw had a foreign celebrity received such a reception as Su-Lin.' Droves of reporters and newspaper photographers jostled for position. Flash bulbs exploded and people shouted. Officialdom argued and worried. For a human star this is all sweet music, but for a very young animal – and Su-Lin's first milk tooth was only just breaking through as they docked in San Francisco – it can be disastrous. Ruth Harkness had to be constantly on her guard. It was as much as she could do to stop the animal being cuddled literally to death, so strong was its appeal to pent-up maternal urges.

One of the biggest problems was caused by the fact that, like Bernard Shaw, Su-Lin was a carnivore turned vegetarian. Although still subsisting entirely on baby food, the time would come when bamboo shoots would be the order of the day and Mrs Harkness had very wisely collected and brought with her some specimens of these plants from the mountains of Szechuan. It was her intention to present them to botanical experts for examination, so that the best substitute for them could be found before Su-Lin reached bamboo-munching age. Unfortunately, the United States Department of Agriculture officials had other ideas. Finally, after a great deal of controversy, it was agreed that the vital plants could be allowed into the country providing that every speck of dirt was first washed from their roots.

After various mishaps in San Francisco and considerable argument as to which airline was going to have the honour of conveying the animal across the States, Su-Lin and owner eventually managed to board an eastbound train after a wild taxi dash across the city. Two days later the whole circus was repeated in Chicago, but this time zoological experts were present in the shape of zoo director Edward Bean and his son Robert, then curator of mammals. They tried to persuade Mrs Harkness to leave

Su-Lin with them, but this only set off a new type of argument. Ruth Harkness refused to sell the animal, insisting that she would only part with it in exchange for backing for another expedition. She apparently had a horror of being called a commercial animal dealer and drew a subtle but, to her, all-important distinction between the two kinds of payment. More cynical observers pointed out that the only real difference was that backing an expedition would cost more.

Leaving a disappointed Robert Bean at the Chicago Zoo, Su-Lin journeyed on to New York and another battery of flash bulbs. Here the confusion and tension became greater still, and it began to tell on the panda itself. Su-Lin became constipated and it was obvious that the animal needed to be in expert hands. The expert hands themselves were not so sure, however. Much to Mrs Harkness' disgust, the zoo officials in New York approached the subject of the panda's acquisition with some caution. After days of public acclaim and adulation, their guarded, critical attitude came as a severe shock. Why, they wanted to know, were its back legs so much weaker than its front ones? One group of visiting officials pronounced that it must have rickets. Doubts were expressed about how long the little creature would live, after all it had been through. Then there was the question of feeding it, the difficulties of obtaining supplies of the correct bamboo, and the dangers of using diet substitutes.

Later, Ruth Harkness wrote of her exasperation and depression: 'Wherever authorities had written about rare animals, you felt that every zoological society of any note whatever was sighing for a Panda, that life would not be complete until they had one' . . . but . . . 'All seemed afraid of the risk involved in raising such a small specimen to healthy adulthood. And no one of them wanted to back me for another expedition; they offered me only a fraction of what my first one had cost. Time went on, and I became more and more discouraged . . . The whole business looked as though it were going to end in utter failure . . . Was I a little insane, or had I just imagined that bringing a live Panda to America was worth anything to this great rich country of ours? When I had sunk to the lowest point of discouragement, the only thing I could think of that I wanted to do was to pack everything up, take Su-Lin and go back to the border of Tibet. And perhaps if I'd had sufficient money, I would have done just that.' Luckily for the American public, she was running short of funds and had to stay put.

By now Su-Lin had taken on the role of a panda ambassador and was virtually changing the whole attitude of western civilization towards the species. Clearly it was unthinkable to invade the homeland of such a charming creature and gun it down as a trophy or a museum specimen. A major conversion was achieved as a result of a visit from the original panda-killers, Theodore and Kermit Roosevelt. Su-Lin won them over in a few minutes. When Theodore, sitting on the floor of Ruth Harkness' apartment, with the small animal cradled in his arms, was asked whether he would like to see it eventually mounted and added to his panda group in the Chicago Field Museum, he retorted 'I'd as soon think of mounting my own son as I would this baby.'

The Roosevelts were followed by other famous panda hunters, paying homage at Su-Lin's court. Brooke Dolan of the Philadelphia Academy of Natural Sciences paid a visit, as did Dean Sage and his wife. Like the others, Sage became an immediate convert declaring: 'Mrs Harkness, I'd never be able to shoot another Panda.'

At about this time Ruth Harkness was honoured by the New York Explorer's Club. A staunchly masculine organization, it made the first exception to its all-male rule in inviting her to be guest of honour at its 33rd annual banquet. The dinner was held at the Plaza Hotel and Su-Lin was provided with a complete suite where all the windows could be thrown open to counteract the fierce blast of New York central heating. When the meal was over, the diminutive panda was carried ceremonially into the dining hall and on to the speaker's platform where, to the delight

Su-Lin poses with her life-story. (Chicago Zool. Soc.)

of the 500 gentlemen explorers, it performed the ritual of broadcasting a few disgruntled bleats to the waiting American nation.

Despite the more ludicrous aspects of this and other such occasions, it is true to say that the growth of the panda cult surrounding Su-Lin added a very important nail to the coffin of the 'huntin' and shootin' epoch'. True, it still goes on today wherever the preferred quarry (other men) is not available. But, like war, it has lost a great deal of its glamour. Su-Lin was perhaps becoming not so much a Hairy Shirley Temple as a Furry Billy Graham.

For Ruth Harkness, however, the dilemma of what to do with a growing panda remained. In the end, fed up with the attitude of zoo officials in New York, she offered the animal to Chicago as a guest. They accepted with pleasure and Su-Lin was soon installed in the first-aid station of Brookfield Zoo, being looked after day and night by Robert Bean and his sister Mary.

The move to Chicago took place on 8th February 1937, making this the earliest date on which any zoo had housed a living giant panda. In a Chicago hotel room that night Mrs Ruth Harkness awoke at midnight to give Su-Lin the usual nightly feed, remembered sleepily that after three months of turmoil she was at last alone, and returned weeping to her bed.

Two months later, in April, the Brookfield Zoo purchased Su-Lin, or, rather, 'contributed' to Mrs Harkness' next expedition. Although she had only just recovered from the strain of the first ordeal, she was already preparing to repeat the whole process in order to acquire a mate for Su-Lin. Unfortunately she, and everyone else, still held the view that Su-Lin was a female. There was no doubt in their minds. As we have already mentioned, the post mortem eventually revealed that they had all been mistaken and she was, in fact, a he. With her newly acquired expedition funds in her bag Mrs Harkness was therefore sallying forth to secure a young male panda as a mate for a young male panda. (Although she was the first to make this mistake she was by no means the last, as we shall see later.)

With Su-Lin steadily putting on weight at a rate of 5 pounds a month and continuing to make friends and influence people, Ruth Harkness made her return journey to the bamboo forests in the Szechuan mountains. There, in Wassu country again, she trekked and trailed for three long months in search of a male panda. She found two live cubs, but to her great disappointment they both turned out to be females. One of them, named Diana, she brought successfully back to Chicago where she was able to introduce it to Su-Lin.

Although Diana had been caught in 1937, this panda did not reach Chicago Zoo until 18th February 1938. Su-Lin's weight in the meantime

Ruth Harkness introduces Diana (foreground) to Su-Lin at Brookfield Zoo

had shot up from 14 pounds to over 100 pounds, and when the two were put together the pioneer panda dwarfed the new arrival. Eventually, it was hoped, they would settle down quietly together, as Diana gradually caught up with the bulky Su-Lin. But unhappily in six short weeks Su-Lin was dead. The post mortem revealed that a piece of wood had become lodged in the animal's throat. The cause of death was not a hopeless, inevitably lethal disease, just a freak accident. As if this were not bad enough, the zoo officials also learned from the dissection that, instead of two females, they had had a potential breeding pair. But on this score at least they need not have worried for, when Diana herself succumbed on 3rd August 1942, she too proved to be a he.

Before this second sex-error was discovered, however, Mrs Harkness was already off to the mountains again to find a young male panda as a mate for the now solitary Diana, commissioned to do so once more by the Chicago Zoo authorities. She left in the spring of 1938 and arrived at Chengtu at the beginning of June. A newspaper report from there a week later stated that she was about 'to take possession of a 40-pound female panda cub captured for her by Quentin Young, a youthful Chinese-American. Young is reported to have a male panda staked, out in the

Diana in congenial surroundings at Chicago Zoo.
(Chicago Zool. Soc.)

hills.' Ironically, it then adds: 'With females in the majority, gentleman pandas are now in the heaviest demand.'

Everything appeared to be set fair for Mrs Harkness to achieve her hat-trick, but for some reason the project misfired. Presumably Young's new finds were poor specimens and died before they could be brought out of China. We can find no record of what happened to them. All we know is that by February 1939 Mrs Harkness was in London, probably on her way back to the United States.

Despite her failure on this occasion, the Chicago Zoo did manage to obtain a third specimen, and did so in a rather unusual way. In the summer of 1938 a correspondent of the Chicago *Daily News*, A. T. Steele, made a wild claim that giant pandas were now a glut on the market. From Chengtu he sent his paper a photograph of four pandas sitting on a lawn. He also wrote an article with the heading PANDAS RARE? SOMEONE WAS REALLY KIDDING. As a piece of journalism it certainly struck a new note. When readers are bombarded day after day with the rarity and value of something, a startling and provocative reporting device that is sometimes used is to slant a story completely in the opposite direction. The trick is that there must be *some* facts to support the sudden twist. A photograph of four pandas on a lawn is just enough to trigger off the great switch. On the basis of the previously stressed rarity, four is a crowd. The shock story is under way. From then on it is a case of dragging in every panda going and a few that are only rumoured to be going. With some strong phrasing to help the tale along, the readers, relieved to find a crack at last in the star image, will soon be convinced. Here are some of the things that Steele claimed:

'Unless all signs fail, the United States is about to be glutted with giant pandas. Ever since word got around that the fancy prices paid in Chicago were offered elsewhere for captive pandas, West China has been panda-conscious. The result is that more pandas, dead and alive, are brought to Chengtu than one can shake a stick at . . . Panda pelts are a drug on the market. Yesterday I was offered four, at 8 American dollars apiece, with skulls thrown in. Pandas are not rare. It was not until Mrs William Harkness came out here a couple of years ago that the mountain dwellers realized that the critters were of any use to anybody, and that they could get more fun and profit from chasing pandas than from collecting herbs or bamboo. Colorful tales have been woven for the American public about the supposed perils of panda hunting in Szechuan. As a matter of fact, the trip into the heart of the panda country from here is no more dangerous or difficult than a journey to the depths of the Wisconsin woods. The panda region . . . can be reached in two days by bus and horse – if one is in a hurry.'

Steele goes on to explain that visitors no longer bother to hunt the pandas, they simply buy them from the locals. 'The buyer getting to the hunter first with the fattest bank roll gets the panda. Giant panda prices, f.o.b. (freight on board) Chengtu, range between 25 and 180 dollars per head, although the latter is regarded locally as fabulously high.'

This shattering information naturally met with more than just a surprised whistle at the offices of the Brookfield Zoo, Chicago. They had paid out hefty sums for their two pandas, enough at least to finance two expeditions to China, and they were not unreasonably annoyed at the suggestion that they had been duped. They immediately contacted the editor of the *Daily News*, Colonel Knox, and threw down the gauntlet. If pandas were so cheap and plentiful, they argued, he would presumably be quite prepared to present them with a third one for the Chicago Zoo. He agreed and straight away cabled Steele in Chengtu, instructing him to secure a giant panda and despatch it without delay to Chicago.

The interesting fact that emerges from this incident is that, although Steele had exaggerated wildly when he used words like 'glut' and 'drug on the market', his anti-rare, anti-exotic theme was not without some foundation. This was proved by the fact that, although he could not produce a panda by return of post, he did contrive to do so eventually. The archives show that it was 17 months and 8 days after his inflammatory article that he finally managed to complete the Chicago hat-trick that Ruth Harkness had been unable to achieve.

This third panda's name was Mei-Lan, meaning 'pretty flower'. Again it was a rather unsuitable title, for like the other two, Mei-Lan was ultimately proved to be a male. As a two-month old cub it had been carried 150 miles to Chengtu by a native hunter. Once there it had spent seven months in the grounds of the West China Union University. During that time four other pandas were brought in, but only Mei-Lan and one other survived. Although it is not possible to give an accurate date of birth, it seems likely that Mei-Lan was born towards the end of 1938. It was caught early in 1939, spent the summer in Chengtu and was flown out to Hong Kong in the autumn in the care of American photographer Roy Scott. From there it sailed for San Francisco on the *President Cleveland*, arriving early in November. On the way to Chicago it stopped off for a four-day visit in Hollywood where its star status was carefully enhanced by an encounter with Dorothy Lamour and a garden party on the lawn of the Hotel Ambassador.

On 16th November it finally reached its new home, was greeted at the station by a fanfare from the Chinese Boy Scout drum corps, and met the resident panda Diana, now re-christened Mei-Mei. Mei-Lan, being nearly a year old at this point weighed about 80 pounds, but once again the newcomer was dwarfed by the resident, Mei-Mei now tipping the scales at 250 pounds.

From the beginning Mei-Lan was a sturdy, tough specimen, and went on to break all panda records for longevity in captivity (a record that lasted nearly twenty years), living contentedly at Brookfield throughout World War II and on into the fifties. The exact date of death was 5th September 1953, giving a zoo life of 13 years and 10 months and a total life span of nearly 15 years.

For their pioneer role in the panda story the Brookfield Zoo, Chicago, deserves the highest praise. It is easy to smile at their errors over the sexes of the pandas, easy, that is, for anyone who has not actually attempted to sex one. The external differences between the male and female are so subtle that, even today, errors are still being made by skilled anatomists when faced with the living animal. Had it not been for the foresight of the Chicago officials, Su-Lin might well have died in New York and such an event could easily have frightened off the zoo world and prevented them from making efforts to obtain further specimens. A great deal of our present-day knowledge of – and respect for – the giant panda would be lacking if this had been so.

New York's part in this story is harder to understand. It was for them that William Harkness had successfully acquired Komodo dragons and

Diana, re-christened Mei-Mei, settles down to life in Chicago.
(Chicago Zool. Soc.)

for them that he had set out again for panda country. It is rather surprising then that they did not snap up Su-Lin for their collection at the Bronx
Zoo. Whatever their reasons, there can be little doubt that they were
rather crestfallen when Chicago's gamble succeeded so brilliantly, for
after a while they started negotiating with China to see what could be done
for panda-less New York. It was probably the arrival of Chicago's second
panda Diana/Mei-Mei that really roused them to action because we know
that it was only a matter of a week or two after this that they began to
tackle the problem in earnest.

The initiator of the scheme that was to bring them their first captive
specimen was Dean Sage, a trustee of the New York Zoological Society.
In March 1938 he suggested to Edward Cunningham of the University
faculty that it would be mutually beneficial to the University of New York
and to the West China Union University at Chengtu if it could be
arranged for these two institutions to 'join forces in a co-operative educational venture'. Chengtu, he argued, 'was situated at the very edge of one
of the richest areas for the collection of scientific material of all sorts in
the whole world. They also had a trained staff capable of making collections. In addition, there was the valuable factor of their close and friendly
relationship with the central government, which would enable them to
export materials collected. All this work could be done by them at low
cost and the fruits of a rich and hitherto unexploited field could be made

available to scientific institutions in this country, which had neither the
financial means nor the political influence necessary for sending out
expensive expeditions ... '.

In return, New York would aid Chengtu with 'educational and scientific material such as films, technical journals, lantern slides, current scientific books, scientific instruments etc.', and the general development of
their scientific department.

To the idealists this sounded like an inspired plan for improving international goodwill and education. To the cynics it sounded like a clever
scheme for acquiring a cheap panda. When he wrote off to Chengtu
University, Dean Sage admits that 'In my letter I did not forget to
mention that the one thing I wanted first of all was a live giant panda cub,
if possible a pair of cubs, male and female.' He goes on to say that 'It had
been, ever since my return from China, my desire to obtain one of these
animals for the Zoological Society, and although efforts on my part had
thus far been unavailing, I felt that here at last was the opportunity that
would materialize.' We could perhaps feel a little more sympathy for him
in his earlier difficulties, were it not for the fact that fifteen months earlier
he had sat in Ruth Harkness' New York apartment playing with Su-Lin at
a time when she was desperately trying to find a good home for the little
animal.

Be that as it may, the Chengtu authorities welcomed the exchange
scheme and immediately sent word out to the native hunters in the hills.
Frank Dickinson, a missionary at the West China Union University was in
charge of the project, but it was his wife who made the vital contact. She
was on a sketching trip at Kwanhsien, a village about sixty miles from
Chengtu, when she was approached at her work by a Chinese woman who
told her that a baby panda had been caught somewhere further west and
was being brought into the village. Mrs Dickinson went into action, the
hunter was soon found, and before long the young panda was playing
quietly in the Dickinson's home at the University. During its three weeks
as the Dickinson family pet it acquired the nickname of Pandora. Dr Roy
C. Spooner, a colleague of Frank Dickinson's, was due for home leave
and agreed to accompany the animal to the United States. They flew to
Hong Kong in a small four-seater China National Airways plane, leaving
Chengtu on 18th May 1938, but not before a last-minute panic about
clearance papers. These were finally obtained from the Commissioner of
Education – sitting on his veranda still wearing his dressing gown – at
6 am on the actual morning of the flight. Pandora sailed for America on
the *President Cleveland* (the same ship that, the following year, was to
transport Mei-Lan to the United States), arriving at San Francisco 9th
June, where she was met by Dean Sage himself. Sage rushed her on to a

plane and had her safely in New York by the following afternoon.

And so, on 10th June 1938, New York was able to join Chicago as the second member of the highly exclusive 'zoo-panda club'. New Yorkers responded overwhelmingly and, after eight hectic weeks of Pandora, an exhausted zoo patrolman was quoted as saying 'Thirty thousand people asked me the way to the panda yesterday. Two men wanted to know where the okapi was, and a woman said she'd always wanted to see an aardvark.'

From the start Pandora had been referred to as a female and for once the identification was correct. Furthermore, when the Bronx Zoo set out to obtain a mate for her they managed to hit the right sex again. However, although they had been lucky with sexes, they were less fortunate with temperament. The new male, called Pan, weighed about 70 pounds on arrival (twice as much as Pandora when she made her debut) and was decidedly anti-social. Lee Crandall of the Bronx Zoo writes: 'Pan was unlike the other young pandas received here in that he was unfriendly, even surly, in his actions to his keepers. Although his weight increased from 72.5 pounds on arrival to 170 pounds at the time of his death on May 5th, 1940, he never adapted fully to captivity conditions.' Pan had been caught by the same Chinese skin-collector, an ex-preacher called Den Wei-han, as had found Pandora a year previously. The animal was presented to New York this time by Mrs Dean Sage, again with the help of the West China Union University, and reached the zoo on 1st May 1939. His short life span in captivity, therefore, was only one year and four days. Pandora outlived him by a year, dying of undetermined causes on 13th May 1941.

With the summer of 1941, New York found itself once again panda-less, and it remained so until the winter. On 30th December 1941, a pair of young pandas landed in New York, but they were the last to grace the Bronx Zoo and, indeed, the last to come out of China before the end of World War II. Their names, selected, as Lee Crandall put it, 'through the sometimes unfortunate medium of a public contest' were Pan-dee and Pan-dah. They were thought to be a true pair and hopes were high that, as they were fairly well matched in weight (Pan-dee 62 pounds, Pan-dah 57 pounds), they would one day breed and provide New York with a zoo-man's dream: a panda family group complete with home-grown cub. A record first breeding of this species would easily have regained the prestige which New York had lost to Chicago over the Su-Lin affair. But their luck over panda-sexing had deserted them. Pan-dee was thought to be the male and Pan-dah the female, but when they died they both turned out to be females. The external differences which the Bronx officials must have studied were obviously individual characters rather than true sexual ones.

Once again this is ample proof of the extraordinary difficulties there are in sexing this species, even when more than one animal can be examined at the same time.

With the political situation in China far from serene, the actual acquisition of Pan-dee and Pan-dah had proved to be a somewhat hazardous affair. Early in the summer of 1941 the Chinese government approached Dr David Crockett Graham of the West China Union University with a request that he should do everything in his power to secure a panda for the wife of the Chinese leader. It was Mme Chiang Kai-shek's intention to make a present of the animal to the American people in appreciation of their gifts to China through United China Relief.

Graham had played an important role in the acquisition of the previous two New York pandas, Pandora and Pan, and was the ideal person for the task. The ex-preacher Den Wei-han was contacted once again and he engaged two groups of hunters, one at Wei Chow and the other at Tsaopo. Between July and August the hunters made their first catch, but the animal fought loose and escaped. Urgent messages were sent to Dr Graham pressing him to speed up the capture. He agreed to do what he could and went himself into panda country to help, but it was summer and the Chinese farmers were more interested in their crops. Also the vegetation was so dense at this time of year that it made hunting extremely difficult.

Dr Graham gathered up Den Wei-han and together they toured the best panda centres, offering large rewards for live pandas. Seven bands of farmers stopped their work and trekked off into the hills. Eventually seventy hunters and forty dogs were out on the panda trail in seven different localities, and the biggest panda hunt in history was in progress. At Tsaopo they prayed to the hunter's god for success and a catch of three live pandas, promising him the sacrifice of a chicken and a pig if he answered their prayers. If he did not answer them, then they would whip him with sticks or throw him on the ground.

After some days Dr Graham was able to buy a cub weighing 42 pounds from a local official, a Mr Yang. He rushed back with it to Chengtu, arriving there on 30th September, although by this time he was tired, weak, and ill. A few days after his return, the hunters captured a second panda. Graham records that 'While the animal was being pursued by men and dogs, one of the hunters ran up, seized it, and overpowered it with his bare hands. His clothing was torn but otherwise he escaped without injury.' This panda, weighing nearly 60 pounds, arrived at Chengtu to join the first one on 13th October.

Graham, who was convinced that the first one was a female and the second a male, kept the 'pair' carefully at his home in Chengtu for a month while waiting for them to be collected. During this time his house was virtually a panda 'court', with a daily stream of visitors, including the Chinese governors of the provinces of Szechuan, Fukien and Shansi.

As an honoured gift from China to America, the two pandas were to be collected in person by John Tee-Van (an American, not a Chinaman, despite his name) of the Bronx Zoo. With the war in China going badly, Tee-Van had to make an incredibly roundabout trip, his total distance covered adding up to 34,868 miles by sea, air and rail. His outward trip went from New York via San Francisco, New Zealand, Australia, the East Indies, Singapore, Bangkok, Rangoon, the Burma Road and 'thence to Chungking, war-battered but unbowed capital of China, and finally to Chengtu, ancient cultural center and capital of Szechuan province, where the pandas awaited me. Newly established war regulations made the journey an endless performance of laboriously filling our documents, sometimes in sextuplicate, of supplying photographs and occasionally fingerprints'. At Chengtu airfield 'A decoy plane, made of bamboo covered with burlap and canvas, was mute evidence that the long tentacles of war reached this distant city.' After collecting the pandas from Dr Graham, a Douglas aircraft 'brought us to the flagstoned runway of the mid-river island airport of Chungking... As the plane came onto the runway, swung over to the alighting place, and its door opened, the pandas were met by the shining nozzles of cameras. To the accompaniment of whirring film and clicking shutters, they were rapidly cleared through customs, placed on a sampan, ferried across the Yangtze-Kiang, and shouldered by coolies up the 324 steep stone steps to the Lin Sen Road... During the pandas' stay in Chungking they were visited by thousands and it was necessary to have three policemen on constant duty to control the crowd and guard the pandas. Only a dozen or so visitors had ever seen a panda before, for in China pandas are as little known as they are in America.'

Shortly after their arrival in the wartime capital, the young animals were formally handed over. In a broadcast speech, Mme Chiang Kai-shek sent the following message to the American people:

'Through the United China Relief, you, our American friends, are alleviating the suffering of our people and are binding the wounds which have been wantonly inflicted upon them through no fault of their own. As a very small way of saying "Thank you", we would like to present to America, through you, Mr Tee-Van, this pair of comical, black-and-white, furry pandas. We hope that their cute antics will bring as much joy to the American children as American friendship has brought to our Chinese people.'

The time was 4 am. The place was the bomb-scarred but newly re-opened radio station in Chungking. John Tee-Van suddenly realized that

Mei-Lan as an adult at Chicago Zoo.
(Chicago Zool. Soc.)

he was responsible for the safety not just of a pair of cubs, but of a symbol of international friendship. He had known this before, of course, but it was only now that the true weight of his responsibility dawned upon him.

On 14th November, complete with living clumps of bamboo, they took off to fly the 770 miles to Hong Kong, in a blacked-out plane and over Japanese-held territory. Landing in a darkened Kowloon, alive with air-raid wardens, they bedded the pandas down comfortably at midnight. 'A day later, pandas, bamboo and luggage went back to the airfield, which was soon to be bombed and captured by the Japanese, and were loaded on board the Hong Kong Clipper for the 758 mile journey over the China Sea to Cavite and Manila in the Philippines.'

Pan-dee and Pan-dah were the first – and probably the last – giant pandas ever to set paw in the Philippines. Bamboo was forthcoming, but the problem was heat. Because of the state of the war the pandas were going to have to sail south, across the Equator, and then double back again up towards the west coast of the United States. The nightmare of keeping mountain animals with heavy pelts alive in the shimmering heat of the South Pacific was haunting John Tee-Van. 'On November 27th, early in the morning before the intense midday heat asserted itself, and ten days before Japan attacked Hawaii, the pandas boarded ship at Manila to begin their long journey . . . On shipboard the pandas lived on the upper deck where breezes blew and where they could be kept as cool as possible. Except for the first four days out of Manila, when they almost died of heat and an intestinal disturbance, their health was perfect. Probably the only thing that kept me from jumping overboard in despair during those four days was the fact that I would have to write a telegram saying that the animals were ill or had died and I could not find the proper words . . . Midway of the voyage to Hawaii war began, and camouflaging of the ship was immediately started. The chief officer threatened to camouflage the pandas, for he asserted that their black and white coloration was entirely too conspicuous.' One of the animals managed to achieve the desired effect accidentally by biting the legs of one of the sailors who was painting the camouflage markings on to the ship. In the chaos that followed, the characteristic starkness of the typical panda patterning became somewhat modified.

After a stop-off at Hawaii, the pandas eventually reached San Francisco without further mishap. On their way across the States to their final destination, they paused in Chicago just long enough for Mei-Mei and Mei-Lan to send them a little reminder, in the form of 'cakes with super-imposed sugar-coated greetings of welcome to the newest pandas to come to America', that the Chicago animals were really the senior citizens where American zoo pandas were concerned.

Pan-dee and Pan-dah entered the Bronx Zoo on 30th December 1941. During the war they gave a great deal of quiet, escapist pleasure to New Yorkers anxious to have their minds taken off the grimmer matters of the early forties. Pan-dee died after nearly four years, with intestinal trouble, just as the world was emerging into peace again, but Pan-dah lived on into the fifties, succumbing after nearly ten years at the Bronx, on 31st October 1951. During the past twenty years New York has once more been panda-less.

The only other American city to enjoy resident pandas before the end of World War II, apart from Chicago and New York, was St Louis. They possessed two specimens, a male called Happy and a female by the name of Pao-Pei. Happy was purchased from a German animal dealer on 24th June 1939, just in the nick of time before war broke out in Europe. Unlike most of the other captive pandas, he was a sturdy adult of 240 pounds when he arrived at the St Louis Zoo. His age was unknown, but he resided there for nearly seven years, apparently living up to his nickname and quietly sharing his enclosure with his young mate Pao-Pei. The latter, brought from Chengtu to Hong Kong in the late summer of 1939 by Dr Gordon Campbell, as a companion for Happy, weighed only 60 pounds on her first day at the zoo and the staff decided that the wedding would have to wait until the following year. By then, Pao-Pei had tripled her bulk and the introduction went ahead without any hitches. Pao-Pei was one of the best adjusted of all captive pandas, nearly rivalling Mei-Lan for longevity. She lived in St Louis for twelve years and nine months, dying eventually on 24th June 1952.

With the final deaths of New York's Pan-dah in 1951, St Louis's Pao-Pei in 1952 and, last of all, Chicago's Mei-Lan in 1953, the dawn of 1954 saw the whole of the New World without a living panda to call its own.

Up until this time, despite Mr A. T. Steele's predictions about pandas becoming a glut on the market, there had, in fact, only been nine living specimens on American soil. All of these had entered the States in the five years from 1936 to 1941, and between them spanned only seventeen years of American history. During that time, however, they not only gave pleasure to millions of people, but inspired the launch of a soft toy industry and injected a new image into American reflections on animals.

This was not to be the end of panda-keeping in the USA, but for eighteen years it was uninhabited by pandas and, for the time being, Europe became the centre of activity.

the london pandas

One name conspicuously absent from the last chapter is that of Floyd Tangier Smith. We left him, back in 1937, fuming at Ruth Harkness' success and avowing that he would soon be acquiring 'bigger and better pandas' with which to startle the western world. He was dogged by set-back after set-back, but refused to give in. If we are to believe all the records, he managed to obtain the astonishing total of thirteen live giant pandas during his lifetime. This makes him the undisputed panda king, but thirteen is an unlucky number. From this whole assembly only four were destined to be successfully delivered and sold by Tangier Smith, and even then he was not able to enjoy his long-awaited triumph, for he was by that time a dying man. His first panda sales were his last and he succumbed to TB within months of completing the transaction.

From the outset his story was an unhappy one. Years of searching had failed to secure a living panda and then, in 1936, Ruth Harkness had marched in and walked off with the prize from the very heart of Tangier Smith territory. According to his own testimony he had even ear-marked the actual specimen for himself. Later, after securing two more, he lost them both, one dying at Chungking and the other at sea. After bringing other livestock to England in 1937 he returned to China and started panda-hunting with an almost desperate intensity. By the spring of 1938 he had caught no less than five, but one had already died. At Chengtu he now boasted three males and one female. By June one of the males had also succumbed, but further intensive collecting must have produced another five specimens because we know from his own writings that by the time he left China in the autumn he had presented two to the Chinese Government which 'were the first live specimens in the Chinese Zoological Gardens' and had added three more to the two males and a female still surviving at Chengtu. With these six animals he set sail for England in the Blue Funnel liner *Antenor*. One of the six animals died on the voyage and yet another expired seventeen days after its arrival in London. The other four, however, were in reasonably good shape and at least enabled

Chiang Yee's version of the Tangier Smith pandas setting sail for London. (From *The Story of Ming*)

Tangier Smith to go to his death-bed with the knowledge that he had, despite his many losses and disasters, achieved the distinction of bringing to the western world the largest group of giant pandas ever seen alive.

The boat trip was comparatively quiet and restful after the chaos of the exodus from China. Tangier had already been a seriously sick man back in Chengtu. So much so, that he had been forced to call on his wife Elizabeth to take charge of the final stages of the operation: 'On this occasion the difficulties of the expedition were complicated by the war in China. Instead of making the trip from the interior to Shanghai by river boat, we had to put all our cages and equipment on lorries and do a journey of 35 days to Hong Kong on roads that were often nearly impassable through bandit-infested country. I say "we", but in fact I was ill and had to fly to Hong Kong while my wife took charge of the expedition. This was the first time she had gone exploring and much of my success was due to her courage and pertinacity. While my wife was bringing the lorries to Hong Kong, one of them tipped over and rolled down an embankment, setting loose two or three pandas. Happily they were quite willing to be caught again, and the incident led to the loss of nothing more than a day.'

On board ship the pandas, according to a member of the crew, became friendly pets. They were chained to their open cages and spent a great deal of time lazing about on deck. Tangier Smith's health must have been badly in need of the sea breezes and deck chairs, but he had a whole collection of animals to look after, including rarities such as the blue sheep, musk deer, Szechuan marmots, and a young golden snub-nosed monkey. To make matters worse, they were heading into the dead of winter.

Dr Geoffrey Vevers, who was then the superintendent of London Zoo, remembers the pandas' arrival vividly to this day. The *Antenor* docked in a snow-storm on Christmas eve 1938 and Vevers hurried across a tinsel-laden London in the freezing cold for his first glimpse of a giant panda. At the London docks he made straight for the *Antenor*'s berth and there, on the ship's deck, with the snow swirling around him, he saw the tall, gaunt figure of Major Tangier Smith wrapped tightly in a long fur overcoat and hugging to his bosom a tiny, golden monkey. The great collector hardly spoke. He was emaciated and obviously seriously ill. Vevers' medical training told him that something had to be done quickly and he immediately started making arrangements to have Tangier Smith admitted to hospital. Like its owner, the little golden monkey – the first of its kind ever seen alive in the West – was riddled with TB. As the man was rushed to the Brompton Hospital, so the monkey was taken to the zoo's animal hospital, but neither survived. Tangier Smith's health did improve sufficiently for his wife to be able to take him back home to the United States, but he died there after only a few months. For him the panda game was played out, but for Londoners it was just beginning.

At first the five pandas were kept behind the scenes at Regent's Park, while the zoo officials examined them and tried to decide how many to buy. There was an old female called Grandma who did not look too hopeful. She was rejected and was still the property of the unfortunate Tangier Smith when she died of double pneumonia on 9th January 1939, without ever having been seen by the British public. Then there were three other adults, a male called Happy and a pair called Grumpy and Dopey. Finally, there was a very young female panda called Baby, estimated to be under a year old and weighing less than 60 pounds.

The London Zoo eventually agreed to purchase the pair and the baby. Happy was sent to Germany on 26th January where he was sold to a German dealer and touted round the Continental zoos. He was the same 'Happy' that we mentioned in the last chapter as being the first giant panda to grace the St Louis Zoo in the USA, but before arriving there on 24th June 1939 he covered a lot of ground. During his five months in a tortured Europe, with the war-clouds growing darker and darker, he was trundled back and forth between the major zoos of Nazi Germany, calling at Hanover, Berlin, Frankfurt, Munich, Leipzig, Nürnberg and Cologne. With World War II only twelve weeks off, the first travelling panda show in history came to an end at the Vincennes Park in Paris.

From there Happy was moved to Cherbourg, where he once again boarded ship for a long sea voyage. Two weeks later he arrived in America and settled in his final home at St Louis.

Happy retained his original nickname throughout his captive life, but the London Zoo trio was re-christened with exotic titles more suited to their oriental origins. The older pair became Sung and Tang, while the baby was re-named Ming.

Ming was first put on show at the zoo shortly after Christmas, but was taken behind the scenes again after only a week. It was the zoo's intention to keep her under special observation until she was a little stronger and then to launch her, like an animal débutante, when the zoo 'season' got into full swing at Easter. But the zoo officials had reckoned without the panda magic. For any other animal this would have been an acceptable scheme, but the public, after only a week's exposure to the panda mystique, was not going to be fobbed off with a three-month wait. According to an *Express* headline: 'Panda Fans phone: "Don't hide him".' Protests poured into the zoo. Hundreds of telephone calls jammed the switchboard and extra staff had to be drafted in to deal with them. The zoo was 'overwhelmed' and a special meeting was called to discuss the situation. It was decided that the young animal would have to go on show again straight away, despite the risks involved, in order to satisfy the extraordinary public demand. But it was agreed that she should only be exposed to the clamour of mass adulation for three hours each day – from noon until 3 pm. The rest of the time was to be spent in the peace and quiet of the zoo's quarantine station in Camden Town. Every day just before midday a car was sent from the zoo to the station to collect the young animal. Ming was then driven in state to her specially erected enclosure in the converted tea pavilion.

As the days passed the crowds grew thicker and thicker. By February it was agreed to extend Ming's daily appearances by one hour. She now held court from noon until 4 pm. By early March she had attracted an extra 7500 people to the zoological gardens and her appeal was still growing. Commercial enterprises were being launched almost daily. There were panda postcards (£96 worth sold at the zoo within a few weeks), panda toys (almost obliterating the teddy bear for a brief period), panda novelties, panda strip-cartoons, panda brooches, and panda hats (made of white ermine with black fox ears and eyes). The panda craze that had struck Chicago in 1937 was now sweeping London.

As the cult proliferated, so the news of Ming's every twitch became stop press. The trivialities of her private life became as essential to Fleet Street as Hitler's rumblings across the Channel. It was eagerly announced that she was beginning to show signs of a romantic interest in the large

From the sublime to the ridiculous. (Left) Ming meets the Princesses Elizabeth and Margaret, spring 1939. (Right) The only panda ride in history?

male panda, Tang. He and his female Sung lived in the quarantine station alongside Ming and the young female had to pass their dens on her way to her public each day. At first she had growled angrily as she passed their cages, but now a change had overcome her. On 2nd March the *Telegraph* excitedly reported that: '...she is making it clear that her anger is directed only against Sung the female giant panda. She pauses at Tang's den as if inclined to pay him a visit, and then she runs on, but looks back coyly and does not growl. Tang is definitely friendly towards Ming and it is hoped that they can be exhibited together. But the affair cannot be hurried.'

In fact, the affair was never consummated and Ming later died a solitary spinster. But in March 1939 she weighed less than 100 pounds and was not yet half-grown. Long before she matured, however, both Tang and Sung had succumbed to London life, so that by the time she was ready to be mated, there was no one to share her den.

Interest in the young panda had by now spread to the Palace and on 10th March it was reported that '...Ming gave audience to Queen Mary, the Princess Royal and Viscount Lascelles on Sunday afternoon. Detectives were present to see that Ming did not play any pranks... The Royal party actually went into the enclosure and Queen Mary asked whether it would be safe to fondle this amusing creature who had captured her fancy.

When she approached, however, Ming, who has a fondness for human ankles, made a determined dive for Queen Mary's umbrella . . . Her Majesty laughed heartily at the incident, but she was even more amused when Ming, tickled on the tummy "giggled" helplessly and covered her curious black-ringed eyes with her paws.' With this, the adulation of Ming rose to a crescendo and vast queues formed at Regent's Park to snatch a glimpse of the sacred form. But across the Channel the news was becoming more and more sombre, and the frenzied interest in a small cuddly animal was sooner or later bound to turn someone's stomach. On 12th April Montague Smith threw up on the pages of the *Daily Mail* with these words: 'The zoo visitors . . . have rubber-necked this monstrosity until their eyes ached. Nor does the matter end there. The sickly sentimental panda plague has infected far more people than can ever hope to see it in the flesh. Hundreds of thousands of postcard pictures of the panda are being sold and a recent film of its idiotic activities filled the newsreel theatres. Children are hugging panda dolls. China images of it occupy mantel pieces where formerly a not quite so hideous "present from Margate" had the place of honour. Would-be fashionable young women are carrying panda mascots. Books, pictures, wallpaper, cigarette cases, jewellery and jokes featuring the panda are making the lives of normal citizens hideous. And now the most nauseating of all symptoms of animal worship is making its appearance. The incorrigibly foolish are beginning to credit the panda with a soul.'

The incorrigibly foolish were furious about this article and the *Daily Mail* was inundated with complaints. The most thoughtful protest came from a young boxer who commented that 'There are so many brutal things about in the world today that it is attractive to find something that you can really have an affection for.'

Montague Smith's objections were swept aside and as the spring of 1939 wore on, Ming continued to hold court at Regent's Park. On 10th May Princess Elizabeth and Princess Margaret visited the panda enclosure and all through the summer the pilgrimage continued. Sung had been sent off to Whipsnade in an attempt to attract crowds there too, and Tang had moved into quarters near those of young Ming in Regent's Park. Being larger, neither Sung nor Tang had the playful appeal of Ming and they did nothing to diminish the smaller animal's hold over the public.

With ample supplies of fresh bamboo shoots coming in from all over Britain, Ming was growing rapidly. By August she weighed 150 pounds, three times her size on arrival. She was now so large that she had to be transported about the zoo in a wheelbarrow, as she was too heavy to carry and too destructive to the car that used to transport her.

On 18th August 1939 Ming appeared on B.B.C. television in one of the earliest of all TV 'outside broadcasts'. There is little doubt that she would have gone on to become a great TV star, but exactly two weeks later she was being unceremoniously bundled on to a zoo lorry and carted off to Whipsnade, along with Tang and Ba-Bar, a baby elephant. War was imminent and the pandas were receiving V.I.P. treatment as priority evacuees. Two days after their safe arrival at the London Zoo's secluded country home thirty miles north of the city, war was declared.

After two autumn months at Whipsnade, Ming had put on so much weight that she was now nearly fully grown. In November Whipsnade shut its gates for the four cold months of winter and the three pandas enjoyed the privacy, the spaciousness, and the (for them) ideal climate high up on the Dunstable Downs. But even in these excellent conditions one of the pandas was weakening. Something was wrong with Sung. At first, it was thought that she must be hibernating, but later the authorities became alarmed and returned her to the Regent's Park sanatorium where she could come under the close observation of the zoo's pathologist.

Sung had always been a rather forlorn creature and had persistently refused to eat bamboo, feeding instead on cereals and porridge. Now she seemed unable to move about without great difficulty. During the first half of December, back at Regent's Park, she showed additional alarming signs, her whole body being shaken at intervals by convulsive movements. On the afternoon of 18th December Sung died. She was embalmed and sent to the Royal College of Surgeons for dissection. From there it was announced that the animal had some kind of long-standing disease of the spine, probably dating back to her days in China. The College also commented that the earlier panda death (Grandma) followed similar lines. Both animals were believed to have died of pneumonia, but this did not explain the convulsions. At first we wondered if these were two of the animals thrown out of the crashing Tangier Smith lorry on the long trip across China. It seemed reasonable to suppose that, as the lorry rolled over and over, the pandas were badly tossed about and they may easily have damaged their backs during this episode, resulting in the disease recorded by the Royal College.

But in the following years three more panda deaths at London Zoo were preceded by fits of some description, and the post mortems on these animals brought us no closer to understanding why. It may be that some unidentified factor in the animals' husbandry – perhaps the diet – was the cause, or that the nervous system of diseased pandas is particularly easily damaged. In fact, our first idea might still be valid for Sung and Grandma but it seemed increasingly likely that pandas were prone to fits. What causes this problem is still a mystery.

Another statement from the Royal College of Surgeons echoed similar reports at American zoos. Sung had been wrongly sexed. She was a he. Little wonder that the zoo had found it impossible to keep the 'pair' together.

Whereas the death of Grandma had been a private affair, Sung's demise was the first 'public' panda fatality. This gave the press a new interest in the species and despite the fact that the country was on the threshold of a bloody war, grave notices were penned and sentimental poems composed. Part of one poem that was published on the day following her death read as follows:

> *Sung, the Panda died today.*
> *At the Zoo she's lying stark.*
> *She'll be mourned in far Cathay*
> *And the wilds of Regent's Park.*
>
> *That's the message of the tapes:*
> *Sad-eyed Sung won't prank again –*
> *No more somersaults and japes*
> *To refresh the minds of men.*
>
> *Sung from China, peace to thee!*
> *'Tis a gloomy song I sing.*
> *Death hath taken one from three*
> *Left us only Tang and Ming.*

As before, the over-emotional climate led to some biting sarcasm. The following day an anonymous comment was made under the heading of 'Dumb Friend's Corner': 'Owing to the war the funeral of Sung, the Zoo panda, will be semi-state, we were told in Whitehall yesterday. The Island Race will be permitted to attend the lying-in-state at Regent's Park, but no mass demonstrations of public grief will be permitted. A deputation of representative modern thinkers will deposit a wreath and funeral orations will be delivered by Sloggers J..d and H.xl.y, dealing partly with the panda and partly with themselves. The notable silence of the Dean of Westminster is being freely commented on.'

Ming, in the meantime, was going from strength to strength and by March had tipped the scales at 200 pounds. After a pleasant winter rolling around in the Whipsnade snow-drifts, she was now on her way back to Regent's Park to meet the Easter crowds again. With her return in mid-March came a note of uncertainty about her true sex. After the error with Sung, the authorities were presumably having second thoughts about Ming's femininity as well. (But in this case they need not have worried, she really was a she.) A month later, with Ming dutifully boosting the

*As the bombs fell,
so did Ming's hair*

morale of wartime Londoners, the adult male Tang started throwing fits
similar to those of Sung and Grandma and died after a short illness, on
23rd April 1940.

Ming was now alone, the sole panda survivor in the whole of war-torn
Europe. During the next four years she became something of a symbol – a
bit of fun in a funless, burning city. She was something exotically unreal
in an epoch that was having its fill of reality. Soldiers visited her on leave,
and she was shunted back and forth between Whipsnade and Regent's
Park, according to the fortunes and misfortunes of the war in the air over
London. Bombs fell on the zoo, but Ming was unscathed. She was not,
however, in the best of health. Her hair was thinning unnaturally and in
the summer of 1943 she started walking backwards: 'After lumbering
around the cage in normal fashion she suddenly goes into reverse. Without troubling to turn round she retraces her steps backwards, continuing

Ming, stuffed, as the taxidermist's centre-piece

until she comes up against the rear wall with a bump.' For a wartime symbol this is the kind of action that is hardly calculated to inspire the troops. Worse still: 'When tired of this the panda sits at the bars and, facing the crowd, places both paws over her eyes.' It was as if the great symbol was saying 'I give up'. This was in 1943. Early in 1944 the zoo wisely took her off exhibition and started a course of serious treatment in an attempt to restore her hair.

Every day Ming was attended by the zoo doctors who increased her vitamin intake, applied coconut oil to her thinning coat and sprayed her with 'a special hair-nourishing liquid'. Throughout 1944 she managed to hold her own, although she was said to be 'dispirited and unwilling to entertain the public'. Then, exactly six years (to the very day) after her arrival at London docks, she fell seriously ill. In a few days she was dead. According to an official zoo statement, her keeper, returning from his Christmas celebrations, found her cold in her cage. The London *Times* published a non-satirical obituary of her, headed simply MING:

'Ming, the Panda, who made her first appearance at the London Zoo on Christmas eve 1938, died in her sleep on Boxing Day – she had been ailing for some time, and English-grown bamboos would seem to lack the vitamins of the Tibetan plant . . . she could die happy in the knowledge that she had gladdened the universal heart, and, even in the stress of war, her death should not go unnoticed . . . She had the air of being the embodiment of some inspired nursery rhyme, and her proper habitation was less a prosaic cage than, in Mr Walter De La Mare's words, "some celestial happy medium between what is sense and what is nonsense." . . . If there had been no panda we should surely have invented one . . . she will live in song and story as a fable, a superior kind of teddy bear become miraculously alive.'

It would be pleasant to end her story here, on this note of passionate acclaim, but it seems that the tale of her death was improved for public consumption. Following a seizure, her legs became highly uncoordinated and she frequently fell over and was unable to stand again. It was a bitterly sad ending for one who had created so much amusement during her short life. Veterinary records reveal that, in fact, Ming was destroyed; and it must have been decided that the British public could not cope sensibly with this news, so they were spared the details and a more demure demise was invented. And there is a sting in the tail yet to come. In January 1945 her body was presented to the Royal College of Surgeons and it was announced that it would be preserved in the John Hunter Museum where it could be made available to anatomical research workers. It appears, however, that this applied only to her internal organs for, as the war drew to an end in the spring of 1945, her stuffed pelt set off on a new career of making-friends-and-influencing-people. A large photograph of a taxidermized Ming appeared in the magazine *Illustrated*, with the following caption:

'Ming, the girl with the two lovely black eyes, is dead. But she's not lying down. Stuffed, she is travelling around the country carrying on with her job of entertaining the children . . . Recently she has been the centre of attraction at a big Liverpool store. Ming is quite a traveller and moves on to other places after about a fortnight's stay in one town. Ming, alive, was valued at £2,000. Her present owner, Mr Gerrard of Gerrard's Natural History Studios, would not sell her. Ming, dead, is priceless.' Such are the extraordinary contradictions of the world of the giant panda.

CHAPTER 7

post-war
pandas

Ma Teh arrives in London with Lien-Ho, the first of the post-war pandas

The close of World War II saw Europe once again panda-less. In an epoch of enforced austerity, of shortages, and peace-time ration-cards, there was a burning need for a few symbolic luxury items to brighten the dull routine. The London Zoo had no doubts about how it was going to solve this problem. It was obvious that a replacement for Ming had to be found and found quickly. But how? The old-time collectors like Tangier Smith had been swept away by the war.

The answer came unexpectedly over dinner one night at the Savile Club in Mayfair. Professor Edward Hindle, then Scientific Director of the Zoological Society of London, happened to mention casually to Dr George K. C. Yeh of the Chinese Embassy that the zoo was seeking a contact to enable them to acquire another panda. Dr Yeh promised to do what he could to help and dispatched an official letter to the Chinese Government.

His request was eventually passed to the governor of the province of Szechuan at Chengtu, General Chang Chun, who agreed to have not one, but a pair of giant pandas captured and sent as a gesture of goodwill and unity between Great Britain and China.

To repay this kindness, a rather unusual bargain was sealed. For each of the pandas the London Zoo agreed to provide a year's fellowship in England for a young Chinese biologist, all expenses paid. The university authorities at Chengtu were asked to select two suitable candidates for this imaginative offer and to prepare them for their special roles as panda chaperons. Dr Kwo, the Minister of Education for the Szechuan Government, was inundated with applications from eager Chengtu University students. His number one selection was an earnest young lecturer in zoology, Dr Ma Teh. If a second panda was caught, it was to be brought to England by a young botanist, Miss Hu Shih Yih, who had made a special study of the plants chosen as food by wild pandas.

Ma Teh was given the task of organizing the panda hunt and, with the thought of the London trip spurring him on, soon had half the local population out scouring the bamboo hills. Some reports claimed that there were over 200 people involved in the search. Panda territory was combed systematically by farmers and professional hunters in groups of ten, until at last an animal was sighted. It took two months of this intensive searching to locate and capture a young panda. For five weeks they saw nothing; then they made contact with one, but it managed to elude them. For a further three weeks they sighted it every day, but it always escaped. Then, finally, on 31st December 1945, it was driven into a tree by the hunters' dogs. When the men arrived, they surrounded the tree and began the delicate operation of lassoing the panda with a soft rope. To do this, one hunter had to climb a neighbouring tree with a long stick, to which was attached a rope with a noose. The problem was to get the noose over the animal's front legs as well as the head. If it fell only around the neck, then there was a danger that the panda might strangle itself.

The operation proved to be rather more difficult than was expected. According to Ma Teh, the animal 'was extremely intelligent. Time after time she caught the noose and threw it off her body'. Eventually she was secured and a second hunter climbed up to her, forced her down, and placed a bamboo muzzle over her face. The victorious party was then able to indulge in an extra-special New Year's Eve celebration.

Within a week the panda, now known as Lien-Ho (meaning Unity or Union, symbolizing the bond of friendship between China and Britain) had lost all fear of human beings and would come bounding over like a great shaggy dog when Ma Teh called her. She was transported to Chengtu in a specially built wooden crate. Once there, she became the centre of excited attention and the crowds flocking to see her reached such alarming proportions that she was promptly shipped back to Wenchwan, to be hidden at a remote farmstead near the site of her capture.

There she waited in quiet seclusion while all the complex details of her long journey were arranged and finalized. In the meantime the hunt was still on for a mate for Lien-Ho, but as the weeks dragged by the situation looked more and more hopeless and the farmers became anxious to return to their farms. After four months of disappointments it was decided to abandon the search and Lien-Ho began her marathon journey. Unlike the previous London pandas, she was to make the trip by air.

After being carried the seventy miles to Chengtu for a second time, she left there with Ma Teh in a special aircraft made available by Lieutenant General Sir Adrian Carton de Wiart, Prime Minister Attlee's personal representative with Generalissimo Chiang Kai-Shek. On 5th May 1946 the plane touched down at Chungking. Lien-Ho was in high spirits and ate a large meal of gruel honey and bamboo shoots. She was, however, suffering from the increase in temperature and was given a cool room with large fans to make her feel more comfortable. The following morning at dawn they took off again, this time heading towards real heat. The destination was Calcutta, where it was a sweltering 97°F in the shade.

Ma Teh became seriously worried about the panda's welfare, but to the rescue came Spencer's Ice and Cold Storage Plant. As soon as the animal arrived in Calcutta they installed her in a specially assembled cold chamber. There, with life-saving blocks of ice, Lien-Ho was able to sleep while she awaited the next leg of the journey. On a stretcher outside the door of her cold room lay Ma Teh, trying desperately to rest and keep an eye on the thermometer at the same time.

On the 9th May she was whisked out of her icy retreat and rushed through the burning heat to the air base at Bally on the Hooghly River. There her crate was carried by six Indian porters to a waiting motor-boat and raced across the water to a white B.O.A.C. Sunderland flying-boat. By this time the panda was panting hard and showing obvious signs of distress, but inside the aircraft was a reserved compartment amply supplied with massive slabs of ice, and the moment she was aboard she was let out to cool off. Ecstatically she turned over and over on what was virtually a floor of ice. B.O.A.C., who had at first refused to carry her at all, because of official regulations, had not only waived their rules in honour of their V.I.P. cargo, but had rolled out a special iced carpet and had saved the project from almost certain disaster. At 5 pm the flying-boat skimmed over the river and headed for Karachi, where the ice could be renewed; then Cairo, Marseilles and finally Poole harbour in the south of England.

For Ma Teh, B.O.A.C.'s thoughtfulness must have been more than welcome, but in Westminster reactions differed. According to one newspaper report: 'The zoo's new baby panda, due to arrive by air next week, is causing a big stir. Should pandas be flown to London when 11,000 people are awaiting transport? Lord Munster has expressed indignation at the idea in the House of Lords. But neither the Air Ministry, the B.O.A.C., nor officials of the London Zoo are altering their plans. The panda, his bamboo shoots and his Chinese attendant will arrive in spite of Lord Munster.' His Lordship was strongly criticized for his comments in the correspondence columns. '. . . it would have been tactless, undiplomatic and ungracious not to have provided a passage for this generous and imaginative gift from our great ally, China'. But not everyone was prepared to put symbolic gestures before stark realities and back came the acid observation that, 'The departure of Mr Herbert Morrison for America on his mission to secure food for starving millions received less notice . . . than did . . . the Giant Panda with its supply of bamboo shoots to amuse the crowds at London Zoo.' The British public were once again busy with their favourite occupation of putting animals before people and then hating themselves for it.

While this was going on, the Sunderland flying-boat was making steadily and uneventfully towards western Europe. On the afternoon of 11th May it circled the Dorset harbour and came to rest. Immediately tugs and launches filled with reporters, zoo men, photographers and officials of the Chinese Government converging on her. With cameras held high in the bobbing boats they waited poised to record the great moment, as if some notorious film star were about to descend from the plane's doorway. All they saw, in fact, was the handing out of a rather small wooden crate.

The crate was rushed to Bournemouth station where a special freight van was waiting, attached to a fast London train. A group of admirers, alerted presumably by radio reports of Lien-Ho's progress, was by this time gathering at Waterloo station, where she arrived in the early evening. From there she was dashed across London to Regent's Park in a B.O.A.C. van and delivered straight into the stores yard, where curators and vets were waiting to check her in. Passed as fit, she was taken direct to her large Lion House cage, freshly re-painted in a delicate shade of yellow.

This was, in fact, Ming's old cage and perhaps the zoo was hoping that some of Ming's earlier magic would rub off on the newcomer. But they were to be bitterly disappointed. Each panda has its own particular personality and Lien-Ho was no Ming. She proved it on her very first day by refusing to wake up the following morning and face her new public. They had been queuing for over an hour before the zoo gates were due to open and now, curled up in her sleeping den, she simply would not budge.

After hours of coaxing by her new keeper, she finally confirmed her opinion of London life by biting him hard enough to draw blood. Eventually she was persuaded to put in a brief appearance for twenty minutes and was then thankfully back in her dark rear den again. Nor was this exceptional. Her surly and unhappy mood persisted and with it came a storm of protest. Had she gambolled and romped about gaily like Ming there would have been no adverse comment, but she was so clearly upset by her new form of existence that emotions flashed and flared: 'Are we really a civilized nation when we hunt this little wild creature, the panda, take away its freedom and force it to be stared at in the Zoo, though it is so obviously thoroughly bewildered and unhappy?' asked an indignant correspondent in the *Express*.

Even royal visitors were unable to muster much enthusiasm. When the Duchess of Kent took her children, Prince Michael and Princess Alexandra, to meet Lien-Ho, the young prince was quoted as saying, 'Not very big, is she? Have you got anything else new?', and they spent the rest of the visit playing with a common vixen. Asked for his views, her keeper could only comment: 'She just sits there all day or sleeps. She only comes to the front of the cage when we lay a trail of bamboo shoots . . . people just don't seem to appeal to her.'

In attempts to encourage her to more lively pursuits, a Whipsnade husky puppy was brought into the act, and a young boy was hired to keep her active. But the row in the press continued. 'Panda plays as cruelty storm rages' shouted one headline. Apparently hundreds of protest letters were pouring in, but the zoo officials were unrepentant. They even emphasized that they were still going all out for a second one. For Lien-Ho, they announced, a new enclosure would be built in the form of a pagoda on the large central lawn.

Their continued concern for the welfare of the panda finally won through and shifted the public mood. *Punch* helped on 29th May by publishing a statement by Lien-Ho herself. ' . . . One did not feel attracted to this new and vulgar civilization in the West, but it did one no harm. Anything was better than those awful hills, the Eternal snows, with their endless struggle for a livelihood. Here at least there were slaves to minister to one's bodily needs . . . ' H. T. W. Bousfield added, in the *Queen* a few weeks later: 'So frantic do the old women (of both sexes) become about our latest panda that I verily believe they envisage her as a nice young lady, brought up in a country vicarage of the best type, who has been kidnapped. If you explored their clouded minds further, you'd find traces of nursery stories of enchantment. Miss Panda, to them is, half consciously, an enchanted princess of sound Anglican principles.'

By the summer Lien-Ho was settling down to the daily routine on the central lawn and was even lively enough by September to break down a small gate, march across a public walk, invade the zoo's First Aid Hut and terrorize the resident nurse, who was forced to defend herself with a broom and pail while the panda examined the bandages and ointments. With the arrival of autumn, Lien-Ho had discovered that she could climb high up into the top of her cage and lie there amongst the roof-struts, gazing lazily down on disgruntled humanity. For the next few years she lived on, sombrely munching her bamboo and snoozing aloft in the bright light of day. In the music halls Flotsam summed it up with a poem which began:

> I think I understand a
> Giant Panda;
> Why should she, while supplied with
> Bamboo shoots
> Give two hoots?

The interest waned and little more comment was heard until Lien-Ho fell sick at the end of 1949. On 12th January 1950 she was admitted to the animal hospital seriously ill and underwent a course of injections. News of her condition appears to have reached the Nationalist Chinese Government. In *Time* magazine on 16th January we read that Dr Cheng Tien-hsi, the Chinese ambassador in London, was summoned to the foreign office to hear from the Minister of State that Britain recognized Communist China and that the Nationalist Chinese Envoy was dismissed. Cheng and his staff were given three months to vacate the Chinese Embassy in Portland Place before the Communists moved in. *Time* comments: 'He had one last ambassadorial duty to perform. On orders from Formosa, he gave £20 towards medical expenses for ailing Lien-Ho, the giant panda presented to the London Zoo in 1946 by Nationalist China as a token of friendship.'

Like Sung and Grandma before her, Lien-Ho was attacked by epileptic fits. The hospital's treatment failed, however, and on 22nd February she died of pneumonia: 'A keeper who found her sitting up in the sanatorium walked right up to her before he realized she was dead.' In a bizarre way the death of this panda mimicked the death of the régime which had presented it. Like Lien-Ho, the Nationalist Chinese Government was effectively dead, but was still sitting propped up in the 'sanatorium' of Formosa (now Taiwan).

The London Zoo announced that 'we do not plan to replace Lien-Ho.

Pandas, though a big box office draw, are perhaps best left in their native forests'. Worried by the outbursts following Lien-Ho's arrival and her subsequently gloomy personality, the council of the Zoological Society agreed to put giant pandas on a zoo 'black list' for all time. If they feared the loss of a box office species in taking this action, they need not have lost any sleep, for, as Lien-Ho's body was being taken away to the post mortem slab (where, almost inevitably by now, she proved to be a he), a tiny polar bear cub aged twelve weeks, called Brumas, was just being weighed for the first time. Within a few hectic weeks Lien-Ho was forgotten and Brumas was breaking all zoo records.

Three and a half years later, the last of the American pandas, Chicago's Mei-Lan, died and the dawn of 1954 saw the whole of the western world without a living specimen of a giant panda. With China still trying to sort out her massive economic re-organization under the new communist régime, panda prospects for the future looked bleak. Also, many zoos, like London, felt that the wild panda population was too small and valuable to be whittled down any further. But at this stage the Chinese themselves took a hand.

The information then available from China is somewhat obscure, but we now know that the new government had started to take a serious interest in Chinese fauna and the Chinese zoos, so that by 1955 the Peking Zoological Gardens could boast three young female giant pandas. Their names were Ping-Ping, Hsing-Hsing and Chi-Chi. By 1956 two more had been added, a female called Ssu-Mao and a large un-named male who died shortly afterwards. In July 1957 Ping-Ping was sent to Russia by Mao Tse Tung as a gift to the Soviet people and was given a new home in the Moscow Zoo. (She was to be followed later, in 1959, by a male called An'-An'.) Then, in December 1957, a very young female was caught by a team of animal-trappers in Szechuan and was moved successfully to Peking Zoo in January 1958. There she was looked after with great care by a Chinese girl and grew rapidly. Like one of the 1955 females this baby was also called Chi-Chi.

For several years an Austrian animal dealer called Heini Demmer had been trying to persuade the Chinese authorities to agree to release a panda in exchange for a collection of African big game. Peking Zoo was badly in need of re-stocking and Demmer's list, including as it did such things as giraffes and rhinos, was too attractive to ignore. They agreed that if he brought the animals to China he could select a panda and take it away with him.

Demmer and his wife left their Nairobi collecting station in April 1958 with three giraffes, two rhinos, two hippos and two zebras, and travelled to Peking via India, Thailand and Hong Kong, arriving in May: 'The

Director and all his staff were most kind and did their utmost to make our stay there as enjoyable as possible. The Zoological Garden of Peking is a wonderful park and has been rebuilt during the last few years in a remarkable way; it is now very modern indeed.'

When Demmer was shown to the house containing the giant pandas he saw not four, but only three specimens. One, called Chi-Chi, was much smaller than the other two. It seems likely that the original Chi-Chi must have died and that its nick-name was passed on to the young newcomer in 1958. (This is a common practice with zoo nick-names.) Demmer records that 'The Director was kind enough to give me complete freedom to choose one of their three pandas, which I thought was more than courteous. So, for about one week I more or less lived in this house and watched all three animals very carefully, and after a few days I made up my mind and asked the Director whether he would mind if I accepted Chi-Chi, the smallest of the trio, but definitely the liveliest and naughtiest of them.' The bargain was struck and Demmer and his wife took off with Chi-Chi in a Russian jet plane for Moscow. There they were greeted by the director of the Moscow Zoo who made a large compound available for Chi-Chi. In her new enclosure the young panda was rested for a week before making the next lap of her journey, to East Berlin.

Berlin, being a split city has two major zoos and Chi-Chi visited both, her transfer from the East Berlin Zoo to the one in West Berlin being the most difficult stage in the whole journey. Or so it seemed at the time. But worse was yet to come. Chi-Chi had been provisionally sold to an American Zoo for the staggering sum of 25,000 dollars, but at the last minute the American authorities clamped down. The U.S. Treasury Department pointed out that as America did not officially recognize Communist China, there was an embargo on all trade with that country. Asked to make an exception in what was obviously an exceptional case, they flatly refused. The American zoo officials were frustrated and helpless. Demmer was stranded and dollar-less.

Frankfurt Zoo came to the rescue by offering to give Chi-Chi a free temporary home while Demmer continued negotiating, hoping, as he put it, that 'some high person in Washington may close one eye and give Chi-Chi permission to enter and remain in the U.S.A., despite her communist background'. But the high persons of Washington were unbending and in the end Demmer was driven to repeat a performance that had been the lot of the panda Happy and his owners twenty years previously. He started up the second great travelling panda-show, hiring Chi-Chi out to European zoos by the week.

Copenhagen was visited and then London. At Regent's Park the crowds turned out again to see the famous giant panda that had become the victim of international politics. For many, the memory of Lien-Ho was a glum one and they expected little. But they were pleasantly surprised. Chi-Chi was much more like the original Ming in personality and was soon sending out great waves of the original panda magic. She suffered the indignities of a bubble bath and provided ample copy for Fleet Street by escaping twice from her enclosure. On the first occasion she climbed over a low fence surrounding the lawn where she had been taken for photographs. On the second, she scrambled out of her large pit while warm water was being tipped into her now famous tub. This time she managed to cause havoc by lumbering into a crowd of on-lookers and biting a startled lady who was promptly rushed off to hospital, where she had three stitches in her damaged leg. Chi-Chi meanwhile was testing out her new hut, installed to give her shelter from the September sun. Her weight – 122 pounds – was too much for it and it collapsed. For the on-lookers, Chi-Chi was rapidly developing an attractively wicked personality, and the London Zoo started to think hard about the possibility of buying her.

In reaching a decision they had to consider two conflicting aspects of her case. On the one hand she was obviously a great attraction, and the crowds were so great that a specially enlarged circular platform had to be constructed around her enclosure to give more people a clear view of her. Also, if anyone was going to give her a permanent home, then it should be London, as that was the only European zoo with previous detailed knowledge of caring for this difficult species. On the other hand, the zoo's council had black-listed pandas for all time as being too hot to handle, and there was the difficult question of the large sum of money that Demmer was demanding for the animal.

Chi-Chi had arrived in London on the 5th September 1958 for a three-week visit and a decision had to be reached before that time was up, or Demmer would have to take her on to another zoo for another brief stay. After lengthy discussions it was decided that she must stay in Regent's Park, even if the cost was heavy. The original 'no-panda' dictum had referred to attempts to take more pandas away from the wild state, but this specimen was already here. The London Zoo had in no way been instrumental in removing Chi-Chi from the wild. This had already been done by the Chinese, and the Zoo's real responsibility was now to ensure that the young animal had the very best possible treatment in captivity.

The financial problem was solved thanks to the assistance of the Granada television company, which agreed to pay £10,000 of the £12,000 purchase price. Chi-Chi became zoo property on the 26th September 1958, and Heini Demmer was able to breathe again. America's loss was London's gain and yet another panda epoch was about to begin.

The pattern was much the same as before and does not bear repeating in detail. There were television programmes, picture postcards, books, photographs and all the usual paraphernalia of animal stardom. A new 75-foot long enclosure was prepared complete with swimming pool, mist spray, weighing platform, suspended rubber tyres, and a pile of logs. Blocks of ice were placed in the enclosure on warm days for the panda to sprawl on, and the mist from the spray wafted gently down to cool her face. Behind the scenes there was a special kitchen where her meals were meticulously prepared, a bamboo store to keep her favourite food fresh and moist, an air purification installation to drive cleansed air through her indoor quarters, and her wood-lined sleeping den. A new keeper was taken on exclusively to tend to her minute-by-minute needs and to play with her when she became bored.

Chi-Chi eased herself gracefully into this life of luxury and steadily put on weight. She received royalty in the approved panda manner and relaxed. When there were heavy London fogs, she retired to her air-conditioned den and breathed more freely and comfortably than any of London's other ten million inhabitants. But she lacked one important ingredient in her life that they did not: a prospective mate. As the years passed and she approached sexual maturity, the problem became more and more acute. By the autumn of 1960, when she was just over three years old, she showed signs of coming into sexual heat for the first time. Her mood changed, she began calling and running around her enclosure, and she started to leave scent-marks on her 'territory'. She refused all food except the softest bamboo shoots.

The sexual mood passed, but returned in the spring of 1961 and again in the autumn. Each period of heat was a potential infant panda wasted and in January 1962 the Zoological Society sent an urgent plea to Peking asking whether they could help. In March, Tsui Chan-p'ing, the director of Peking Zoo replied, and we will quote him at length, because his comments are an important reflection on China's early official policy for the conservation of pandas:

'As you will know, the distribution of the giant panda is extremely limited and in its natural habitat its existence is also limited by the particular natural conditions. Furthermore, in its natural environment, it suffers from the depredations of beasts of prey and, as you will well understand, its numbers may also have decreased since the development of communications.

'But from the establishment of our nation (The People's Republic of China), measures have rapidly been taken to protect the giant panda; regulations for the protection and hunting of it have been promulgated and put into effect. In order that the giant panda shall not decrease

*Chi-Chi at play – the antics which
drew the crowds to London Zoo.
(Granada TV)*

further in its natural habitat, hunting is prohibited for the time being, and for this reason we are at present unable to meet your wishes.

'We are confident that, thanks to the attention paid by our government and the research work undertaken by our zoologists in this field, the giant panda will not become extinct in its natural habitat.'

There the matter rested, and the Chinese could not be blamed for their attitude. For years they had seen their panda territory plundered by westerners and now they had called a halt. If this seems unreasonable, it is a worthwhile exercise to imagine the roles reversed. Supposing a French priest, strolling on the shores of Loch Ness, discovered the Loch Ness Monster. Then suppose teams of Chinese hunters arrived and shot every Loch Ness Monster that they could find; following them, a Chinese lady who found a baby Monster and, without any official blessing, tried to get it out of the country to exhibit it in a Chinese Zoo; following her, more and more foreign collectors taking every living Loch Ness Monster they could find. It seems just possible that somewhere along the line the natives would have raised a faint protest against this course of events. Viewed through these spectacles, the panda scene takes on an entirely different appearance, and the Chinese emerge as unbelievably patient.

All this, however, was no comfort to Chi-Chi, whose periods of heat were becoming more and more intense, frequent and prolonged. In the autumn of 1963 she began a sexual phase that persisted for week after week. As she hardly ever ate anything when she was on heat, the situation became desperate. Two months passed and she was beginning to lose weight. The zoo vet was called in and administered a heavy dose of tranquillizers. By mid-December she had calmed down and was munching away on her bamboo again as if nothing had happened.

In January 1964, the Zoological Society again approached the Chinese authorities, but to no avail. It looked very much as though Chi-Chi was going to have to face an annual round of heats and tranquillizers. In the spring, she scratched her eye on a piece of bamboo and was admitted to the animal hospital. Oliver Graham-Jones, the zoo's Senior Veterinary Officer, had the unenviable task of being the first person to be faced with the prospect of anaesthetizing a giant panda. Chi-Chi squinted at him from her cage in the hospital's operating theatre, as if defying him to calculate the correct dosage. With a deep breath he went into action and in a short while the western world's greatest animal star was sprawled out comfortably on the operating table. Everything worked perfectly and Graham-Jones was able to make good use of the opportunity to carry out a thorough medical examination of the animal. The eye was treated (and soon afterwards was completely healed), saliva and blood samples were taken, pulse rate was checked, and the fur was examined for any possible infections.

Most important, it was possible – perhaps for the first time – to make a close study of the sex organs of a living adult giant panda. After all the mistakes that had been made in the past, it was particularly interesting to see if anything definite could be established during life, given an anaesthetized panda. Chi-Chi had arrived at the zoo as a female and had always given the impression of being one, in her general behaviour. But back in August 1959 a famous anatomist had examined her as best he could in her zoo enclosure and pronounced that, once again, she was a he. He did not, of course, have a chance to examine her very closely and, in addition, she was still immature at the time. As she grew older, her keepers became more and more confirmed in their opinions that she really was a she. Now, at last, on the hospital operating table, it was possible to make sure. Animal breeding experts had been alerted and together carried out an examination that left them in no doubt. Chi-Chi whose title apparently means 'naughty little girl', had been well named: she was a she.

Chi-Chi recovered easily from her anaesthetic and by the next morning was active and lively again. Two months later, in June, she entered another period of heat and the zoo kept its fingers crossed. But to everyone's pleasant surprise, she came out of it in little over a week. Just as it seemed that everything was back to normal, she shattered the peace in a completely unexpected way by savaging one of her young keepers.

Although she weighed 230 pounds and was no longer a playful cub, Chi-Chi had never been treated as a 'wild' animal. All through her career at the zoo, she had had the company of her keepers, and they thought nothing of working in her enclosure with her looking on. Occasionally, during a bad spell of sexual frustration, she had become ill-tempered and taken a swipe at them, but she had never shown any signs of a really serious intent to attack them. Now, out of the blue, came this assault on sixteen year-old Christopher Madden. Chi-Chi had knocked him down and, as he lay helpless on his back, had sat on him and started savaging his right leg. Ken Alliborne, a keeper from the Monkey House nearby, heard his screams and without a moment's hesitation leapt into the enclosure (from which there was no escape for either man or panda) and ran towards the boy on the ground. Picking up Madden's broom, he tried as hard as he could to lever Chi-Chi off the boy, but she refused to budge. Blood was pouring from Madden's leg and Alliborne was forced to take drastic action. He clouted the panda on the head with the broom and Chi-Chi looked up, startled, just long enough for him to pull Madden clear. Chi-Chi then turned her attention to the newcomer and advanced threateningly towards Alliborne, her mouth covered with blood and mucous, growling angrily. Using the broom, he threatened back and managed to keep her at bay until help came and she could be shut away in her sleeping den.

Alliborne was awarded the Zoological Society's Bronze Medal for his bravery. Madden's leg slowly healed in hospital, while its owner worried about whether the zoo would let him have his old job back, working with the panda. Naturally the zoo was delighted, but Chi-Chi had other ideas. To Head Keeper Sam Morton's astonishment, she recognized Madden again instantly and started growling and pacing angrily up and down her enclosure as soon as the young keeper re-appeared. The strange feature of this reaction was that it took seven months for Madden's leg to heal sufficiently for him to return to work, so that, after knowing the boy for only a matter of weeks, Chi-Chi had remembered him as an individual after a considerable period of time. Although this feat was a credit to the panda's intelligence, it meant that Madden's ambition to return to his old post could not be realized.

Chi-Chi now had to be treated as a 'wild' animal. She showed little change in her behaviour, and there were no further indications of increased aggressiveness. In early September 1964 she started coming into heat again, but in a perfectly normal way. It was at this point that new hope dawned for the possible consummation of her sexual urges. Press reports from Moscow indicated that the zoo authorities there might perhaps be prepared to consider an East-West honeymoon between their male panda An'-An' and London's Chi-Chi. Immediately London Zoo sent the following cable:

'From press reports we are delighted to hear that you are interested in possible mating of Moscow and London pandas. We are happy to do anything to help this valuable zoological project. London Zoo officials prepared visit Moscow any time for discussions or we would welcome you as our guests here in London. We await your reply with great interest and hope that this will lead to greater friendship and co-operation between our two zoos.'

In addition, letters were sent offering to have An'-An' as a guest panda in Regent's Park or to transport Chi-Chi to Moscow at the London Zoo's expense. Shortly afterwards pressmen in Moscow were told that there were difficulties and that the 'manliness' of the Russian panda was in doubt. This led to a great deal of speculation and a variety of interpretations, some more serious than others.

It was suggested that perhaps An'-An' was sick, or that he was considered too dangerous, or that he was thought to be too valuable to risk in a mating attempt that might prove to be rather violent. In certain quarters it was felt that perhaps the Russians were not sure of the sex of their panda and were reluctant to admit this fact.

It emerged later that all these interpretations were incorrect. The truth was that the Moscow Zoo authorities were unhappy about the degree of isolation that both An'-An' and Chi-Chi had experienced during their adult lives. Neither had lived with another member of their species since they left China and it was feared that they would simply fail to respond appropriately to a panda of the opposite sex. The mating attempt was not on.

China came back into the picture briefly a few days later, when an animal dealer rang up the London Zoo and offered a Chinese zoo panda for sale. The price was a mere £27,500, including delivery to London. The animal was said to be available through a Chinese animal dealer, the only one who was permitted to enter and leave China freely without difficulty. The sex of the panda was unknown, but it was stressed very strongly that the animal was in good condition and that its export was entirely legal and above-board. This seemed very strange, after all the difficulties that had been encountered during the past few years, and London Zoo demanded official documents from the Chinese authorities before proceeding with any further discussions. These were not forthcoming and negotiations ceased. But the matter did not end there. News began to filter through that an American animal dealer was now offering a giant panda to the Los Angeles Zoo for something in the region of 100,000 dollars. Once again, its official status was stressed. Rumour had it that it was a 90-pound male and that the Chinese zoo involved was none other than Peking itself.

It is hard to know what to make of these fragments of information. Los Angeles reacted in the same way as London, demanding proof of legality. No further details became available, however, and so far as we know the mystery panda never appeared in the western world. So for Chi-Chi there seemed no hope of finding a mate.

Early in 1965 An'-An' reared his head again. A report from Moscow indicated that he was showing signs of a sexual awakening and that Moscow Zoo might after all consider a mating for him with Chi-Chi. Michael Frayn in the *Observer* commented satirically: 'Perhaps a long holiday together for the two pandas might be arranged. Friends of the happy couple believe they would choose Ibiza, or possibly Corfu, and mingle unnoticed among the crowds like any other holiday makers ... Commentators in London point out that any meeting of the pandas would have to be preceded by a meeting at the tapir or wallaby level to prepare the ground ...'.

In fact, it seemed unlikely that Moscow was seriously reconsidering the project, but London Zoo wrote again, to make sure, repeating the earlier offer.

It was a good move; Moscow Zoo was interested, but it took nearly a year before any progress was obvious. Igor Sosnovsky, director at Moscow, invited an official from London to come and discuss the possible mating of An'-An' and Chi-Chi. London Zoo's Curator of Mammals flew to meet Sosnovsky on 4th February 1966. Sosnovsky agreed to Chi-Chi visiting An'-An' in the spring and, because Moscow's interest in the mating was purely scientific, he said that any offspring from the union would belong to London Zoo. The information about An'-An' suggested that, like Chi-Chi, he had two periods of sexual excitement each year – a strong one from February to May and a weaker one in the autumn. During these phases he would scent-mark more often than usual, bleat like a sheep and 'go off' his food. At 339 pounds, he was thought to be about 40 pounds overweight for a male, possibly because there was no bamboo in his diet, but An'-An' was healthy and had obvious testicular swellings, so hopes were set on a successful mating.

British European Airways was especially helpful and modified one of its Vanguard aircraft to carry Chi-Chi to the USSR. On 11th March 1966 she was flown out to Moscow, with her head keeper, Sam Morton, his wife and child, and the zoo's vet, Oliver Graham-Jones.

Chi-Chi was first given time to settle into her new surroundings. Then, on the 26th March, the pandas were allowed to meet, while still separated by a wire partition. They responded by barking, and were very curious of each other. Five days later, after they had become used to each other's presence, they were put together in an outside enclosure. 'We could see almost immediately there was going to be no mating today', Morton told the press; for Chi-Chi and An'-An' began circling and snarling at each other and then started fighting and had to be separated. Chi-Chi was not in heat, and so may have been considered an intruder in the male panda's 'territory'. In fact, she did not come into heat that spring, perhaps having been upset by her journey to Moscow, so London Zoo's officials flew home leaving Chi-Chi to recover in time for autumnal nuptials.

Then, on 1st October Moscow Zoo staff noticed that Chi-Chi's appetite was waning. Two days later she refused her morning feed and, moving to the bars of her cage, presented her rear-end to her keeper. There was panic: all systems were go, and Moscow cabled London asking for a team to fly out. So, on 4th October, the Curator of Mammals flew out again, this time with Victor Manton, the vet from Whipsnade Zoo, and Michael Lyster, London Zoo's photographer. All of An'-An's systems were go, too; he had started to bleat, and Chi-Chi had presented her rear to him through the bars of the adjoining grille.

Arrangements for the pandas' meeting were finally completed by 6th October, and at 1.00 pm the whole zoo was closed to the public. With water hoses, wooden shields and anaesthetic gun standing-by, Chi-Chi and An'-An' were put together for an experimental hour. At first they fought briefly, barking, and cuffing each other. They separated, but An'-An'

Chi-Chi and An'-An', in Moscow showing no signs of international friendship.
(Zool. Soc. Lond.)

persistently approached his partner, occasionally bleating, while she equally persistently barked and swiped at him, forcing his strategic retreat. Eventually he mounted her, but without an erection; so they were parted.

On their second meeting, next morning, the scenario was the same. In the afternoon, however, they met again and Chi-Chi began to assert herself, not waiting to be pursued but approaching An'-An' with barks and swipes. At least there was no serious fighting. So the pair was left together for the night, under constant watch. Both animals slept, but then Chi-Chi began pacing; she paced restlessly for hours. As dawn broke An'-An' made his first serious mating attempt. He seized Chi-Chi by the scruff of the neck and held her down; he achieved an erection but she would not raise her tail, and the coup was doomed. From then on the marriage went rapidly downhill.

Chi-Chi drove the Russian male off, and the pandas were separated. Neither had eaten much for two days, and An'-An' now took his feed but Chi-Chi refused even the bamboo specially flown out for her. She roared violently when driven from her inner den at 5 pm, then roared at An'-An' who was outside, waiting, but she quietened down and, apart from the occasional bark, it was a quiet and uneventful night. The most telling event occurred at 7 am when the animals were separated; Chi-Chi again presented herself sexually to her human observers. When pushed outside, later on, by her Russian keeper she adopted the full mating posture to him, curving her back and raising her tail, but once she was in the outside enclosure she would not let An'-An' near.

Two days of separation changed nothing. Chi-Chi continued her aggression to the male panda but often presented herself to her keeper, even with An'-An' 10 feet away. Every indication was that, because she had been raised by humans, without seeing another panda, Chi-Chi was humanized, not even recognizing An'-An' as the same species. It seemed that, in spite of strong sexual motivation, prolonged familiarization with An'-An' (56 hours together), and his persistent, unaggressive, sexual approaches, Chi-Chi was not prepared to mate with him. So the attempt was abandoned, and on 17th October 1966 Chi-Chi was flown back to London.

Hoping against hope, London at once asked Moscow about the possibility of a return-match. Perhaps, in the comfort of her own home Chi-Chi might be more receptive; it was worth a try. But over a year passed before Moscow Zoo agreed to send An'-An' to London. He arrived in the special BEA Vanguard on 1st September 1968, supposedly in time for Chi-Chi's autumn oestrus.

By stages, the two pandas were introduced to each other. At first, each was allowed, in turn, to explore the outside paddock, and picked up the smells of the other. Then they were allowed to see and smell each other through a mesh fence. Finally, as in Moscow, the two were given the same den to sleep in at night. There were many skirmishes, although none was serious, and Chi-Chi never relaxed in the male's presence. In the paddock she kept her distance from him but was more settled than she was in the dens; if An'-An' came near her she would snarl or strike him a warning blow. Unfortunately, Chi-Chi's unease in her intended's presence led to her losing condition, so they could not be left together for more than a few days at a time.

In spite of all the care that was taken, however, there was no mating (although An'-An' made several attempts) for Chi-Chi did not come into heat. An'-An' was due back in Moscow so, in November, while negotiations to prolong the sojourn were under way an attempt was made to stimulate oestrus in Chi-Chi, using hormones. Within six days she lost interest in food and showed indications of a mild 'heat'. An'-An' pursued her but she would not present herself, and he was not very persistent. On 1st December he attacked Chi-Chi, biting her on the back and mounting mid-back. She became extremely distressed, walking around and yelping pitifully, and the couple had to be separated. After 16th December she showed no more signs of heat. Moscow then agreed to extend An'-An's stay to the spring.

Now it was feared that the hormone injection would have upset Chi-Chi's natural oestrus cycle, so on 4th February 1969 she was dosed with hormones once more. The heat induced was weak again, and still Chi-Chi was unreceptive to her Soviet wooer. Each would bark or bleat. Occasionally there were skirmishes; more often, An'-An' would receive a blow to the nose; and sometimes he chased Chi-Chi hard for short periods. But there was no mating.

Michael Brambell, London Zoo's Curator of Mammals throughout this second episode, concluded that Chi-Chi probably never came fully into oestrus during An'-An's visit – the condition in which she would be prepared to accept a male and have a mature egg capable of being fertilized. In any case, the experiment was over and An'-An' had to go home; Brambell delivered him back to Moscow Zoo on 21st May 1969.

Breeding pandas in captivity was clearly not a simple matter. The Chi-Chi affair had consumed four years and made no progress, perhaps because she was humanized and unable to respond suitably to An'-An's amorous approaches; or perhaps because they were growing old for pandas, Chi-Chi being thirteen years old and An'-An' twelve when the return-match commenced.

In Peking Zoo, however, events had been far more cheerful; in fact, they had made international zoo history by breeding giant pandas in

Li-Li with her first baby, Ming-Ming, at Peking Zoo. (WWF)

captivity. They achieved this feat in September 1963, by which time they had had more than ten pandas under study in the zoological gardens, and had gained a great deal of experience. We mentioned earlier that in 1955 they had acquired three females, then another female and a male in 1956. In 1957 they obtained a young female called Li-Li who was destined to become the mother of the zoo-born baby. Later that year young Chi-Chi was caught and taken to Peking early in 1958. In 1961, when Ivor Montagu visited the gardens, he saw only one pair of adults, Li-Li and her husband. They had been living together amicably for some years, but without producing any offspring. Then, in 1962 a new male called Pi-Pi was brought in from the zoo's Animal Husbandry Station, where he had been living since 1959. Pi-Pi was mated up with Li-Li and this time the combination worked. At dawn on 9th September 1963, Li-Li gave birth to a 5-ounce male cub.

Ouyang Kan and Tung Shu-Hua, described officially as the pandas' 'chief feeder' and 'feeder' respectively, reported that: 'We named the new-born panda Ming-Ming, meaning "brilliant" in Chinese. Li-Li means "beautiful", while Pi-Pi, the baby's father, means "mischievous".' The birth was kept secret for three months because zoo staff feared that a massive influx of visitors might upset the female panda.

Li-Li with female baby, Lin-Lin. (Peking Zoo/WWF)

Li-Li proved to be a model mother, cradling Ming-Ming in her arms: 'His mother at first held him on her lap or in her arms day and night, not putting him down for a moment, neither when eating nor when sleeping. After the first month, Li-Li became less anxious and permitted the keeper to handle Ming-Ming.' Later, 'When the baby was two months old, Li-Li would play with him by tossing him from one arm to the other. When Ming-Ming grew impatient, she would soothe him with her paw just like a mother caressing a child. At three months Ming-Ming could manage to walk. The world was a novelty to him. He frequently wandered away from his mother during her nap. Recently Ming-Ming has started playing alone outside his room. He wanders in the enclosure, nuzzling anything that comes his way. He forgets to return until his mother brings him back.'

Almost exactly a year later, on 4th September 1964, Li-Li produced a second infant. Ming-Ming by this time was separated from his mother and growing rapidly. The new addition was a female and was called Lin-Lin, meaning 'pretty jade'. Rumour has it that the original male Pi-Pi, the father of Ming-Ming, had died, and that a new male had been brought in to provide Li-Li with yet another mate. If this is true, the new male could well have come from Chengtu, which was traditionally the stopping-off place for expeditions into panda country, and where the zoo is now known to be the main clearing-house for pandas under veterinary care and en route to other zoological collections. In fact, this seems likely to be the 'Animal Husbandry Station' connected with Peking Zoo, that we referred to earlier; a speculation supported by a recent statement by the World Wildlife Fund, saying that most pandas in Chinese zoos and all those in foreign zoos have spent time in 'Chengdu' (ie what we and previous authors have called Chengtu).

Detailed information on pandas in Chinese zoos is difficult to come by (only Peking regularly submits data to the *International Zoo Yearbook*), and it is hard even to estimate accurately how many captive giant pandas there are or have been in China. When Ivor Montagu, a fellow of the Zoological Society of London, visited the Peking Zoo in April 1961, he was told that there were pandas in Shanghai, Nanking, Kunming (Yunnan) and Shensu. Between them, these four zoos were said to have a total of five specimens, although it was not clear which one had two. This information was published in the *International Zoo Yearbook*, but Montagu later commented that Shensu should probably be written Chengdu. So, gradually, the picture was becoming clear. In 1964, Al Oeming, of the Alberta Game Farm in Canada, went to China and was able to see both Peking and Shanghai Zoos. He saw three giant pandas at each and was also informed that there was one at Pinkiang (Harbin) in the north-east and a trio at Chengtu.

Information also reached the office of the *Zoo Yearbook* in 1964 that two captive giant pandas had been seen that year, down in the south of China, in Canton Zoo, where a great deal of re-building and development was in progress. By 1966 the *Yearbook* staff had heard reports of three giant pandas at Canton, three at Chengtu, at least one at Chungking, a female at Hangchow, a male at Harbin, a female at Nanking, a male and two females at Shanghai, three males and four females (including the zoo-born Ming-Ming and Lin-Lin) at Peking and a pair at Pyongyang in

North Korea. Furthermore it seems that, all over China, reconstruction and modernization of zoological gardens was actively under way, and more panda births were to be expected.

Indeed, at Peking meanwhile, the third birth had already taken place. It is not clear who the father was, but on 10th October 1965 a female called Chiao-Chiao gave birth to a male cub, named Hua-Hua. The most remarkable aspect of this birth was that, according to Maurice Burton writing in the *Illustrated London News*, 'There was no mating, the new arrivals being the result of artificial insemination.' Burton used the plural 'arrivals' because his postulation was that not only Hua-Hua but also Ming-Ming and Lin-Lin were conceived by human intervention. Although we have seen no supporting evidence of this suggestion it is certainly not necessarily invalid: there is no obvious reason why the principles of artificial insemination as it is applied to domestic animals should not be applied to giant pandas. In fact, as the science of wild animal husbandry has progressed, the use of artificial insemination as a tool has become more widely practised, although it is still in its early stages of development, and although purists still regard any tampering of this nature as 'playing God'. But, as we shall see later, playing God produces pandas, even though we do not yet understand exactly how, which is why it is not always successful.

When Chi-Chi and An'-An' failed to consummate their marriage of convenience in 1969, a number of people suggested artificial insemination as the answer to the problem. For the most part they overlooked the problem of first collecting semen from a male, and at that time there seemed little chance of the Russians or the Chinese attempting this, so far as the West was aware; considerations of the technical difficulties of ensuring that the semen was good, storing it so that it would be usable, and transporting it, would have been premature. So Chi-Chi remained childless.

For three years after returning to London, Chi-Chi appeared normal and healthy, except for her occasional loss of appetite, which was presumed to be associated with oestrus. But early in March 1972 her head keeper reported that she had had a fit, and she was admitted to London Zoo's Hospital for observation. Here she seemed to be fine, was eating well, and behaving vigorously, so on 14th March she was discharged back to the collection. A visitor to the zoo was looking at her three days later when the panda started frothing at the mouth and champing her jaws, fell on her back and became quite rigid. It would have been a disturbing spectacle in any animal, but in the famous and attractive Chi-Chi it must have made frightening viewing. Quickly the visitor called a keeper and within a few minutes a vet was present. By now Chi-Chi was walking again, but her back legs were weak and poorly co-ordinated. At once echoes of previous pandas rang around the Zoo Hospital and records of them revealed that convulsions presaged a terminal illness by up to five weeks.

Treatment for Chi-Chi started immediately, but failed to stop the fits, each lasting a few minutes, which now occurred about every other day. On 30th April she suffered a particularly severe attack, lasting over thirty minutes. A thorough examination would obviously be necessary so, for the second time in her career, Chi-Chi was admitted to the Hospital and anaesthetized. Her heart, eyes, abdomen and limbs all seemed normal, and there was no evidence of a brain tumour or of parasites. Nor was the opportunity wasted to collect samples for investigation by outside experts, both of Chi-Chi's health and of panda classification, but the cause of her illness was still a puzzle and it remains so now.

Her return to the public gaze was uneventful and for the time being all seemed well, because the fits had stopped. When they struck again, however, it was with a vengeance. On 21st July Chi-Chi suffered six severe convulsions in two hours, and on one occasion was left unable to use her hind legs. To relieve her suffering she was heavily sedated and the Curator of Mammals agreed to stay with her during the night. Fortunately, perhaps, Chi-Chi never woke again; at 3.00 am she died in her sleep.

Twelve weeks later, on 12th October 1972, An'-An' died in Moscow, reportedly of a 'heart disease'. The *Cyprus Mail* remarked: 'An'-An' died on Sunday and his passing went unmarked by obituaries in Pravda, in sharp contrast to the splash treatment given by the British Press to the death of Chi-Chi.'

The press was not aware of it at the time, but Chi-Chi deserved special acclaim for setting a new longevity record for captive pandas. She had been caught in December 1957 in Szechuan, and was then believed to be seven months old, so that at her death she would have reached the grand old age of fifteen years and three months. But An'-An' was not far behind. When he came to Moscow in August 1959 he was thought to be at least two years old, and he must have lived at least fifteen years and two months. Both animals, then, way outstripped the previous record of fourteen years eight months set by Mei-Lan in 1953.

As we have mentioned, the advanced age of these two pandas may well have been a significant factor in their failure to mate. When Chi-Chi died, the post mortem carried out on her was extensive and, according to veterinary reports, the appearance of the ovaries provided convincing evidence of senility. The Zoological Society of London published a report of the scientific study of Chi-Chi stating that: '... the ovaries contained little evidence of function other than some secretory activity by the corpora lutea in the left ovary. Apart from this, no hint of cyclical activity could be obtained.' In other words, she did not appear capable of coming fully into heat. Whether this was so just three years earlier we shall never know.

In a way, the deaths of Chi-Chi and An'-An' celebrated the birth of a new era. Panda numbers in Chinese zoos had been steadily growing (although we do not know exactly how many pandas were born in captivity) and things were going so well that China decided, once again, to allow pandas out of the country. But this time they would only be exported by the Government.

Even as Chi-Chi was falling ill in London, a pair of pandas was on its way out of China, heading for Washington DC, to be the first American Ailuropods for eighteen years.

pandas today

Although pandas were valuable when London Zoo bought Chi-Chi in 1958, they rapidly became priceless. After An'-An' was exported from Peking to Moscow just a year later, no more pandas were released to the West. Hunting giant pandas was banned, and they could not be obtained for love nor money. Outside the Far East were only the hesitant An'-An' and the unconsenting Chi-Chi. Consequently the status value of owning a panda in the West was immeasurably high. In China, meanwhile, there were at least twenty pandas in zoological gardens, and as China is the only country where the specimen lives in the wild it has come to be a symbol of Chinese wildlife. Zoos all over the world were clamouring for specimens, so the giant panda was also an obvious candidate for presentation by the People's Republic of China to other nations as a gesture of goodwill.

In honour of President Richard Nixon's visit to China, in 1972, Chairman Mao gave a pair of young pandas to the US National Zoo, in Washington D.C. They arrived there on the 16th April 1972, a male called Hsing-Hsing and a female by the name of Ling-Ling. The latter was the older animal, weighing 136 pounds and believed to have been born in November 1970, making her eighteen months old. Hsing-Hsing was half her weight, at 74 pounds, although he was only six months younger. On the recommendation of Peking Zoo the animals were housed separately, as in Peking this has proved the best management practice, and the male and female there were allowed together only when she was in oestrus.

At Washington, the two pandas were clearly frustrated by being able to see each other through the wire-mesh but unable to reach the other; both animals would bite at the wire fence that separated them and, according to Susan Wilson and Devra Kleiman who studied their behaviour, 'the female especially would dig at the gravel next to the fence.' But they played a great deal and made themselves as popular as any previous pandas. Somersaulting or rolling over sideways seem to have been particularly popular exercises for the pandas and were apparently ways of inviting the other to play, but sometimes they would stop halfway, as if having just remembered something. This meant the animal often ended-up doing a headstand but with its feet still on the floor. In fact headstands and handstands were also favourite manoeuvres, but to achieve these the pandas would usually cheat and use some vertical surface for support. Sometimes they played with toys such as basketballs, plastic hoops and metal barrels, butting them or swatting them with a forepaw, and would even play with their own tails or hind limbs, pulling or mouthing them. In monkeys this behaviour is often thought to result from a neurosis that may be caused by boredom, but it did not seem so in these young carnivores. If they played together one would often run to and from its partner, toss or shake its head or twist its body. But Wilson and Kleiman found that when the two were introduced they were less inclined to roll around and swatting with the paws suddenly became the most fun.

Such frolicsome, animated creatures could not fail to please the American public; the old black-and-white magic was back. Most important of all, there was not just one panda, as in the old days of panda-keeping, but a pair, with a chance of breeding.

The aim of breeding was obviously uppermost in the minds of the Chinese donors too, because all their future gifts were to be pairs of pandas.

Ueno Zoo in Tokyo, Japan, was next to benefit from the generosity of the People's Republic of China. The ambassadors to Tokyo were Lan-Lan, a four-year-old female, and Kang-Kang, a two-year-old male. Both had been caught in Szechuan and they arrived at Ueno on 28th October 1972. Like the animals at Peking and Washington, the pair were kept separated to avoid fighting, and so that they could be introduced as soon as the female came into heat.

In Tokyo, it was not at all certain when this was likely to be. Information coming from China indicated that the timing of oestrus varied from one location to another: in Peking it was April/May, in Shanghai, to the south-east, it was in March. Interestingly, neither zoo reported an autumnal oestrus, only an annual breeding season in the spring. Whether this is because they did not witness any second 'heat' in their female pandas or because they considered it too weak to be significant is not yet absolutely clear. Lan-Lan in Ueno appears only once to have shown signs of oestrus late in the year, in September/October 1975. Her spring oestrus that year was particularly late, and hardly in the spring; the signs lasted for only three days in mid-July. Compared with her April/May heat the previous year this seems extraordinary, but perhaps this was a period of adjustment to her new latitude, environment or diet. We really cannot say. At any rate, in 1976 she showed no signs of oestrus at all. Shigeharu Asakura,

Director of Ueno Zoo, tells us that the signs of sexual activity shown by Lan-Lan were much the same as we saw in Chi-Chi: a lower intake of food, an increase in bleating, an increase in scent-marking and presentation to the male (or, in Chi-Chi's case, to the keeper), and an increase in body-cooling activity.

In 1977 Lan-Lan did not show these signs until 25th May. Immediately she was run with Kang-Kang and, to everybody's great delight, she presented herself to him and they copulated. The heat lasted just two weeks and the animals were then confined to their own quarters again while the zoo staff patiently awaited the results. But they waited in vain. There was no panda birth.

The following year Lan-Lan's oestrus began on 8th May: it lasted only eleven days but that was long enough for Kang-Kang once again to do his duty as a panda, and hopes of the first panda birth outside China ran high. But once again the zoo staff were to be disappointed. How was it that Peking could breed pandas and nobody else could? What was the secret? As it turned out, Tokyo Zoo had stumbled upon it. On 11th May 1979 Lan-Lan began her regular annual oestrus and was soon allowed to meet Kang-Kang. They were not seen to copulate until 25th May; it was a close-run thing, because two days later she showed no more signs of willingness to mate. All was fine, though, and it was just a matter of waiting. In the middle of August Lan-Lan's appetite was decreasing again, and her food intake dropped by one third. Could this be a sign of pregnancy or was she beginning a second heat, throwing all hope to the wind? Presently her nipples became reddish and swollen as if preparing for an imminent birth, she was inactive, seemed depressed and would hardly eat. Then on 31st August she collapsed, making quiet vocalizations, began frothing at the mouth and fell unconscious.

The signs were all too familiar, and the vets acted fast. But, in spite of their eager therapy, Lan-Lan died on 4th September, apparently from a disease of the kidneys. Ironically, the post mortem on Lan-Lan revealed that she was indeed pregnant, carrying a foetus 10.5cm (4 inches) long and weighing 42.6gm (1½ ounces), a tiny baby by any standards.

A Chinese magazine bore the news that on hearing of Lan-Lan's death children in Japan cried, people sent wreaths and memorial meetings were held. The Japanese people had clearly been as enchanted by their representatives from China, as any westerner might be.

It was quickly realized, in China, that progress had been made in Tokyo and that Lan-Lan's death was a stroke of extreme ill-fortune. In consequence, China did not delay in making arrangements for Ueno Zoo to receive another giant panda. The seven-year-old female, Huan-Huan, came from Baoxing in Szechuan, arriving at Ueno on 29th January 1980.

Probably because of this disturbance, she showed no signs of oestrus that year. In 1981, however, she had a very early heat period, starting on 23rd March, for three weeks, and, as we write, we wonder if this will settle down to a regular date in May, or if the variation is not latitudinal at all. For Huan-Huan the point is purely academic since disaster struck again at Tokyo just a few months after her arrival. Kang-Kang died on 30th June 1980, reportedly of congestive heart failure, a doubly bitter blow because he was a proven breeding male. As this book goes to press Ueno's new female is still waiting to discover what her fate will be.

Tokyo, however, was only the second in a series of capital cities to receive pandas from the People's Republic of China since 1972. In the following year a male called Li-Li (therefore not the same Li-Li that mothered Peking's first panda-birth) and his mate Yen-Yen arrived at the Parc Zoologique in Paris, on the 8th December, in celebration of George Pompidou's sojourn in China three months earlier. A comment in the *Daily Mail* observed that, 'quite apart from the fun of owning a pair of the world's rarest animals, French diplomats have been busy reading all sorts of prestige into them. They soberly note that Mao gave President Nixon only one panda. How much more, then, he must think of Pompidou!'

It does not much matter that the giant panda is not the rarest animal or that Nixon actually received two specimens; great political status was clearly accorded the owner of pandas. Any nation which possesses them carries not only one of the most valuable and sought-after zoological attractions but also living proof of a friendly association with China.

The male, Li-Li, was just one year old when he arrived in Paris, and Yen-Yen was already 5½ years. So it seems that like the American and Japanese pairs before them, the male was younger than his bride. Whether there is any significance to be read into this, such as an improvement of breeding probability, is unclear, but seems unlikely. The pair were normally kept apart, any attempt at promoting communal living never lasting more than ten minutes before they became intolerant of each other. In retrospect this is not surprising, not only because of the experience of other zoos with mixing pairs but also because in 1978 the Paris Zoo authorities concluded that Yen-Yen was also male. By this time, however, disaster had already hit Paris just as it had Tokyo, for on 20th April 1974, only five months after his arrival, Li-Li died. A month before he had been found lying sprawled out on the ground, instead of in his normal resting position rolled into a ball lying on his platform. He refused to eat bamboo and had a very sensitive abdomen, which proved to be the result of a large tumour in his pancreas.

All this must have been galling enough for the French diplomats who had so gloated over the arrival of their Chinese gift, but worse was to come. According to the *Guardian* newspaper in March 1976, the import of the two pandas had been blamed for an epidemic of the rare and fatal bone marrow disease *meliodosis*, for which there is no cure. Tests had been carried out by the Pasteur Institute, which identified the disease, and the floor of the pandas' enclosure was said to be contaminated. The entire zoo had to close for three months while disinfection was carried out as best it could be.

Across the Channel, Chi-Chi, as one newspaper reported was 'back in good shape'; she had been stuffed and in December 1972 was put on exhibition in the Natural History Museum, South Kensington where she sits as a permanent reminder of the evolutionary controversy to which she has contributed. Dead pandas, on the other hand, lack the charm and attraction of their living brothers and sisters, and London Zoo was desperately missing the presence of giant pandas. Fortunately, the Zoological Society of London also possessed a species that was highly prized in China – Père David's deer, that had become extinct in China during the Boxer Rebellion and had been bred in large numbers, meanwhile, in the U.K, notably at Woburn Deer Park and at Whipsnade, London's country zoo. So in 1973 four of these unusual deer were handed over from Whipsnade to Peking Zoo and the visit of Prime Minister Edward Heath to China soon afterwards clinched the deal.

On 14th September 1974 a female panda celebrating in the name of Ching-Ching (meaning 'crystal bright') and a male called Chia-Chia (meaning 'excellent') were delivered to London Zoo. Born in September and October 1972, respectively, they were only two years old, still very playful, and drew the crowds with an almost magnetic seduction. From the time of their arrival they were kept together, a fact which must have added considerably to their allurement, and there was no major problem until a year after their arrival. In October 1974 Ching-Ching began to eat less, but as there were no strong signs of oestrus this was probably not the cause. She began to lose weight, and the problem was obviously serious. Luckily it was not medical: a close examination of her behaviour showed that in the male's presence she was feeling stressed and her feeding was inhibited. As soon as a régime of separate feeding was started Ching-Ching began to gain weight again.

Since then the pair has only been together at times of her oestrus. She first showed signs of being 'on heat' at the age of 2½ years, in March 1975, and then again in October, but the indications were weak, as they were in April and December the following year; but by 1977 the signs of oestrus were more marked. The Zoo Hospital tested samples of her urine for hormone levels, and confirmed that Ching-Ching was, indeed, in

Chia-Chia and Ching-Ching (bottom) at play. (Zool. Soc. Lond.)

mating condition. It seemed, then, that she had become sexually mature at 4½ years old.

In Washington too, Ling-Ling had shown signs of heat since 2½ years of age, in 1973, but unlike the symptoms shown by Ching-Ching the onset of oestrus was always conspicuous from the start. Devra Kleiman and her co-workers at the US National Zoo record a 'decreased food consumption, increased scent-marking, backwards walking, and vocalizing (bleating)'. But the major impetus for beginning encounters between Ling-Ling and her mate, Hsing-Hsing, 'has usually been a dramatic increase in anogenital rubbing or masturbation by the female (on objects or with the paw) or an increase in interactions at sites where the two animals can see and sniff each other'. It was also noticed at Washington that the male's behaviour changed before that of the female, and it looked as if he might be coming into rut each year. If this was so, perhaps the secret of successful mating was to ensure that male and female sexual activity coincided – if the male activity was triggered by the female then this should not be a problem, but if not the panda breeders still had much work to do. It would make sense if, in the wild, a male panda was stimulated to mate by the presence of a sexually receptive female. Otherwise their hope for long term survival seemed slim. Many authorities, however, still do not believe that there is a male rut, only a reaction to the presence of a suitably prepared female, but we must remember that An'-An' had two annual periods of sexual excitement without there being any female pandas within miles.

Hsing-Hsing appeared to be in every respect a fine healthy panda but he had what is politely called an orientation problem when it came to mating. He simply was unable to position himself in the right place to copulate. When this became evident, in 1979, London Zoo offered the use of Chia-Chia as a partner for Ling-Ling, but Washington had another plan to try first. They collected semen from Hsing-Hsing and when Ling-Ling came into season in spring 1980 she was anaesthetized and artificially inseminated. This was the first time that AI had ever been attempted on a giant panda outside the Far East and unfortunately it failed. And it failed again when she was inseminated in the autumn. This technique has, therefore, yet to be perfected.

Meanwhile, in London, the affairs of pandas had taken a perilous turn for the worse. In early 1980 Ching-Ching was going off her food, which, by now, was clearly a sign of change in a giant panda. She rapidly became critically ill and lost over a third in weight. The zoo vets had to act fast. They anaesthetized the sick panda and carried out an exploratory operation that lasted for three hours, after which they felt sure she would not last long. A bacterial infection had caused a digestive malfunction which prevented Ching-Ching from absorbing the vital protein in her diet. In the fight to save her life, outside help was called in: tissue samples were sent for examination at University College and King's College Hospitals in London, and the Zoo also contacted the famous Great Ormond Street Hospital for Sick Children. The zoo's senior vet, David Jones, told the *Daily Mail* newspaper, 'Malabsorption of protein is a typical children's medical problem so we've asked doctors there (at Great Ormond St) if they can help.'

A treatment was formulated, and Ching-Ching was kept under intensive care at London Zoo's Hospital. 'For three hours a day', the *Daily Mail* reported on 3rd April, 'Ching-Ching is sedated in the operating theatre and drip-fed a special fluid rich in protein, sugars and fats . . . Her condition has improved enough for her to sit up and eat from a bowl of rice and eggs – but she is not too keen on the charcoal biscuits which will help her stomach problem, Mr Jones said yesterday.' Her chances of survival were only fifty/fifty, but she finally pulled through the worst. Having conquered that problem, however, she was still not a healthy animal.

A year after her first serious set-back, Ching-Ching suffered another. On 17th March 1981 she was rushed into the University College Hospital for a radio-isotope scan. Anticipating complaints of preferential treatment for pandas, perhaps, the hospital made it clear to the press that, 'Technical staff in the scanner room carried out the investigation voluntarily after their working hours.' They revealed some reaction in the upper gut. Chronic peritonitis was the sickness this time and a great deal of fluid had to be drained off the abdomen. Ching-Ching responded to treatment, but even as we write she is not well. 'She has not been right for three years', David Jones told us. Her weight was not at its optimum in 1978 and has shown a great deal of fluctuation, changing by as much as 20 pounds in a week. Jones now believes that there have been long term changes in her gut wall, although there is no apparent damage. So the Zoo Hospital is still carrying out tests.

For treatment of her ailments Ching-Ching has been anaesthetized over seventy times. 'This must be the most looked-at panda in history', remarked Jones. Indeed it must, and a great deal is being learnt about panda biology from Ching-Ching. What is not at all plain is that she will ever be fit to breed.

London Zoo had an inkling of this back in 1979 when they approached Washington. In preparation for the 1981 breeding season, the US National Zoo began discussions with the authorities both in London and in Paris where the twelve-year-old Yen-Yen was living a solitary existence. But hopes were still high in France that a female might be forthcoming, so for the time being they decided not to be involved. It strikes us that Yen-Yen is not young for a western panda, and that time is running out to make use of him as a breeding animal. If a female arrived in Paris now it might not be long before she became solitary. (Having said that, we should mention that *inside* China the longevity record is much higher than outside. Li-Li, the mother of Ming-Ming, lived to be at least twenty-two!)

In London it was plain that Ching-Ching would not be good for mating in 1981, so a cooperative effort with Washington was definitely on the cards. Finally it was agreed that Britain's male should fly to meet America's female in time for her spring oestrus. Certainly Chia-Chia had previously attempted to mate with Ching-Ching, so his virility was not in question.

The question arose, of course, of who would own the baby panda that might result from the meeting. It is a gratifying fact that many zoos are becoming less obsessed with owning animals and more concerned with doing the best thing for the species. Washington and London can be counted amongst these. They are effectively managing their four pandas as one group, and have decided that neither shall have the exclusive right to any progeny. The task was first to produce that progeny.

Chia-Chia left London on 5th March 1981, to give him plenty of time to settle-in to his temporary lodgings. As it turned out, Ling-Ling showed signs of heat earlier than expected: in the second week of April. To test that she was ready for mating, Hsing-Hsing, her usual suitor, was allowed to meet her. She was certainly amenable but Hsing-Hsing had his usual problem – he was completely disoriented – so had to make way for the younger panda. Chia-Chia and Ling-Ling were introduced and set about striking another blow against zoo matchmaking. The male chased the American, tried biting her legs, and they fought seriously. Finally they had to be separated, and Ling-Ling remained chaste. Only a few days after she had come into oestrus, on the 17th April she showed no more signs, and the third international panda 'love-mission' (as the *Daily Telegraph* called it) had failed.

Chia-Chia was to remain in Washington until the end of May, just in case Ling-Ling came into oestrus again. The chances are slim, but the zoos do not give up hope easily. That is how things stand at the time of writing.

Meanwhile, in Mexico, the first western panda has been born. Chapultepec Zoo in Mexico City received its gift from the People's Republic of China on 10th September 1975, in celebration of the state visit to Mexico of Vice-Premier Chen Yua Kui. The male, Pe-Pe, was ten months old and weighed only 46 pounds, while the female, Ying-Ying was just a month older and weighed 57 pounds. Both had been caught in

Jean F. Schoch, Director of Chapultepec Zoo with Pe-Pe and Ying-Ying just after their arrival in Mexico City (Chapultepec Zoo)

Szechuan three months before.

The panda house at Chapultepec had been built especially for keeping the two animals apart, on the advice of Chinese zoologists. In practice it was not necessary to keep them in separate enclosures for at least three years; and in fact they became distressed if parted from each other. Quite apart from the pandas appearing to enjoy each other's company, the zoo authorities expressed their belief (in the *International Zoo Yearbook*) that, 'by not separating the pair it will be easier to detect when they are ready to mate, and that breeding could be facilitated by the fact that the animals are accustomed to each other's presence'.

At three years of age, Ying-Ying showed signs of her first oestrus, but Pe-Pe was not interested. This was in October 1977 which, interestingly, lends support to the idea that there is an autumn oestrus. Pe-Pe, in fact, showed no sexual interest until early in 1978, and although we should not read too much into this one example, the obvious thought is that perhaps males do mature later than females (as in many other species), in which case it would be expedient to keep a female with an older male if the animals are young and every opportunity for mating is to be taken.

We are not certain that Mexico was still keeping the pair permanently together when they mated in spring 1980. No doubt this information will be published in due course, and it will be very interesting to see if this has been possible, but it seems unlikely. The early tolerance probably stems from the animals' immaturity.

Whatever the circumstances, on 11th August 1980 a panda cub was born in Mexico City, the first ever in the western world. But the ill-fortune that has always accompanied captive pandas in the West was not to be readily overcome. The cub, Xeng-Li, was just one week old when the inexperienced Ying-Ying, in her sleepy way, rolled over and crushed her cub. When you know that the unfortunate infant was only 4 inches long this episode is less surprising!

The West, then, has still to rear a giant panda and the enigma of breeding is not yet conquered. With each pair of pandas that comes into a zoo, of course, the chances of captive breeding are increased, but this has to be weighed against the substantial benefits from the conservation viewpoint of leaving them alone in the wild. As we shall see, however, there are important reasons why pandas sometimes need to be kept in captivity. If they are to be kept then it is to everyone's advantage if they live long and breed well.

In the past few years only two pairs have been sent to the West, and of course the Ueno female Huan-Huan. Madrid received the female Shao-Shao and the male Chang-Chang on 24th December 1978, and West Berlin Zoo received a male, Bao-Bao, and a female Tian-Tian on 5th November 1980. No progress has yet been reported with these. Spain's

Ying-Ying and baby three days after its birth. (Chapultepec Zoo)

female is of particular interest, because she was born in captivity in Peking, from a mating at Shanghai Zoo in spring 1975.

According to Gordon Woodroffe, in *Wildlife Conservation and the Modern Zoo*, Mexico, Shanghai and Peking are the only zoos in the world to have bred giant pandas. Of these, the most outstanding is unquestionably Peking. The only zoo to have raised cubs beyond infancy, it first bred pandas in 1963 and has done so regularly since then, although it must be admitted that even there the birth-rate is low. Of course, Peking has had a greater opportunity than any other zoo, but the achievement is not less significant for that. As they have gained in knowledge in recent years, Chinese zoologists at Peking Zoo have made their information available to outsiders. Indeed, their experiences form the basis of nearly all present knowledge of panda breeding. Much of this is summarized in the next chapter.

Several births at Peking are reported to be the result of artificial insemination. We have already mentioned Maurice Burton's report that the first three pandas born in captivity were conceived this way. Others have been reported in recent publications of the World Wildlife Fund and in the press but unfortunately there are no particulars. The West has yet to see details of the preliminary scientific work carried out in China, but when it becomes available it will be extremely important for zoo pandas and may resolve the problem of aggression by precluding the necessity of mating. However, we understand from oral reports that artificially inseminated females have subsequently been introduced to a male, although this might not be true in every case. It does stimulate many questions, which we hope will soon be answered.

Information from Peking is that there are usually two cubs in a litter, but it is unknown for more than one to survive and even hand-rearing has proved unable to salvage the second animal. Woodroffe says that of ten litters born at Peking Zoo only seven youngsters have survived.

Numbers of pandas in Chinese zoos, however, have also been increased from wild sources. In April 1973 the *Times* reported the capture of a male baby, two feet long, that was caught by a hunter in Szechuan and donated to Peking Zoo.

Michael Brambell, who keeps the zoos' studbook for giant pandas, tells us that one was caught, that year, aged about three months, and called Wey-Wey (perhaps the same animal). Wey-Wey joined the Shanghai Panda Circus on tour in Japan from February to May 1981. The exploits of Wey-Wey had hit the British headlines three years before, in May 1978. The *Sunday Telegraph* then reported him in the circus at Shanghai doing a balancing act; the versatility of pandas was obviously considerable. Wey-Wey could 'lie on his back and span a barrel with all four paws, turn somersaults and ride in a dogcart while blowing a horn'.

Other animals had left China on loan only. From March to June 1980, Canton Zoo loaned a male, Shan-Shan, and a female Pao-rin to Fukoka Municipal Zoo in Japan. Pao-rin, owing to some linguistic entanglement, is probably the female, Baoling, that Ocean Park, Hong Kong had reported on loan from Canton with another female Baoli, in 1979.

The total number of captive pandas in China now appears to be about forty, according to information received at the *International Zoo Yearbook* office from James Dolan of San Diego Zoo, who visited China recently.

The question of how many giant pandas live in the wild is harder to answer: their inhospitable territory makes any estimate of total population extremely difficult. In the past there have been only 'guesstimates', ranging from just forty animals up to several thousand. In 1974 the People's Republic of China took steps to answer the question, beginning a national survey of panda numbers. In any one day, between two and three thousand people participated in the survey. Analysis of the preliminary results indicates that the surveyors outnumbered the pandas by up to three against one. The most optimistic figures indicate that there are about one thousand giant pandas remaining in the main populations, but the number could actually be only half that many.

Pandas can also suffer severe setbacks. In the winter of 1975/76, nearly one hundred and fifty pandas were found dead. They had died not from cold but from starvation because of the extraordinary life cycle of their staple food, the bamboo.

There are many species of bamboo but the main species in panda country – fountain, umbrella and arrow bamboos – belong to the genus *Sinarundinaria* and *Thamnocalamus*. In many species, and notably those eaten by pandas, reproduction is normally asexual; no transfer of pollen is required. But eventually the entire bamboo stand will come into flower and within a few months will wither and die, leaving no bamboo until the new stand grows up from the seeds of the now-dead plants. In these species, this event is believed to happen about every one hundred years. This is what happened in 1975/76 over more than 5000 square kilometres (1900 square miles) of China. For pandas, this phenomenon is more important now than it was in the past when pandas could move from one stand to another, lived in less fragmented populations and were, in any case, more widespread.

Many more pandas must have died in 1975 than were ever found by humans: total numbers may have been reduced by anything up to one quarter. The Chinese Government and biologists reacted quickly, and immediately took measures to prevent human destruction of the remaining bamboo, investigate the biology of the bamboo and the needs of the panda and to increase the number of plant species available to the pandas. (According to local peasants, the animals turned to eating grasses, wheat and corn.)

Already, many reserves had been established and more still were set up for the protection of the pandas' habitat from other pressures. In all, seventy-five reserves existed in China by 1981 and there are plans to increase this to three hundred areas, covering 1 per cent of China's land area. Wherever pandas live, they are officially protected from hunting, and wherever practicable the area has been designated a reserve. There are at least ten special reserves for giant pandas, totalling about 600,000ha (nearly 1½ million acres). In Szechuan seven are administered locally. The Ministry of Forests administers three key reserves: Wolong in Szechuan, Foping in Shensi, and Buisha River in Kansu.

The first of these, Wolong Natural Reserve, is the centre of one of the most exceptional conservation efforts of this era, not only in terms of ambition and cost, but also because it is a joint project of a government, the People's Republic of China, and a non-governmental organization, the World Wildlife Fund (WWF).

WWF, it should be remembered, has a special interest in the giant panda because this animal has been the Fund's symbol since its foundation in 1961. That symbol was drawn by Sir Peter Scott, the Chairman of WWF International. In September 1979 he led a delegation to Peking to discuss problems of wildlife conservation in China. The discussions led to an agreement in October between WWF and the People's Republic of China, setting up 'the WWF/China Joint Committee' of six conservationists and scientists, three from each signatory. As its first priority China decided to make every effort to save the panda.

Although only a fifth of Wolong Natural Reserve is suitable for giant pandas, this is the largest of the specially protected areas, covering about 2000 square kilometres, and it was decided to set up a research and conservation centre there. Sir Peter Scott was invited to lead a delegation of western scientists to visit Wolong in May 1980. These were the first westerners to visit this part of China, in western Szechuan, since the 1930s, and the first *ever* to be invited there.

The scheme was to set up a massive research station at Wolong with living accommodation for its staff. There would be a panda breeding unit, a wildlife research laboratory and a hydro-electric power station. The breeding unit would also be used as a holding station for pandas brought in in the event of a bamboo die-off, since it is predicted that this will occur in Wolong within the next ten years.

WWF set to work finding technical help and deciding on its own com-

Sir Peter Scott, Chairman of WWF-International with
a semi-wild panda at Yingxionggou, the site of the new research centre.
(WWF/Philippa Scott)

mitment. It was to be substantial. On 30th June 1980, at the Soestdijk Palace in the Netherlands, WWF International and the People's Republic of China signed a Protocol in which WWF pledged to contribute U.S.$1 million towards the cost of the new Centre. The total needed would be some U.S.$4.5 million, so China's own commitment was momentous.

Plans forged ahead, and the Chinese authorities have gladly sought western expertise to help in the preparation. From New York Zoo, director William Conway advised on the design of the panda breeding facility. From London Zoo, John Hearn and Keith Hodges from the Institute of Zoology advised on the laboratory set-up.

Building has already started and the design was specially adapted to blend with local architecture. The laboratories will be fitted out for work on reproductive physiology, nutrition, behaviour and veterinary science. Significantly, the behavioural research is already well under way.

George Schaller has been seconded to the World Wildlife Fund from New York Zoological Society where he is director of the Animal Research and Conservation Center. He is renowned in the zoological world for his pioneering work on the study of animal behaviour, notably on mountain gorillas, and he accompanied Peter Scott to Wolong in May 1980. Seven

Sketch of the proposed research station at Wolong.
(WWF)

months later he was back there, this time to study the giant panda in the wild. He would be working with Professor Hu Jin Chu of Nanchong Teachers' College, probably Szechuan's best naturalist.

Their base camp is at Wuyipeng, and the difficulty of their task is indicated by the experience of other researchers; a team that had been in the area since 1978 had seen only sixteen pandas in all the time they were there. In 1981 it was particularly difficult for Hu and Schaller because the January snows failed, making it hard to follow tracks. As Schaller reported in a letter to the WWF, 'One of our tasks is to find out if pandas select certain parts of the bamboo and, if they do, how much of their preferred food is available at various seasons. Are the selected portions more nutritious than the others? Samples must be collected, dried and weighed for later analysis.' Pan Wen Shi, a biologist from Beijing University, and Wang Xue Quan, a wildlife expert from the Northeast Forestry College, in Harbin, are working on this problem in particular and have been collecting bamboo samples.

In February the snows occasionally fell, and Hu and Schaller were out tracking in the bitterly cold weather of the Chinese winter. In February, they were joined by Howard Quigley, a researcher from New York Zoo,

*George Schaller, Wang Meng
Hu of China's Forestry Ministry
and Professor Hu Jin Chu
examine giant panda tracks in
Szechuan. (WWF/Nancy Nash)*

and a new phase of the work began. Quigley is an expert in radio-telemetry, and the aim was to put a radio collar on a panda and follow its every move without disturbing it. 'Traps were baited', reported Schaller. 'Day after day we made our tedious and far-flung rounds to check traps, but without result. Our traps are in good locations where pandas can logically be expected to walk. But panda logic and human logic do not necessarily coincide, and the traps remained monotonously empty. Still, there were moments of intense expectations. Once Wong Lian Ke saw a panda ambling towards a trap, but with a few metres to go it sensed its human observer and bolted. Another time a panda circled a trap, unable to reach the bait because a yellow-throated marten had earlier triggered and closed the trap door.' Their frustration continued and their traps remained empty, but it was important to fit the collars before the breeding season started so that they did not disturb the pandas during this crucial period.

Satisfaction was provided in other ways. 'A lone spruce rises tall and straight from a bamboo thicket. Near the top of a bough, some 15m above ground, crouches a small panda, perhaps 3 years old. Below, among the lower limbs, sits a massive panda. Hu and I infer that the youngster has sought refuge in the tree after being chased by the adult, but, being unable to determine the sex of the animals, we do not know the basis for the antipathy. Twice the young panda sends a long-drawn hoot plaintively across the silent and snowbound hills. We see the adult panda slide down the tree hindfeet first and disappear, and we watch the youngster seek a secure seat before dusk and fog obscure our view.

'As we turn toward Wuyipeng, we grin at each other with pleasure.'

But patience and dogged persistence were rewarded and, in a letter to WWF received on 26th March, Schaller reported a young male panda and an old female with radio collars attached.

Thanks to the People's Republic of China and the World Wildlife Fund, George Schaller and Hu Jin Chu are breaking virgin ground in one of the most exciting and important wildlife conservation projects to be conceived, to dispel the ignorance of more than a century about a large wild mammal that would otherwise certainly be threatened with extinction.

the zoology of the panda

Despite its colourful history, we have discovered remarkably little about the biology of the giant panda in the one hundred and twelve years since its discovery or, for that matter, about the biology of its small cousin, the red panda. Until George Schaller and Professor Hu Jin Chu started their work, in 1980, there had been no detailed field study of the giant panda by any professional zoologist, and so far as we know the lesser panda is still awaiting study. It is not hard to see why this is so, for both animals inhabit regions extremely inhospitable to humans. As we write these pages the field study is still at an early stage; its completion will undoubtedly fill a great many gaps in our zoological knowledge. But in the meantime we are not completely ignorant. Scraps of information, a piece here and a piece there, have become available over the years and we can glean some idea of the panda's natural existence by assembling these hard-won fragments.

Forty-four years of keeping giant pandas in zoos have also given us certain information about their behaviour, anatomy and physiology, most of which has only become available in the last twenty years, but which throws a flood of light on the picture.

Firstly, where do pandas live? It has already emerged that they are confined to the Himalayan range of Central Asia, but what is their exact geographical range? The red covers a wider area than the giant panda, being found all along the forested slopes of the Himalayan mountains, through Nepal, Sikkim, northern Burma and into western China. At the eastern end of its range it becomes larger and sturdier, and this Chinese race is known as Styan's panda (*Ailurus fulgens styani*) after the man who discovered it in 1897, F. W. Styan. It is found right through northern Yunnan and up into Szechuan, almost to the borders of Kansu. Its distribution therefore overlaps considerably with that of the giant panda.

Both species live at high altitudes, typically between 5000 and 10,000 feet, but they may wander even higher, to as much as 12,000 feet.

The stronghold of the giant panda is undoubtedly Szechuan, but the

Map of China showing main populations of the giant panda.
(From *Trans. Zool. Soc. Lond. 1976* (33))

studies of Chinese scientists indicate that the main distribution extends into at least two other provinces. There now appear to be three main populations, which may adjoin each other. The best known of these is in central and northern Szechuan, and reaches north into southern Kansu (or Gansu). The Russian explorer Berezovski, approaching panda territory from the north, encountered it here in the mountain range that forms the border between Kansu and Szechuan. This is nearly 500 miles north of Yehli, where the Roosevelts shot their giant panda. The second population inhabits the Liang-shan mountains of south-eastern Szechuan, and the third occurs to the north-east of Szechuan, in southern Shensi Province (also called Shaanxi) on the south-facing slopes of the Ching Ling mountains. Some sightings of pandas certainly occur outside these areas but the present view in China, expressed by Michael Brambell in the London Zoo study of Chi-Chi, seems to be that these stragglers are not significant in any estimate of total numbers.

Even without these outlying pandas, however, the territory they cover is enormous, but it is only a small part of their former range. Only a few thousand years ago giant pandas roamed throughout much of eastern

China; their range was diminished largely by the destruction of their natural habitat.

Hung-Shou Pen, along with other members of a Natural Resources Exploration Expedition, encountered a mother with two cubs far away to the west, on the Tibetan plateau. It was early morning on 10th June 1940, when they saw them. The party was near the twin lakes of Tsaring Nor and Ngoring Nor in the Tsinghai province of north-eastern Tibet. The expedition guide was the first to spot them, sauntering along on the opposite side of a river. The explorers quickly forded the river on horseback and were then able to watch as the mother panda munched her breakfast. 'The colour of the two cubs was paler than that of the mother animal. They followed and sucked their mother as does a little pig or calf. Later they turned back and suddenly flashed before us in all their beauty. Our guide and bodyguards drove them away by shouting. They were then frightened and hurried away.'

Hung-Shou Pen was naturally excited about this observation, since the nearest known giant panda country was over 175 miles away to the east, and he began to make enquiries to try and ascertain whether his observation had been a freak case. Perhaps these animals were isolated, displaced pandas, a long way off their normal beat. But this did not appear to be the case. He was informed that: 'The fur of the panda is rarely to be found in the market at Sining, the capital of Chinghai province. It does not fetch such a good price as that of the blue bear, as the fur is considered rather coarse.' In other words, pandas were well known enough in Tibet for the qualities of their fur to be weighed against that of the local bears. So the species certainly exists in small numbers on the Tibetan plateau of western China, although perhaps only in isolated pockets.

Altogether, then, this adds up to a formidable Asiatic distribution, extending from Tsinghai in the north-west to Shensi in the north-east to Yunnan in the south, making a triangle with sides of 500 miles (approximate maximum longitudes: 97-107°; approximate maximum latitudes: 27-35°). As there are many unexplored mountainous regions adjacent to this area, we may yet see the panda's realm expand still further in the textbooks of the future. The three main populations, however, already cover some 11,500 square miles (30,000 square kilometres), and it seems improbable that any other major population will come to light.

For all their vast range, pandas, like other animals, are not evenly scattered throughout their homeland. They are limited by their biological requirements. As we have seen from earlier chapters, the typical giant panda habitat is the almost impenetrable bamboo forest on the steep mountain slopes. This bamboo belt gives way, higher up, to the rhododendron forest, and into this the animal does not normally venture. Only two exceptions to this rule were noted by the members of the Sage West China Expedition: 'In one case we found unmistakable panda droppings high on the Chen Lliang Shan range, 1000 feet above the rhododendron forest, and probably 1500 feet above the nearest bamboo. It was interesting to find that on occasion the panda must travel above its regular habitat to the bare grasslands of the blue sheep country. In another instance I saw where a giant panda had climbed a small pine tree just above the village of Tsapei on Chengou River. It was located 300 feet above the river bottom on an open slope, with the nearest bamboos across the valley.'

Hung-Shou Pen's Tibetan observation is, of course, another exception, for he saw his animals on the open steppe of the high plateau. The mother panda was clearly seen to be feeding on a variety of succulent plants that were plentiful at the time. Pen argues that perhaps there is an annual east-west panda migration, determined by the fluctuating food supplies. He points out that in the winter the plateau would be too bleak and the animals would descend eastwards to the bamboo slopes of the mountains, across the border in Kansu. There they would spend the winter months and then trek back to the west again at the end of the following spring: 'This westward migration will lead the animal through an open valley where the Ma Chu or the uppermost part of the Yellow River passes through. Along this stream there is a great abundance of water and vegetables. The winter and spring are severely cold on the plateau; while in the forests of the high mountains the weather is less rigorous and bamboo shoots are thickly growing and provide the panda with its staple food. In the summer the conditions are reversed in these two habitats: in the plateau nutritious vegetables are to be found everywhere, besides a plentiful supply of mouse-hares and fishes. At that time the accumulated snow in the forests is still there unmelted and the succulent bamboo shoots have already grown into bamboo thickets no longer palatable. Other vegetables are covered by snow as on the plateau in winter. That is the reason why the panda has to migrate to the Tibetan plateau in summer.'

Although this is an ingenious idea it is perhaps dangerous to accept it too readily on the basis of Pen's slender information. It may well apply to those pandas living near the Tibetan border, but it is doubtful if all the Chinese specimens from further east set off on a regular summer migration of this kind.

The most important aspect of Pen's report is that it proves something about wild pandas that zoo men had already discovered with their captive specimens, namely that they can survive – for a while at least – on a completely bamboo-less diet. Strangely enough this fact is mentioned by Père David in the very first published notes on the giant panda's way of life, but seems to have been overlooked by later writers. They were so absorbed by the bamboo-eating specializations of the species that they automatically assumed it ate nothing else. It was Sheldon who finally sealed the error in 1937, with his authoritative statement that 'Not only is the giant panda entirely herbivorous, but it is known to live on the dwarf bamboo of the northeastern spur of the Himalayas to the exclusion of *all* other vegetable matter.' From that date onwards the giant panda was looked upon as a totally bamboo-bound species, like the koala in its gum trees, but Hung-Shou Pen's female panda was happily tucking in to gentians, irises, crocuses, Chinese vines (*Lycium chinense*), and tufted grasses such as tice-grass and bent-grass. The plants were apparently grubbed up by the female who then ate them, roots, bulbs, leaves, and all.

The local Tibetan inhabitants claimed that the giant panda also occasionally hunted fish, pikas (mouse-hares) and small rodents, but Pen was unable to back this up with personal observations. Père David had been told a similar story seventy years before: 'It is said that it does not refuse meat when the occasion presents itself.' It is surprising therefore to read in Dwight Davis' monograph in 1964 that 'They refuse meat in captivity.' It is not only surprising, it is also untrue. Chi-Chi luxuriated on morsels of roast chicken as a diet supplement from the time of her arrival at London Zoo in 1958 up until her death fourteen years later.

Despite these comments it must be admitted that bamboo *is* the principal, basic diet of the giant panda and it is interesting to see just how the animal deals with such an unfriendly food. The main bamboo in question goes by the name of *Sinarundinaria* and it grows in dense thickets to a height of 10 to 12 feet. (Some idea of the density can be gained from one of Schaller's comments, 'To trace the route of a panda for 2km (1¼ miles) may take all day'.) The culms are slender, rarely exceeding an inch-and-a-half in diameter. Naturally, the panda prefers the thinner, younger and more succulent shoots to the older, tougher stems, but these alone would be insufficient for its needs. In addition it breaks off the bigger, hardened culms and devours these too. By examining the remains of panda feasts in the field, Ernst Schaefer was able to conclude that 'The bulk of its nourishment consists . . . of stone-hard bamboo stems thicker than a finger. With its powerful molar teeth the panda bites off the 3 to 6m. long stems about 20 to 40cm. above the ground, lays them down and eats the middle part up to the beginning of the leaves, while it regularly rejects the lower, hard part and lets it lie. Such chewed places are not particularly hard to find, although they are always concealed in the middle of the jungle. Usually they are not larger than one to two square metres. In these places perhaps 15 to 20 stems are bitten off, and the rejected parts cover the ground.'

Perhaps this is just a passing snack, for George Schaller has found that much larger quantities can be devoured. In a letter to the World Wildlife Fund, written from Wuyipeng in February 1981, he explained, 'With fingers so numb from cold that they can barely hold a pencil and shivering in our sodden clothes we record the age of each stem and measure the remnants. One feeding site revealed that the panda had consumed two hundred and thirteen stems. Having measured and weighed various bamboo parts, we can calculate that the animal ate about 3kg (6½ pounds) in one casual meal.'

In the act of eating, the giant panda brings into play its specialized front feet. We have already referred to the famous 'sixth claw' that enables it to grasp with precision even the most slender stalks and carry them to the mouth. This is not really a claw at all, but an elongated wrist-bone (35mm. in length) covered in a tough, fleshy pad. It functions exactly like an opposable thumb. For some reason the real thumb was not employed in this evolutionary development. It lies quietly alongside the other four digits and acts *with* them, not against them as in man. The mobility of the panda's pseudo-thumb is not passive. It is capable of active, powerful grasping, thanks to the fact that during the course of evolution it has stolen some of the muscles normally running to the real thumb. These have shifted over and become attached to the enlarged wrist-bone, endowing it with powerful 'opening' and 'closing' movements that provide the hand of the panda with a strong forceps grasp.

The pseudo-thumb bone is known technically as the radial sesamoid

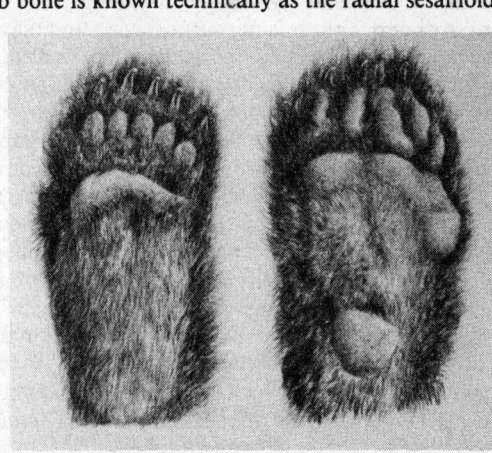

The claws of the giant panda, showing the pseudo thumb (far right)

and it is interesting that this same bone is also enlarged, but not to such a great extent, in the red panda. This animal can also use it to grasp bamboo shoots, but there is obviously less power involved. It would seem that, as the giant panda grew bigger during the course of evolution, and began to feed on larger and tougher stems of bamboo, its grasping mechanism managed to keep pace by becoming more and more sturdy and muscular, until it developed into the unique pseudo-thumb that we see today. Throughout the whole animal kingdom there is nothing exactly like it.

Having this dextrous ability, the giant panda can sit back and enjoy its meal in a relaxed posture. In fact, it always carries the bamboo up to its mouth, rather than lowering the mouth to the food. In this way its feeding movements and postures are superficially extremely human.

When the bamboo stalk is brought up to the mouth, it is grasped by the teeth and the tough outer layers are stripped off. This is achieved by a sideways turning of the head combined with a twisting movement of the hand. The peeled stalk is then placed sideways into the corner of the mouth, where the massive cheek teeth lie. With a powerful crunch of the heavy jaws a section is then bitten off and laboriously chewed.

The whole head of the giant panda has become modified as a crunching machine. The skull is heavy, the jaws broad and strong, the muscles immense. The cheek teeth are huge, blunt, grinding-stumps. They are adorned with so many ridges and tubercles that drawings of them look like miniature relief maps of the mountainous terrain in which the animal lives.

Even after being battered by the mighty molars, the swallowed bamboo fragments are still formidable objects for any digestive tract to have to deal with. It is not surprising to find that the oesophagus has a horny lining, or that the stomach is thick-walled, muscular and almost gizzard-like. The panda does, however, have a surprise in store for us in its guts. The prediction here would have been that the intestines would be tremendously elongated. This is typically what happens with other herbivorous mammals. But with the giant panda (and the red panda, too, for that matter) the guts are shortened instead of lengthened. This secondary shortening of the intestines connected with a secondary herbivory is as odd and as unique as the panda's pseudo-thumb.

The total length of the unwound intestines of an adult giant panda is only five-and-a-half times its overall body length. In relative terms, this makes it one of the shortest-gutted carnivores in the world today. When one thinks of the indigestible nature of its bamboo diet, it is hard to understand why there has not been some elaboration of the guts to help deal with the situation. A close look at the different sections of the intestines reveals that most of the shortening has taken place in the region next

Typical feeding posture.
(Granada TV)

to the stomach and it has been argued that, at this stage, the food is still largely insoluble. It is thought to be passed quickly through the abbreviated small intestine and on into the comparatively normal large intestine, where it can be acted upon by the gut bacteria and protozoa.

The strange thing about the panda's digestive system is that it is obviously so inefficient that one would think it had only just started to evolve and was not yet properly adapted to the newly acquired plant-eating habits of its originally carnivorous owner. But then one has to cast one's mind back to the extraordinarily efficient development of the bamboo grasping pseudo-thumb. It can hardly be said that that organ is 'just beginning' to develop. And so, for the present, the giant panda's guts must retain their mystery.

One point is certain, namely that they do not retain much of the goodness of the swallowed bamboo. Field observers have always reported that the droppings of giant pandas are remarkable for their size and for the largely undigested matter they contain. William Sheldon managed to make reasonably detailed observations in one particular case, when he was able to follow the track of an adult animal for some distance, shortly after snow had fallen: 'For two miles it wound in and out through the bamboo thickets where the animal had fed, and the surprising detail was that at an average of every hundred yards there were from one to three large droppings (4 to 6 inches long and 2 inches thick, tapering at each end). At a conservative estimate there were 40 droppings when the track was still two hours old. At this point I disturbed the panda, but could not see it because of the dense bamboos. The animal had been resting at the base of a small spruce tree, and must have stopped feeding before 9 am. Below the resting place was a pile of at least 30 more droppings, making a total of 70 excreted between the very early morning and 9 am . . . I pursued the animal for three hours longer, and I found droppings almost as frequently for another four miles, although it had not stopped to feed meanwhile . . . These droppings emerge almost totally undigested. It seems logical to assume that an animal of such large proportions must have to eat tremendous quantities to secure the nourishment that it requires . . . I estimate that they would have to spend from 10 to 12 hours a day feeding in order to secure sufficient for their needs.'

Researchers at Washington Zoo have calculated just how efficient is the panda's digestion of bamboo. Their male panda was experimentally fed on a quantity of bamboo with a potential crude fibre (roughage) content of 1056gm; when the animal's teeth and gut had done their work, the faeces still contained 440gm of crude fibre. So only half of the crude fibre that the panda had eaten was sufficiently chewed to ensure its digestion. Overall, it was estimated that the giant panda uses only 46-66 per cent of the energy content of the bamboo it eats.

The panda in the wild state is therefore a giant food machine of rather poor quality, like the gorilla. Surrounded all day by its natural bamboo larder, it sits munching steadfastly on, hour after hour. Its more lethal relatives – the carnivorous carnivores – would, if they understood, sneer at it as a clumsy, heavy-boned, dim-wit. Instead of hunting down highly nutritious prey every so often and then lying around sunning itself, the panda has waved goodbye to the nimble-minded world of helter-skelter chases, bloated blood-feasts and sprawling cat-naps. Instead it has become (literally) a manual labourer, toiling endlessly at its repetitive bamboo-picking tasks.

In reply, the panda would no doubt point out that life in the bamboo forests is serene and untroubled by sudden deaths and disasters. There are few predators to speak of, and there is an endless supply of food. If one has to be heavy-boned and clumsy in order to crunch it up, it really does not matter, because there is nothing to force one to be un-clumsy. There is no pressure on one to start sprinting, either towards a prey or away from a predator. Life in the bamboo jungle has its compensations.

Moving from wild pandas to zoo-kept specimens, it is not surprising to find them taking greedily to nutritious diet substitutes. With their inefficient digestive systems, a carefully prepared 'porridge' of mixed fruits, vegetables, cereals, minerals and vitamins soon proved most welcome and drastically cut down the amount of time spent feeding. It did not always cut it down enough, however, and some pandas tended to gorge themselves on this new luxury diet and rapidly became over-weight. In some instances they even began to ignore their ancestral bamboo. Zoo officials decided that the only thing to do was to ration the rich substitutes and insist that their pandas ate at least half their daily food in the form of bamboo shoots and stems. This system has worked well ever since and, in the main, the feeding of captive pandas has provided less of a problem than was once feared.

Shortly after Chi-Chi had been purchased by the London Zoo, the veterinary department instituted the following daily food régime for her:

1 lb. boiled rice	½ lb. bread
6 oranges	yeast
6 bananas	2½ oz. chocolate
3 pears	sugar
3 apples	salt
grated carrots	chicken (cooked, every other day)
2 eggs (raw)	vitamin additives
	mineral additives

Half this daily diet was mixed up into a 'porridge' and served in the morning. The other half was mixed and served in the evening. The total daily weight of this food was between 9 and 10 pounds. A constant supply of bamboo was also available, with a minimum of 9 pounds put into the panda's enclosure every day.

At the time when this feeding régime was introduced Chi-Chi weighed about 150 pounds. On the average she consumed about 9 pounds of the porridge and 6 pounds of bamboo every day through her first winter at the zoo. As the months passed and she began to grow, the amounts offered were modified slightly and the components of the porridge were somewhat simplified, but the basic system was retained. At one point, Chi-Chi did start to become over-weight and it was then that the 'fifty-per-cent-bamboo' diet rule was enforced. When she became mature, however, and started to experience her first periods of heat, it was the porridge and not the bamboo that fell out of favour. This is an interesting twist in food preferences. Previously she had been only too eager to demolish her special mixture and, as with other pandas, she was in danger of becoming de-bambooed. But now, with her food intake sinking lower and lower as the sexual mood increased, it was the porridge that was the first to be ignored. At the height of the sexual heat, nothing at all was eaten, but just before and after the peak she would still toy with a bunch of bamboo shoots. It is hard to explain this shift in preferences and we are once again up against the hard fact that we really know next to nothing about the natural feeding habits of the animal. Perhaps there *are* seasonal changes in the kinds of food preferred, as Pen has suggested. In the meantime it is worthless to speculate. We must simply wait patiently for the results of the present field study.

As she became older the diet was modified further still, and was listed by Michael Brambell in the study on Chi-Chi. Where she had been given twelve raw eggs she was later given six boiled ones, 'to avoid the risk of avidin poisoning', and eventually eggs were removed from the diet altogether. Milk and sugar were withdrawn completely, and after 1966 she developed a taste for tea, 'a taste apparently acquired in Moscow'.

In American Zoos the feeding régime has been much the same as at London, with a few minor differences. At Chicago, Robert Bean offered his pandas vegetables, fruit and sliced bread in addition to bamboo. His diet included green corn stalks, green soy bean plants, spinach, chard, raw carrots, apples, milk and porridge. At New York, Pandora was at first also given a wide variety of supplements, including milk, egg, honey, orange juice, fish oil, green corn stalks, willow sprigs, celery, lettuce, chard, beet tops and baked potato. After a while she began to refuse many of these items and by the time she was adult was only taking bamboo and a semi-liquid formula consisting principally of powdered milk, raw eggs, honey, water, and vitamin and mineral additives. Again, one would like to know the exact significance of this change in food preferences, but again we can only record it and await further news from China.

Much of the present diet of the Washington animals, in the way of American diets, is pre-mixed and pre-packed, specially prepared for zoo animals. Hsing-Hsing, for instance, receives 3½ pounds of cooked rice, 2 tablespoons of Vitamin Diet Fortification Mixture, ¾ cup of powdered cottage cheese, 2½ tablespoons of Panda Mineral Premix, 1 tablespoon of soy oil and 2 tablespoons of honey, all mixed together and served twice a day. He also gets half a can of a special zoo diet for carnivores (Zu/ Preem Feline Diet), ¾ pound of apples, 1 pound of carrots and has 25 pounds of bamboo provided. Ling-Ling has slightly less than this, but for all its unnaturalness both animals do very well on this diet.

Diets for giant pandas at other zoos outside China vary only in the details, but have changed little in substance since the days of Chi-Chi.

At Peking Zoo the food régime for pandas appears to be much the same as in the West. In addition to bamboo leaves and shoots they are given milk, sweetened gruel, eggs and biscuits, three times a day, as well as fruits and various supplements including ground bone.

Turning from feeding to breeding, the information is, of course, more fragmentary, but from the many births at Peking we are now getting a much better picture. Most births occur in September. Ming-Ming was born on the 9th and Lin-Lin on the 4th September the following year. The most astonishing fact to emerge is that Ming-Ming weighed no more than 5 ounces (140gm) at birth and looked rather like a small rat: ('One could scarcely recognize him as a giant panda.') His mother Li-Li, at 250 pounds was eight hundred times as heavy as her offspring. But judging by recent data, Ming-Ming was relatively large at birth. The cub born at Chapultepec, as we have mentioned, was only 4 inches long and weighed 100gm (3½ ounces), and the range of usual weights at birth in Peking is now recorded as 90-130gm, ie 3-4½ ounces.

Growth is rapid for a young panda and after only twelve weeks Ming-Ming had multiplied his bulk by forty times, weighing 12 pounds and measuring 2 feet in length. Three weeks later, on 1st January, he tipped the scales at 15½ pounds and was nearly 2½ feet long. By the end of January he weighed 21 pounds. Lin-Lin showed approximately the same rate of growth, reaching the weight of 22 pounds by 19th February, when she was about 5½ months old.

Two cubs are usually born, sometimes one or three but, as Brambell notes, 'Peking Zoo know of no recorded instance of a mother, in the wild or captivity, rearing more than one cub; the others are left on the ground and die of neglect or from being rolled upon.' Blind and toothless at birth, the infant pandas have a pale red skin and only sparse white hair, and they are cradled gently by the mother during the early weeks. Film of Li-Li holding Ming-Ming released from Peking, shows her cuddling and hand-ling the baby in a startlingly human manner. While sitting up with her back leaning against the corner of her zoo den, she hugs and fondles the young animal, holding it to her chest, and frequently licking it. By the age of one month it has acquired its permanent characteristic colour scheme. It is not until it is between three and four months old that the baby is able to crawl.

Li-Li was apparently extremely co-operative with the zoo staff and permitted her offspring to be removed for weighing. Sometimes she posi-tively welcomed visitors, but on other occasions, she turned her back on them, grasping Ming-Ming tightly to her body. Zoo officials noted that Ming-Ming could shout loudly, out of all proportion to her tiny body size, and he 'shrieks at anything that seems threatening and is responsive to sound. If we call out his name two metres away, he never fails to turn back and come to us.'

Ming-Ming had 'cut several teeth' by January 1964. We now know that the milk teeth start to come in at 2½-3 months and are fully-in by the time the young panda is 5-6 months old. It then has, on each side of each jaw, two incisors, one canine and three premolars – that is, twenty-four teeth. By the age of 6 months the cubs should be fully weaned; it leaves its mother and becomes quite independent. From the evidence we have, it seems that the adult dentition begins to erupt at 12-14 months. The adult panda has forty or forty-two teeth, comprising (on each side) three upper and three lower incisors, one upper and one lower canine, three or four upper and four lower premolars, and two upper and three lower molars.

Sexual maturity is not thought to occur before the age of about six years, although there is sure to be a variation between individuals. In Washington, as we have said, Ling-Ling showed signs of her first oestrus at 2½ years; even so, this does not mean she was fit to breed. Both Li-Li in Peking and Ying-Ying in Mexico were six years old when they first produced cubs.

In Peking, oestrus appears clearly in the spring and may last four to fourteen days. If the male and female fight when placed together, they are separated. Persistent, twice-daily introductions seem to pay dividends, however, and when the female is ready she walks backwards towards the male. They mate in a squatting position, and the process may last as little as thirty seconds or up to 4½ minutes. If the mating has been successful the gestation lasts 118-168 days, such a large variation as to indicate that a delay may sometimes occur between the egg being fertilized and it becoming embedded in the wall of the uterus (ie delayed implantation).

Six weeks after the start of pregnancy the female's appetite increases, and a month before birth it drops again until, finally, for a few days before giving birth the mother eats nothing. During these last days, her breasts begin to swell, the nipples protrude and become reddened, ready for supplying milk to the new-born panda. So the birth generally occurs in late summer.

If the mating has not been successful, then weak signs of oestrus are often seen in the autumn in Peking. Not all panda owners agree on this, however. At Washington, Ling-Ling is only reported to have a regular annual oestrus in the spring. With Chi-Chi, though, the indications were unmistakable twice a year.

Ever since Chi-Chi arrived at London Zoo in 1958, Head Keeper Sam Morton kept detailed records of her development and behaviour. By turning his panda diary into a chart, it was possible to show that Chi-Chi's periods of heat followed a characteristic bi-annual rhythm. As we mentioned in Chapter 7, her first period came when she was 3½ years old, in the autumn of 1960. Morton noted that from 1st to 10th October she was off her food for the first time, was bleating and calling and was leaving scent marks on her 'territory'. Her mood also changed and she became more affectionate towards her keepers, pushing her rear end up against their legs if they stood still. The phase passed but re-appeared again the following year, from 12th to 20th February. During this eight-day period she ate nothing but the most tender bamboo shoots. From 7th to 20th October the same thing occurred. In 1962 the spring period of heat did not begin until 12th March but was much longer, lasting until 1st April. The bleating and calling was stronger and more insistent and her passion for her keepers more intense. In the autumn of 1962 a change was noticeable. She came into heat on 20th October, but instead of becoming more friendly, she was 'rather spiteful this time... increasingly vocal, calling and bleating, and shows signs of really looking for a mate... She now shows signs of temper when she is approached. She does not wish to go into her sleeping den at night and it is with great reluctance that she does so.'

It seems as if Chi-Chi, after several unsuccessful sexual seasons, was beginning to become dissatisfied with her environment. When no mate materialized in response to her calls and her scents, her reproductive system went into revolt. As if determined to attract a male at all costs, it began to work overtime. As the chart shows, 1963 saw two spring periods of heat and two in the autumn. In addition, they were more intense and more prolonged. Her spitefulness developed into a 'wicked temper'. Her wanderings through her paddock became more agitated and elaborate.

Towards the end of 1963, the situation became serious. Chi-Chi had been on heat for so long that she was beginning to lose weight. During the earlier, normal heat periods of one to two weeks, her no-food-during-sex rule had resulted in brief but marked dips in the curve of her weight chart, but these were never any cause for alarm. They were quickly rectified as soon as the sexual phase was over. But now, with a period of heat extending over two months and showing no signs of ending, something had to be done. We have already mentioned that the veterinary department was called in and a course of tranquillizers was administered. Chi-Chi began to take a little food, Sam Morton having discovered that he could tempt her with a bar of chocolate. Throughout the first half of December the tranquillizers were continued. She had been on heat since the beginning of October, but now at last she showed signs of calming down. Bamboo came back on the menu, and then dates. By January 1964 she was completely back to normal and was putting on weight again.

During 1964 the spring heat was seriously delayed, as if the reproductive system had worn itself out with its great efforts in 1963. It did not, in fact, appear until the early summer, and was brief, lasting only from 10th to 17th June. In early August there was another mild sexual phase and then a more typical one in September. Happily this proved to be normal in length and intensity and was terminated naturally without any veterinary assistance. Soon after, of course, it was disturbed again by flights to and from Moscow, and by hormone injections to stimulate oestrus. But perhaps Chi-Chi was completely abnormal. One animal is a small sample on which to base any firm conclusions.

But, abnormal or not, her bi-annual season mirrors what has been observed in China. Returning to the question of birth peaks, there is obviously then a possibility of bi-annual birth periods. Every indication is that the spring breeding is the strongest, so that most births come in late summer. This does seem strange, since the cub will be very small, and susceptible to the northern winter that comes only a few months after its birth. Presumably there must be some evolutionary adaptive advantage in being born late in the year, but this is puzzling. It may be that predators are fewer at this time of year in panda habitat, but we will come to that presently.

The situation is similar in Himalayan bears (and bears elsewhere, for that matter): the gestation period is seven to eight months, the young being conceived in the spring or early summer, but not born until the end of the year. In bears, however, the winter dormancy sees them through the winter while the tiny young grow in the den. According to Père David, pandas, on the other hand, are 'not inclined to remain asleep' in the winter and, with an inquisitive cub beginning to crawl around, this is understandable.

As with the bears, young pandas start small and then grow at a furious rate. Brambell has compiled information on the weights of pandas at various ages in different zoos (see graphs) from which we can see the wide range of possibilities even up to the age of sexual maturity. This can be used as a rough guide for working out the age of any particular panda, where its early months were unrecorded.

A guide of average weight to age relationships was drawn up by Brambell for the Chi-Chi study, after much information had become available from Peking Zoo, and using data from the pandas Chia-Chia and Ching-Ching at London. This indicated that our calculations for the first edition of this book were out by two months, so that the following may be a more accurate picture:

birth	90-120gm (3-4½oz)
4 months	3kg (6½lb)
7 months	9kg (20lb)
12 months	27kg (60lb)
14 months	36kg (80lb)
18 months	55kg (121lb)
full grown	90-120kg (198-265lb)

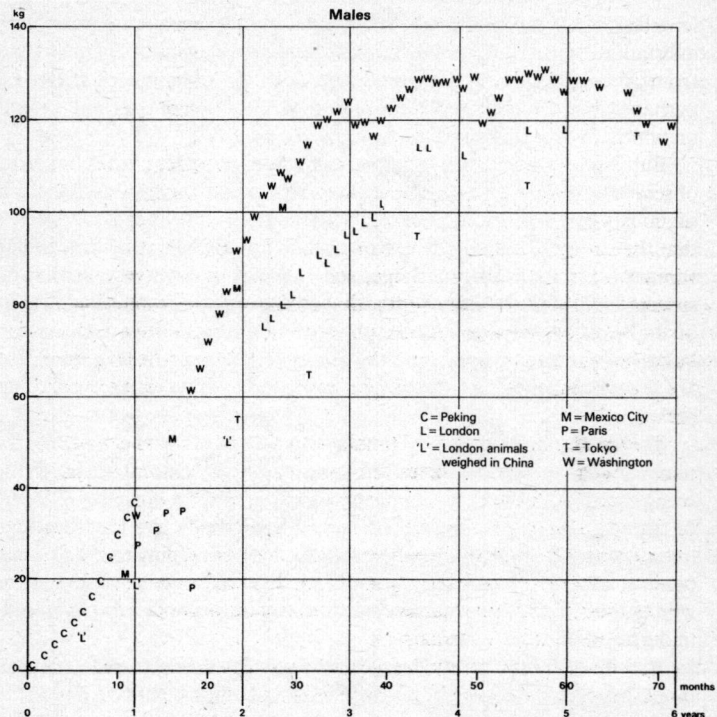

Produced from the register of Giant Pandas, compiled by Dr M R Brambell under the auspices of the
International Zoo Yearbook, Zoological Society of London

Growth rates of male giant pandas.

Although 265 pounds is a good size for an adult panda, they certainly grow much larger – at least under the easy conditions that are provided in zoos. An'-An' was large at 339 pounds, but the highest weight recorded for a giant panda is 399 pounds for Ping-Ping, the earlier Moscow male. Neither of these animals was fed on bamboo, which might have accounted for their great mass, but New York's Pan-dah was not far behind at 379 pounds. It is difficult to decide whether these are typical wild panda figures, or whether these animals were grossly overweight. Considering Pan-dah, the facts contradict one another. If one looks at her adult weight curve alongside those for Pan-dee and Chi-Chi, the big animal certainly seems to have a healthy enough curve. It almost appears as if the other two females became abnormally slowed down in their

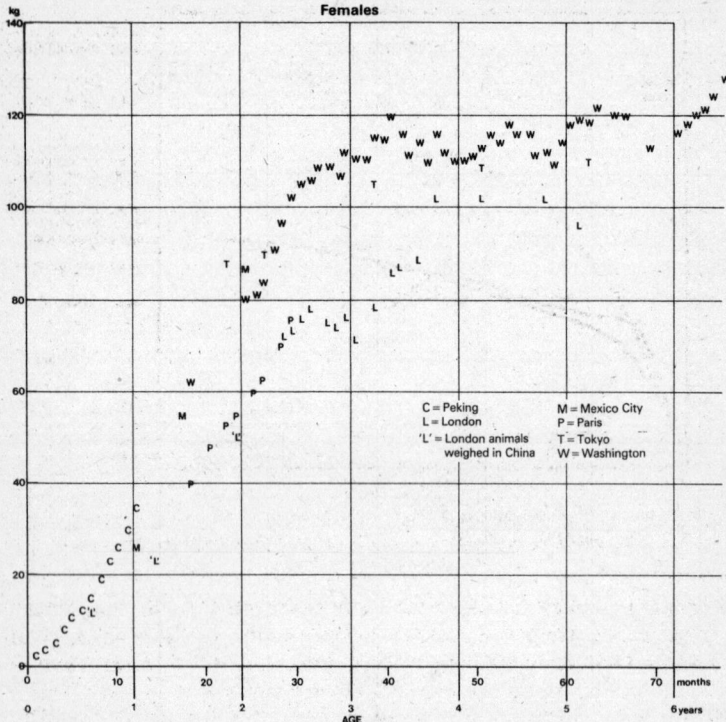

*Produced from the register of Giant Pandas, compiled by Dr M R Brambell under the auspices of the
International Zoo Yearbook, Zoological Society of London*

Growth rates of female giant pandas

growth, just after passing the 150 pound mark. But if one then looks at
the table of maximum recorded weights for nine of the adult captive
pandas, it looks more as though it is Pan-dah who was abnormal. Certainly, the two longest-lived specimens, Mei-Lan and Pao-Pei, did not
become so massive.

If one ignores Pan-dah and the Moscow males, then the top three
males bunch together at between 280 and 300 pounds, while the top three
females group together at between 230 and 250 pounds. Until we have
accumulated more detailed information, these are probably the best
figures to take as the average weights for adult male and female giant
pandas.

They are not, however, reliable enough to be of any value in attempting

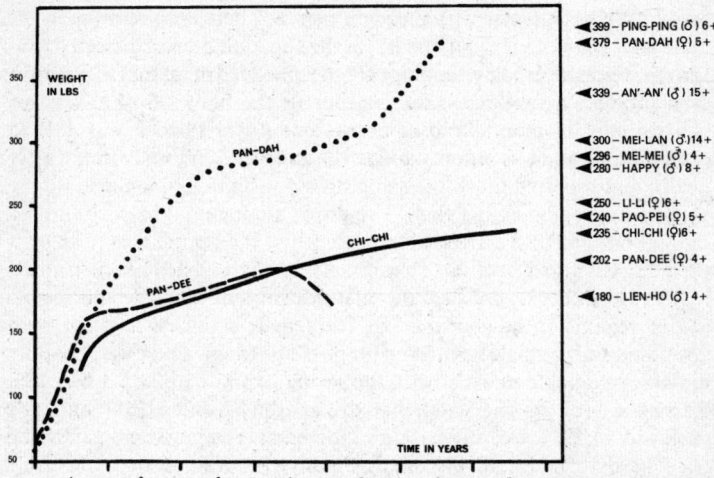

Giant panda weight curves. Arrows to right of chart indicate maximum weights for eleven captive adults. Figures following names give sex and age in years.

to sex an adult animal. As the history of captive pandas has already revealed, determining the sex of a member of this species at any age is an extremely difficult task. Of the fifteen giant pandas that had arrived alive in the western world before 1970, only ten were correctly sexed. One in three were only assigned their true gender after post mortem. Su-Lin, Mei-Mei, Sung and Lien-Ho were all believed to be females, but proved later to be males. Pan-dee was thought to be a male, but was in fact a female. In addition to these, Chi-Chi was for a while held to be a male. As we have already explained, she arrived as a female, was then examined by a learned anatomist and declared masculine. Later, when she had to be sent to hospital for minor eye treatment it was discovered that, on closer examination, her original designation had been the correct one. Why is there such difficulty in this seemingly simple matter? Even of the fifteen giant pandas that have been given to zoos outside China since 1970, one already, Yen-Yen, changed his designation to male after being kept for five years at Paris Zoo.

Many people imagine that all mammals show recognizable external differences in anatomy between the sexes, and that any expert can tell at a glance whether he is dealing with a male or a female. But this is far from true. In many species the sex organs are normally hidden and it is only during the mating act, when the penis is extruded, that it is possible to be certain. This is the case with the giant panda. There is no scrotum in the male and, to quote Dwight Davis, 'in the subadult animal dissected (Su-Lin) the testes and their wrappings are so embedded in fat that they do not even produce a swelling in the contour of the body'. Su-Lin was, of course, only 17 months old at death, but Royal Pocock was able to examine the adult London pandas (Grandma, Sung and Tang) after death, and reported much the same state of affairs. He summed up the situation by commenting that 'The testes are inguinal in position and there is nothing in the external appearance of the genital area to suggest their descent into a scrotum. The animal looks as if it had been castrated.'

In 1941 Pocock published the first drawings of the male and female genital regions of the giant panda. The female details were taken from Grandma and the male from Sung (or possibly Tang). These were the only drawings available to assist with the sexing of Chi-Chi, and it was with Pocock's book in one hand that the anatomist entered the animal's enclosure in 1959. Peering back and forth between book and panda, he tried hard to make up his mind. Finally, he decided that Chi-Chi's genitalia matched up better with Pocock's masculine drawing and pronounced the animal male.

Chi-Chi was two years old at the time and had not yet started to exhibit sexual behaviour patterns. When this did occur, during the following years, it seemed once again as though she must be a female. She adopted the female copulation posture (lordosis) typical of many mammals, with her back arched down and her tail held high, and, as we have already mentioned, pushed her rear end up against the legs of her keepers.

Even at this point, however, one could not be certain, for sexually frustrated male mammals will often adopt 'pseudo-female' sexual postures, just as frustrated females will sometimes mount. In a second attempt to clear up the mystery, efforts were made to obtain a close-up photograph of the genital region of the giant panda. It was argued that now she was sexually mature there would be a better chance of identifying the sexual anatomical details. A picture was obtained in the spring of 1962, when Chi-Chi was five years old. Photo-copies were also made of the Pocock drawings and the three documents were then shown to a number of experts, labelled only A, B, and C. A and B were the two drawings and C was the Chi-Chi photograph. The experts were asked to match C with either A or B. They were, in effect, being put in the same position as the anatomist who had entered the panda enclosure, except that they had a better view of Chi-Chi's genital region and, of course, it was now sexually mature. Despite this, opinion was divided and several authorities refused to commit themselves at all on the basis of the evidence offered them.

In all three cases, one thing is clear; namely, that there is a large expanse of naked, glandular skin surrounding the ano-genital region. Pocock summarizes by saying that although this 'skin is generally highly glandular . . . the pair of anal glands, normally developed in Carnivora, appears to be aborted as in bears. But no bear has a trace of the glandular area described'. This tallies with observed behaviour differences between Chi-Chi and the various bear species. Chi-Chi frequently backed up to special rubbing points in her enclosure, arched her back, raised her tail and rubbed her ano-genital skin region on to the hard surface. This deposits sticky glandular secretions and leaves a strong personal scent. It is a method of stamping the individual's identity on to its territory. Zoo bears have never been seen to do this. We shall have more to say about it later, but for the moment it is interesting to note simply that the ano-genital region has a triple rather than a dual function; it is not only concerned with defecation and copulation, but also with territorial behaviour.

In 1964, when Chi-Chi was seven years old she was, as already described, anaesthetized and examined in detail. More photographs were taken, and one of these showed clearly that the large *central* area of naked skin shown in the previous photograph does, in fact, open to reveal the female sexual orifice. This is, then, the vulvular region. This did not emerge clearly from the earlier photograph, and the *lower* area of naked skin had the appearance of a heart-shaped swelling similar to that drawn by Pocock for the male.

Unfortunately, Pocock's drawing exaggerated certain meaningless differences and concealed several meaningful ones. We now have a much

Pocock's drawings of the genital region of the giant panda, female (left) and male (right). The photograph of Chi-Chi therefore matches the left-hand drawing – could you have seen the difference?

more accurate drawing of the male genital region (of Su-Lin) published by Dwight Davis. For future reference it will be best to use this one and the later Chi-Chi photograph, rather than the earlier pictures.

There is some evidence that with older males the problem of sex determination may become easier. All the early sexing problems have come with juveniles or young adults. Even 'Grandma', who was described as an 'old female', weighed only 170 pounds at death, and it is probable that she, Sung and Tang were, in reality, all young adults that had not yet reached full sexual maturity. Su-Lin, dissected by Davis, was also sub-adult, but he did examine an adult male as well (Mei-Lan) and makes the cryptic comment that 'At sexual maturity the testicles are very evident.' He does not enlarge on this point, or explain it. Ivor Montagu, when he visited the director of Peking Zoo, asked him how the Chinese zoo officials managed to sex their pandas. Tsui Chang-p'ing replied that it was very difficult indeed when the animals were young, but continued: 'Only after about five or six years, with maturity, do the male's organs become visible.' Having heard this, we then checked the ages of all the mis-sexed captive pandas (males that had been thought to be females until after death) and found that none of them had lived more than four years six months in captivity. Perhaps if they had survived longer their masculinity would have begun to reveal itself. Even so, this would not solve the problem of sexing younger pandas, and this is the time when it is most important to establish the gender correctly.

The Peking officials claim to be able to tell the sexes of their pandas by other secondary characters, informing Montagu that 'The female is gentle, the male tends to be ill-tempered. The male is inclined to be moody and easily gets angry, the female is more sociable. The female is more handsome; her fur is better, finer, looks cleaner. The white on the back and even on the belly looks whiter. The belly colour of the male is darker, there is more black.' Asked specifically about differences in sexual behaviour, the Peking Zoo director replied: 'if a male, the animal runs around all the time and will bark. The female will rub her lower parts on stone.' Valuable as these comments are, it must be pointed out that Chi-Chi, a proven female, has been both 'sociable' and 'ill-tempered' at different times. Likewise, she has both run-and-barked and rubbed-on-stones when in sexual condition. (Also, the male Happy was seen to perform the rubbing action when at Leipzig Zoo). There may nevertheless be important differences in the *degree* to which the males and females perform these actions. Only when many more living specimens have been studied and compared, will we be able to say for certain.

In the meantime it is interesting to take a closer look at the way in which Chi-Chi behaved when she was at the peak of one of her periods of heat. To do this we made observations of her movements immediately after she was released into her paddock in the morning. At this point in the day, after being confined to her sleeping den all night, she was always at her most active. When she emerged she soon began to clean herself, patrol her territory, and deposit her scent marks. Records taken on a typical heat-period morning present a clear picture of the sequence of events:

9th September 1964. Chi-Chi released into paddock from den at 09.26.

09.26:	Chi-Chi calling out as she emerges from den door.
09.28:	Walks over to log-pile, climbs up and stretches out.
09.38:	Sits up on logs, scratches one side of face, then the other; then scratches flanks and feet. Sits up and raises her right back foot straight up so that she can rest her chin on it.
09.41:	Scratches face again and gives full yawn. Scratches arms with back feet. Scratches tail with left back foot.
09.43:	Scratches face with back foot and ear with front foot.
09.44:	Leaves log-pile and walks back towards door of sleeping den.
09.45:	Turns round, raises tail and presses ano-genital region against the concrete wall (A) just to the left of the sleeping den door. Rubs against wall with ano-genital region, depositing scent.
09.46:	Walks to wall (B) on the other side of the cave entrance and scent-marks again. Rubbing action applied to wall eight times, during which the animal performs five vigorous head-shakes.
09.48:	Sits up just behind logs and scratches again.
09.49:	Moves over the keeper's door to paddock, sits up against wall by door and scratches again.
09.51:	Returns to (B) and scent-marks – three rubs this time.
09.53:	Walks to the front of the pool, then turns sharply and goes back to pillar in middle of cave entrance. Scratches back against pillar.
09.54:	Walks to (C) and turns, squatting, to place ano-genital region on slight ridge in concrete floor. Rubs on floor ten times. The fifth, sixth and seventh rubs are of lower intensity than the rest and during these three movements Chi-Chi again performs vigorous head-shaking.
09.55:	Walks to tree-stump, sits down and scratches. Then sits holding top of stump with front feet.
09.56:	Moves across to the pool and walks to water's edge. Front feet in the water.

09.57:   Paws at water, 'pulling' it towards her. Sits at water's edge. Slumps forward and stares fixedly at the reflection of her face in the water.

09.59:   Walks back to wall (A) by den door and scent-marks there again, rubbing four times.

10.00:   Starts patrolling territory again, walking right along the 75-foot front and back again.

10.01:   Stops at drain (D) and deposits scent nearby, rubbing three times.

10.02:   Walks right round the back of the enclosure and to the front again, where she sits down and rests.

10.03:   Observation period ends. (Note: On other days, scent-markings were also seen at sites E, F and G on the map.)

*Map of Chi-Chi's movements in her enclosure
during observation period*

The photographs showing these scent-marking actions clearly reveal the strange, high-shouldered posture, with the head held low and the back arched down. This is accompanied by slight movements of the back legs that rub the ano-genital region up and down over the wall or object being marked. The powerful head-shaking and head-tossing actions that appear during the rubbing sequence are associated with a special 'grin-

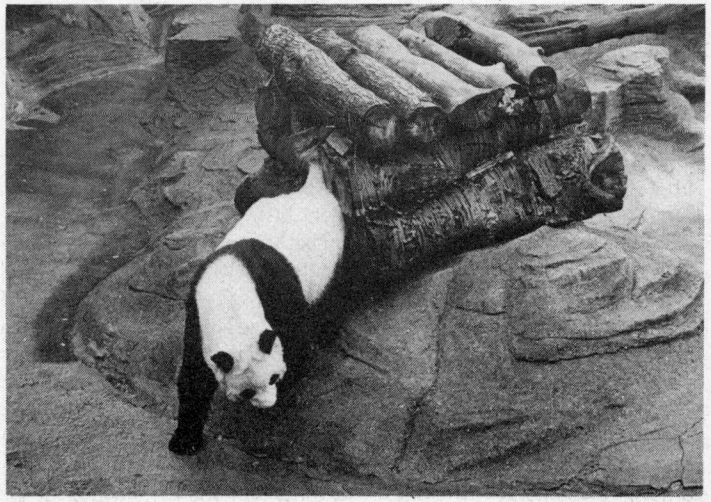

Chi-Chi leaving scent-mark on a log-pile. (Zool. Soc. Lond.)

face', or an open-mouthed expression, and the whole performance gives the impression of a behaviour pattern of high intensity.

It could be argued that the animal was merely attempting to relieve an anal irritation, as domestic dogs will do, or that, in its frustration at being maleless it was trying to masturbate. In view of the fact that the rubbing actions are limited to several distinct sites in the territory, and that these same spots were used day after day and year after year, it seems more likely that the territorial scent-marking explanation is the correct one. Furthermore, although the rubbing actions occurred with greatest frequency during the heat periods, they were by no means entirely absent during the rest of the year. Also, they were closely linked with territorial patrolling and appeared rhythmically at certain times of day. Heavy scent deposits could, in fact, be seen at the points where the rubbings occurred and the animal often sniffed at the spot before marking it.

The patrolling that took place each morning was interspersed with cleaning actions, as the record shows. These are of no particular interest in themselves, except to indicate just how flexible the giant panda's body is. It is able to scratch its tail with its short back leg and can even, while sitting up, scratch the left back foot with the right back foot. Its reclining and resting postures are so varied and extraordinary that they give the animal an almost rubber-boned appearance. We have seen no other species that has thrust its back leg straight up in the air, whilst sitting down, and then rested its chin on it.

Scratching, with either front or back foot, and rubbing the back against hard surfaces are the only cleaning patterns that appeared in Chi-Chi with any frequency. Occasionally she might lick her fur, and sometimes would use a front paw to clear some obstruction from the teeth or rub her eyes. J. Eisenberg and Devra Kleiman, at the US National Zoo, found that, although their pandas spent little time licking, nibbling or scratching, the fur was conditioned by bathing in sand or water. 'When allowed on a grass substitute or supplied with tubs of soil, the panda will rub and writhe while lying on its back on the soil; the underside will be cleaned by rubbing with clods of soil or sod, using the forepaws. When water is available the animal may also bathe daily and it is likely that the absence of both soil and water will result in poor fur condition.'

There is probably much variation in the preferences of individual pandas, because Chi-Chi rarely bathed. Swimming is unheard of, there is no record of a panda swimming voluntarily, and most are reported as refusing to submerge themselves. The most they will do is paddle at the water's edge, or play with water from a hosepipe. Consequently the studbook for giant pandas recommends the provision of a pool only 0.6m (2 feet) deep. A fine spray of water may be accepted on hot days and, if a block of ice is provided, a panda will readily sprawl out on the cool surface.

Zoo pandas sleep sprawled on their bellies with all four legs spread out, or sitting up in a corner with their backs to the wall, or hanging in a fork of a tree, or lying flat on their backs. At night they seem to be more likely to adopt the last of these postures. From his studies of panda country in Szechuan, William Sheldon reported that 'The favourite resting places of pandas are at the bottom of trees, under dead stumps, and in crevices of ledges. Dens under overhanging rocks in the midst of a precipitous slope of bamboos were often seen. Bamboo stalks had been broken and arranged to form a nest, and old piles of droppings gave evidence of frequent use. The natives say that it is in such places that the mother brings forth her young. I saw one instance of a well-used panda bed on the top of a large flat stump in an opening of the bamboo forests.'

Like many mammals, the giant panda appears to be neither diurnal nor nocturnal, but crepuscular; that is, it becomes active in the mornings and again in the evenings, with a sleeping or resting period in the middle of the day and again in the middle of the night. Juvenile pandas are much more active throughout the day than adults and, as we have already seen, this can lead to disappointments for zoo visitors after a playful young panda has matured into a drowsy adult.

Locomotion in giant pandas is very similar to that in bears. There is the same 'diagonal walk', to give it its technical name, and, at higher speeds, a clumsy trot. Unlike bears they have not yet been seen to gallop and hunters have several times commented upon the panda's apparent inability to flee at high speed. Sheldon reported that 'On one occasion at a distance of 350 yards I observed two individuals on the edge of a bamboo jungle. Driven out by four dogs and warned by several high-powered bullets whistling about them, neither animal even broke into a run. The gait was a determined and leisurely walk. Again, Dean Sage and I observed another panda pursued by four dogs. In this instance he *walked* to within eight feet of Dean and was stopped only by bullets . . . During the course of tracking different animals for several miles I never saw a sign of one travelling faster than a walk.'

Sheldon concludes from all this that 'the panda is an extremely stupid beast'. Whether, in fact, his observations reveal panda stupidity, or whether they indicate that the animal's heavy-boned body is incapable of really rapid fleeing, or alternatively that the species is simply not attuned to being hunted and has no panic responses with which to respond to the situation, it is hard to say. All that we can be sure of is that pandas are basically slow-movers.

Once seen, the giant panda's wiggling, pigeon-toed walk is never forgotten. Dwight Davis describes it with great clarity in the following words: 'The head is carried well below the shoulder line, and the tail is closely appressed against the body. The stride is considerably longer than in bears, and as a result the gait is more rolling, with much more lateral rotation of the shoulders and hips than in *Ursus*. This gives a pronounced waddling character to the locomotion. The heavy head is swayed from side to side.'

Pandas often heave themselves up into a standing position against a vertical wall, and sometimes do so in space, away from a vertical surface, but they have never been seen to walk bi-pedally like certain bears. They are also less efficient than bears at climbing. Young pandas will frequently clamber up branches and adults occasionally do so, but their tree-borne actions are extremely clumsy. Against a vertical, or almost vertical, tree-trunk, they will climb in a special way, embracing the wood and progressing by a series of caterpillar movements. When descending they usually come down backwards, tail-first, unless the branch is so near to the horizontal that they can actually walk down.

Despite their awkwardness in the trees, we know from the trappers' tales that giant pandas will take refuge aloft when pursued by dogs. No doubt if the dogs were unaccompanied by human beings the manoeuvre would work. After a while the pack would lose patience and follow up

Chi-Chi standing bipedally during play. (Granada TV)

some new scent. This brings up the whole question of the natural enemies of the panda. Is the species really predator-free or does it have certain killers to fear? The evidence is conflicting. According to the director of Peking Zoo, 'it suffers from the depredations of beasts of prey', but what could these be? There are only four other large carnivores in panda country: the Himalayan, or Asiatic black bear (*Selenarctos thibetanus*), the local race of the brown bear (*Ursus arctos*) known as the Tibetan blue bear, the Asiatic wild dog (*Cuon alpinus*), and the leopard (*Panthera pardus*). The two bears might contest certain territories with the panda, but are never likely to act as panda predators. This leaves only the wild dogs and the leopards (and possibly some of the largest birds of prey). Donald Carter sums it up by saying 'In the dark recesses of the bamboo the animal has few foes except man. Leopards, wild dogs, or a bird of prey might take an occasional young one, but the old animal has little to fear,' and we are inclined to agree with this view. Some authorities specify that the dhole (or Asiatic wild dog) is the main predator of pandas. These carnivores are the size of small wolves and, as they hunt in packs of up to twenty animals, in these numbers they would certainly be capable of surrounding and bringing down a panda if they were prepared to risk it. They do kill very large wild cattle and wild boar but according to Lois Buelear (in *Wild Dogs of the World*), 'dholes probably do not systematically come in violent conflict with other large carnivores', and this perhaps includes pandas. An adult panda might also be a bigger bite than even a leopard would want to chew, but both animals are less than common, and the leopard does not appear a strong candidate as a panda killer.

But the evidence is not conclusive. On the one hand, it is hard to believe that a giant panda, even an adult one 5 feet long, would offer much of a hunting challenge to a hungry leopard or a pack of hungry wild dogs. On the other hand, it is equally difficult to see how the panda could have survived at all if these lethal cats and dogs were a serious threat. As we have already heard, the giant panda is a slow-moving, clumsy, and probably not over-intelligent beast. It is unthinkable that such a cumbersome creature should have persisted to the present time if there were any serious predator pressures working against it. Perhaps in some way which we do not at the moment understand, the animal's environment protects it from its potential enemies. Perhaps the leopards and the wild dogs prefer not to hunt in the bamboo forest for some reason? Once again, we must await the results of the Chinese field studies.

There is one other possibility that is worth examining. Although it would not appear at first sight to be capable of defending itself against a hungry 'professional' animal killer, the giant panda is nevertheless able to inflict serious wounds if given a chance. Sheldon recorded that the specimen shot by his expedition 'hesitated long enough to growl savagely, turn about, and bite one dog through the foot'. We have already mentioned the damage done by Chi-Chi to her keeper, and we have since learned that when the Chicago male Mei-Lan was adult he mauled one of his keepers so severely that the unfortunate man had to have his arm amputated. The actual methods of attack vary according to the intensity of the mood. When mildly aggressive, the giant panda swipes out with a front foot. When it really means business, it runs or thrusts itself at the enemy, grabs out with a front foot, pulls the victim towards itself and at the same time delivers a powerful bite. Jaws that can crush hard bamboo stems can obviously inflict serious damage, and it is just possible that this is the panda's 'secret deterrent'.

Could it be that the panda's answer to the problem lies not in its 'unhuntable' qualities, but in its 'un-killable' qualities once it has been cornered? Its teeth are so massive and its jaws so powerful that it is just feasible that at the end of a comparatively easy pursuit, the unhappy leopard or wild dog pack is faced with the threat of a bite so terrible that it is simply not worth the risk of pressing home the advantage. This would explain three things. First, it would clear up the problem of why the giant panda has not evolved a more rapid form of escape, when sharing the region with potential killers. Second, it would explain why the animals cornered by hunters' dogs did not even *try* to escape. Third, it would provide a reason for the extraordinary colour pattern of the species.

The usual explanation for the black and white markings is that they are cryptic in function and help the animal to conceal itself against its snowy background. To quote George Goodwin: 'As the white-and-black animal moves across the snow where rocks crop out and the trees cast dark shadows, it is often lost against the background.' Photographs of captive pandas taken in the snow tend to back this up, but it is doubtful if anyone has yet made serious observations of this camouflage phenomenon operating in the wild state. Hung-Shou Pen, one of the few men to see living giant pandas in the wild state, wrote that 'they flashed before us in all their beauty'. William Sheldon, well-travelled in panda country, has stressed that 'Other animals with more natural enemies and living in exactly the same habitat are mostly dark in colour and of a uniform shade . . . It is doubtful, therefore, if the characteristic markings of the giant panda are protective.'

To sum up, it seems possible that on certain occasions, at special times of the year, in dim lighting, on particular types of terrain, the black and white markings may act as camouflage. At all other times and places it will probably be dramatically conspicuous. We have only to look to the skunks for a similar state of affairs. These animals have a secret weapon – their anal stink-glands – and they fear few enemies. As with the giant panda, their fur is boldly marked in black and white, and this acts not as a cryptic pattern, but as an advertisement, a warning of their horrible hidden powers. Like the giant panda, they are rather slow and clumsy and not given to rapid fleeing. If harassed, they jog along until the situation becomes too trying, when they turn on their foe and threaten him. If he ignores this, they squirt their foul-smelling, near-blinding liquid at his face and wander safely away. Like the panda, they are not heavily endowed with intelligence; they do not need to be.

The more one thinks about it, the more the skunk-panda comparison fits. Pandas do not have anal stink-glands like the skunks (the ano-genital skin glands used in panda scent-marking are totally different), but if their secret weapon lies in the savage bite they can inflict with their broad jaws, then they would not require the additional aid of 'chemical warfare'.

The wild panda has often been referred to as 'shy' or 'timid', but a better description would be 'retiring and elusive'. Obviously this is not an animal that is going to go looking for trouble, but, on the other hand, when trouble finds it, it has shown remarkably little concern. Its behaviour in the face of human hunters could hardly be described as 'timid'. Furthermore, its zoo personality is one of serenity rather than anxiety.

By and large, then, it would seem that the famous black-and-white markings are most probably a warning pattern. It is interesting to contemplate how this situation could have evolved. If we think of the giant panda as developing from a creature rather like the red panda, then what are the evolutionary steps that would have been taken? If the proto-panda was – like the red panda today – a partial bamboo-feeder, it would only have been able to devour the smallest, tenderest shoots and the leaves. The more massive and heavier-jawed certain specimens became, the larger and larger would become their possible food stems. This would open up a bigger and bigger food supply in the bamboo forests. But, in order to be large enough to consume the heavier stems, the expanding panda would have to grow beyond a point where it could clamber nimbly to the safety of the tree-tops. The moment this ability had been lost, the (now medium-sized) panda would be in trouble. Still too small to defend itself against large killers, and too bulky to escape them, it would quickly die out.

This is apparently exactly what happened and explains why, today, we have only two members in the panda group – one small and nimble and the other large and powerful. The middle-sized pandas that were intermediate between the two were no doubt a rapid failure and became extinct. Only those medium pandas that managed to evolve very quickly into the full-blown giant we know at the present time would have achieved any evolutionary success. Once a certain size had been attained, the already relatively vast crunching teeth would become effective weapons as well as bamboo-destroyers. Their development as feeding equipment would automatically make them secondarily available as defensive equipment as soon as they became absolutely, as well as relatively, huge.

At this point it would have become important to develop a warning coloration to fend off enemies at an early stage in an attack. Leaving it to the last minute to prove your superiority is a dangerous game. Even if you win, you may become damaged in the process. It is far better to have some kind of signal that operates at a safe distance. If the proto-panda was coloured like the present-day red panda, then very little change would be necessary. This small creature already has the black legs and the black marks around the eyes. The face is white and all that is necessary to convert it into a giant-panda-pattern is for the rust-red of the body to be replaced by white. (Reports from Peking Zoo note that new-born giant pandas are only sparsely covered with white hair, so that the overall impression is of the light-red body colour. This seems to hint at the link-up between the two species. On top of that, if one looks closely at the fur of a giant panda one can still see a faint yellowish tinge to the white, as if the process of bleaching was never quite perfected.) True, the marks around the eyes would have to be modified slightly and the dark hairs inside the ears would have to spread over their whole surface, but these are minor modifications. Assuming that the long tail, no longer needed for balancing, had been reduced to the giant's 5-inch white stump, and that the body proportions had become stumpier to support the heavier weight, then, hey presto, there was a giant panda.

Like almost everything connected with the giant panda, however, it is not as simple as this. The above story seems straightforward enough and, we must admit, we believe it to be true. But we must in fairness report that there is a school of thought which firmly states that the two living panda species are not closely related to one another at all. They contend that the similarities between them are entirely due to convergence and that they have only come to look alike and behave alike because they both inhabit the same part of the world and endure similar living conditions.

The arguments put forward for both sides are long and complex and we will only summarize them here. Nearly all previous authors have either strongly stressed one attitude or the other – often rather dogmatically – but we will do our best to summarize both points of view as objectively and fairly as we can, so that you, the reader, can decide which way you wish to vote.

Firstly, what exactly are the rival claims? The *raccoon school* insists that because the red panda is so obviously a member of the raccoon family (*Procyoninae*), and because the giant panda is so obviously a close relative of the red panda, then both the pandas must be placed together inside the raccoon family. This school of thought recognizes that there are certain important differences between the pandas and the other members of the raccoon family and so separates them into two sub-families within the family *Procyonidae*: pandas – sub-family *Ailurinae*; raccoons – sub-family *Procyoninae*. They do not think that the giant panda has any close relationship with the bears.

The *bear school* insists that the giant panda is a true bear and a member of the family *Ursidae*. They agree that the red panda is a member of the raccoon family, and do not therefore believe that it has any close relationship with the giant panda.

Clearly this is no minor squabble over some trivial details. It is a basic argument about the very fundamentals of giant panda evolution. Is the animal really a bear-like panda, or is it a panda-like bear? First, a brief look at the history of the controversy.

We have already described how Père David himself considered the animal to be a black-and-white bear in 1869. He did not appear to object, however, when Milne-Edwards, after studying its bones and teeth, decided it was closer to the lesser panda and the raccoons, and so in 1870 changed its name from *Ursus* to *Ailuropoda*. In the same year Gervais, on the other hand, examined its brain-case and claimed that it *was* a bear. He felt it was nevertheless sufficiently distinct to have a name of its own, and so placed it inside the Ursidae as *Pandarctos*. Later, in 1885, Mivart was forced to place the giant panda with the raccoon family because he found its similarities with the lesser panda inescapable. In 1891 Flower and Lydekker, in their work *Mammals Living and Extinct* reversed the process again and put the giant panda with the bears and the red panda with the raccoons. Winge, in 1895, decided that the giant panda was a bear, but that it belonged to a distinct group within the bear family and that its only close relative was the extinct *Hyenarctos*. In 1901 Lydekker made further skeletal studies and changed his previous view. Now both he and Lankester decided that the pandas belonged together in a special subfamily of the raccoon family. They put forward the two names mentioned earlier – *Ailurinae* and *Procyoninae*. They also changed the popular name of the animal from parti-coloured bear to great panda. In 1902 Beddard, in his *Mammalia*, put the giant panda back with the bears. In 1904, Weber in his work *Die Säugetiere* also placed it with the bears. In 1913 Bardenfleth studied the teeth in great detail and decided that their similarity with those of the red panda was due to convergence as a result of similar bamboo diets. He placed the giant panda with the bears. In 1921 Pocock solved the problem in a novel way by giving the giant panda *and* the red panda a distinct family apiece, thus completely begging the issue of their relationship. In 1936 Gregory and Raven examined the skull and viscera respectively and both concluded that the giant panda belonged with the raccoon family. In 1943 Segall studied the bony auditory region of both pandas and felt that *both* should be associated with the bears. In 1945 Simpson, in his *Classification of the Mammals*, put the pandas into the raccoon family. In 1946 Mettler and Goss (like Gervais in 1870) studied the brain of the giant panda and came to the conclusion that 'the configuration of the brain . . . is identical with that of the bear'. In 1951 Ellerman and Morrison-Scott, in their comprehensive checklist of *Palaearctic and Indian Mammals*, placed both pandas inside the raccoon family. Colbert followed suit in 1955 when he published his *Evolution of the Vertebrates*, commenting that 'modern studies suggest it is a large procyonid that has paralleled the bears'. In 1956 Leone and Wiens made serological tests that 'clearly indicate that the giant panda belongs in the family Ursidae'. In 1964 Davis published his massive anatomical monograph on the giant panda and firmly asserted that '*Ailuropoda* is a bear and therefore belongs in the family Ursidae. This conclusion is not based on one or a few characters, but on a host of similarities, many of them subtle, throughout the anatomy'.

This then is the impressive line-up of big names involved in the panda dispute. If you join the *raccoon school*, you find yourself in the company of Milne-Edwards, Mivart, Lankester, Lydekker, Gregory, Raven, Simpson, Ellerman, Morrison-Scott and Colbert. If you enlist with the *bear school* you are siding with Gervais, Flower, Winge, Beddard, Weber, Bardenfleth, Segall, Mettler, Goss, Leone, Wiens and Davis. Either way, you would belong to a powerful team.

When Chi-Chi fell seriously ill, in 1972, many samples were taken from her for expert examination, and when she died a most comprehensive post mortem was carried out. These two efforts were effected not only in the interest of Chi-Chi's health but also for the rare opportunity that presented itself to compare the anatomy and physiology of pandas with that of bears and raccoons. Thirty-one scientists from the UK and USA were involved in the study and their results were published for the Zoological Society of London in 1976. There were few good clues to help in solving the puzzle. A. D. Dayan examined the nervous system and had to agree with Mettler, Goss and Davis that the panda brain strongly suggested its relationship with the bears. The neurochemistry was carried out by R. B. Ramsey who looked at fatty acids associated with the brain and found them far closer to polar bears than to raccoons. Characteristics of panda milk fat were shared both by raccoons and bears. In the arrangement of Chi-Chi's cranial arteries, G. H. du Boulay found major differences from the raccoons but in each case the arrangement was 'typical of bears'. A serological study carried out by V. M. Sarich again indicated the closeness of giant pandas to bears. So the Chi-Chi study gave no support to the raccoon school.

Whichever clan you consider, on the basis of their respective reputations alone, the choice would be a difficult one. We must take a closer look at the specific arguing points.

No one would deny that *superficially* the giant panda looks very much like a bear. It is the same size and the same general shape. No member of the raccoon family approaches either the weight or the body proportions of the animal. But this is not a very convincing argument. There are many cases of animals that have come to look very similar to one another – at first glance – but which are totally unrelated. Convergent similarities of this sort are so common that not even the most ardent members of the *bear school* would use this as a serious debating point. It is necessary to examine detailed structures or patterns of behaviour to see if there are subtle as well as crude likenesses.

The massive teeth of the giant panda have been a hotly discussed area. Most authors have agreed that they resemble closely only those of the smaller red panda, and that the upper jaws of both differ strongly from the bear in this particular respect. *Bear school* supporters have tried to minimize this difficulty by stressing that both pandas have to chew tough bamboo and that therefore one would expect a strong convergence here. They emphasize that if one considers the cheek teeth as a single unit rather than as a set of separately determined characters, then it is easy to see how a simple genetic change could influence this whole area to produce a kind of dental gigantism. This would not, they argue, involve a mass of minor lengthy changes during evolution, but just a brief, simple enlargement. The *raccoon school* contend, however, that the minute details of the jaw, tooth by tooth, are so different from those of the bears that true affinity must be ruled out.

The *raccoon school* also points out that the panda skull is much shorter in the muzzle, much broader and generally more massive than that of the bears. Their opponents counter that this is merely secondary, following in the wake of the heavy dental developments. If there are to be large teeth, then they must have a suitably swollen housing. If they are to be crunched together effectively, then they must be supplied with enormous muscle-power, and these muscles must have strong attachments, hence a denser, tougher skull. A similar attack is launched against the famous 'sixth claw' on the front foot of the giant panda. This, it is stressed, is simply a very recent adaptation to bamboo-feeding and could have been developed from either a bear ancestor or a raccoon ancestor. The come-back here is that the red panda uses a very similar grip when holding bamboo stems and has the necessary behaviour to provide the starting point for the evolution of a specialized structure like the 'sixth claw'.

The general nature of the giant panda skeleton has been held to be unbear-like in many detailed ways. It is said to give the impression of being the skeleton of a 'fake' bear. This is especially true of the way the limb bones relate to one another. Also there is a generally heavy-boned quality about the panda skeleton. These differences are belittled by the simple device of claiming that, when the animal had to get a heavier head in connection with its feeding habits, it did so by getting a heavier skeletal system in general. Hence, the body passively became more heavy-boned along with the skull and the teeth, even though there was no need for this. It is admitted that the weighty body structure is a hindrance to the panda, but it is felt that, in the 'predator-free' world of the bamboo jungles, this did not matter. If it slowed the beast down, this would not reduce its chances of survival. This is a strange argument, and it certainly seems more reasonable to assume that the giant panda was instead a rapidly enlarged red panda, if one wants to give a plausible explanation of these skeletal features. The point to remember here is that if the giant panda evolved from a bear, then its ancestor did not have to become generally enlarged, only more heavy-headed. As the bears had already evolved an efficient high-speed body, it seems odd that they should have thrown this advantage away. If, on the other hand, the ancestor was a small creature like the red panda, it would have to undergo considerable and rapid enlargement to become a giant panda. The new giant might well be of a clumsy design to start with. Polishing up of the final product of this evolutionary step would take some time. We would expect to have to wait a while to see the body clumsiness swept away. On this basis we feel that the giant panda has more the character of an old time bamboo-eater newly giantized, rather than an old time giant recently bamboozled.

Turning to the alimentary system, the fact that the small intestine is shorter and less complex than that of the bears is very difficult to explain if they are closely related. As even the hardened members of the *bear school* have to admit, one would expect the bear gut to become lengthened if the degree of herbivory were drastically increased. On the other hand, if the entrails were evolving rapidly from those of a much smaller creature, inefficiencies of the kind already referred to would be less surprising. Also the structure of the stomach, the liver, and various other alimentary characters are extremely similar to those of the red panda. These similarities do not appear to be simply the result of bamboo digestion.

In other body systems, such as musculature and respiration, there are striking similarities in detail between the bears and the giant panda. The meticulous dissections of Dwight Davis leave no doubt about this. But these systems do not differ so drastically from carnivore to carnivore and if any two species came to be about the same size and general shape, it seems likely that these systems would also come to resemble one another to a remarkable degree.

In one particular body system there are, however, some startling differences between bears and pandas. This is the genital system, where we find sex organs so astonishingly different that it really is impossible to accept them as having a recent common origin. A bear has a long, straight, tapering, pointed penis that is directed forwards. It is not dissimilar in design to the penis of a dog. The penis of the giant panda, by contrast, is ridiculously short for so large an animal, being less than three inches long in the adult. It is cylindrical, S-shaped and posteriorly directed. It is very similar to that of the red panda. This likeness is extremely difficult to explain if the two species are not closely related, especially as the structure is so unique in its design. Dwight Davis, a staunch member of the *bear school*, found this very difficult to explain, but suggested that perhaps there had been a freak matching of two cases of arrested genital development. It was as if both pandas had become stuck almost at the embryonic stage in this particular respect. Davis comments noncommitally that 'The significance of this convergent "fetalization" of the external genitalia in two remotely related forms is unknown.' It might have been better to admit that, on the basis of this feature at least, the word 'remotely' is unjustified.

We have already pointed out that the large area of naked skin in the ano-genital region of the giant panda is a character that distinguishes it sharply from the bears. Likewise, its scent-marking behaviour is totally un-bearlike. The production of minute offspring, on the other hand, is typically ursine and provides valuable ammunition for the *bear school*. In the case of bears, however, this character is intimately linked with the mother's habit of taking a long, deep winter's sleep – virtually a hibernation. As the panda is reputed to remain active throughout the winter months it is obvious that the whole question of the detailed life cycle involved needs further study. Until this has been carried out, the existence of a 5-ounce or smaller newborn must be noted down as an important bear-like property for the giant panda. It is more reasonable to assume, at our present stage of knowledge, that this character is a hangover from a bear past than from a raccoon cum red panda past.

The vocal efforts of the giant panda have not previously been employed as a taxonomic character, as far as we can ascertain. Barking and bleating have been mentioned, but no one appears to have attempted a serious analysis of the sounds. Head Keeper Sam Morton of the London Zoo has had daily contact with raccoons, pandas and all species of bears for a number of years. When we asked him whether he thought that the giant panda was a bear, his immediate reaction was to comment that 'It doesn't sound like a bear. Bears roar – the panda bleats. It's totally

The S-shaped penis of the giant panda. (After *Dwight Davis*)

different in that way.' He then went on to discuss other panda characters, some pro-bear ('it moves and sits like a bear'), some anti-bear, but it is interesting that his first thoughts were concerned with the animal's vocalizations. In view of this we felt it would be worthwhile preparing some sound spectrograms made from recordings taken during Chi-Chi's intense period of sexual heat in the autumn of 1963. She was so vocal at that time that it was only necessary to open the den door when she was inside her sleeping quarters and hold a microphone towards her to produce repeated loud calling. The cries came in various intensities and several of these have been included here. By themselves they cannot be of assistance to the panda ancestry debate, but when similar spectograms become available for the red panda, the bears and the members of the raccoon family, it will be possible to carry out a detailed scrutiny of the different patterns and perhaps obtain some valuable relationship clues. In the meantime these sound spectrograph pictures provide us with a permanent and precise record of an important giant panda behaviour character, and we are very grateful to Professor D. B. Fry of the Department of Phonetics at University College London for preparing them and making them available to us.

The use of behaviour characters as aids to settling taxonomic disputes is a comparatively new trend. Until the last few decades anatomical features were all-important, but nowadays more and more categories of 'species properties' are being brought into the front line. In addition to behaviour factors, there are also valuable clues to be gathered from such spheres as serological analysis and chromosome studies. In 1956 Charles Leone and Alvin Wiens of Kansas University published the results of a series of serological tests they had carried out using sixteen carnivore species, including the giant panda, the raccoon and the polar bear. The outcome was a serious set-back for the *raccoon school*. The figures showed clearly that 'The serological affinities of the giant panda are with the bears rather than with the raccoons.'

The method used was to inject serum from a particular carnivore into rabbits, where antibodies were produced. This provided a specific anti-serum against which the sera of other carnivore species could be tested. The strength of the reactions was held to indicate the 'blood relationship' of the species concerned. The following table gives the results obtained with the three vital species. (The higher the figure, the closer the relationship is said to be.)

These figures are without doubt the strongest weapon in the armoury of the *bear school* and they are strongly supported by the work of V. M. Sarich of the University of California. Using samples from Chi-Chi, he carried out a serological study, of the type described above, to make

		Serum		
		Giant panda	Polar bear	Raccoon
Anti-serum	Giant panda	100	80	22
	Polar bear	76	100	41
	Raccoon	53	59	100

immunological comparisons of two blood proteins (transferrin and albumin) from giant panda, black bear and raccoon. He did not want to become involved in taxonomic arguments, but his results showed that the giant panda shared an ancestor with the bears far more recently than it did with the raccoons: not only that, but even the red panda appeared to have split off from the bear lineage! (see diagram below).

Against the serological results, the *raccoon school* can place chromosome studies by Professor William Davidson of the Department of Haematology at King's College Hospital Medical School, London. He reports that on the basis of chromosome numbers the giant panda (42) matches the raccoon (42), but not the bears (56 and 74). (He wishes us to point out, however, that until accurate chromosome counts have been obtained for *all* the bears, *all* the members of the raccoon family, and the red panda as well as the giant panda, any conclusions on this point must remain tentative.)

It seems as though at every step there is a strong pointer one way, followed straight away by something pulling in the opposite direction. We would like to be able to settle the matter for you with a final authoritative flourish, but clearly that is not possible. There is still a fascinating detective story here to be pursued in the years to come. Perhaps when lengthy studies have been made of pandas, in the field, the zoo and the laboratory, we shall finally know exactly what this strange creature really is. In the meantime, we can only gaze at it and make a guess. The leaning of specialists in recent years has been very much towards the *bear school*. As we said earlier, we tend to side with the *raccoon school*, but we realize the position is a shaky one. We have been able to scrutinize living specimens of both species of pandas, all seven species of bears and six species of raccoons (the North American raccoon, the crab-eating raccoon, the coati, the kinkajou, the cacomistle and the olingo), over a period of years, and if we are forced to cast an intuitive vote it must be for the *raccoon school*. We cannot avoid a feeling that somehow the giant panda is a

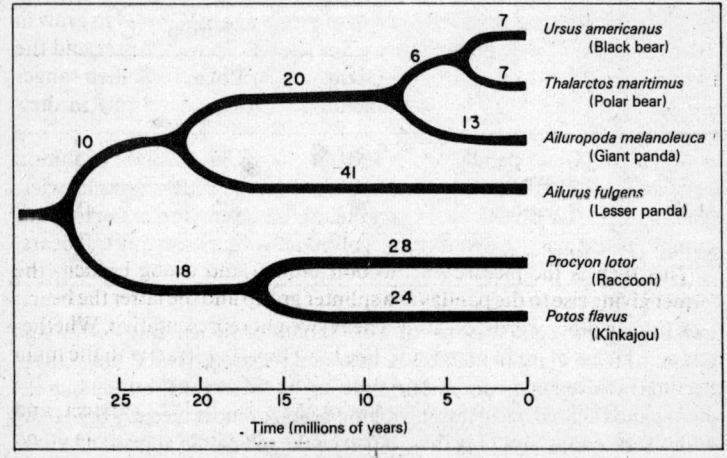

*Evolutionary interpretation of derived lineages of six carnivores
using data of immunological distances (figures shown).*
(After *V. M. Sarich, 1972*)

counterfeit bear rather than a true one.

Along with American palaeontologist Edwin Colbert, we imagine that
the panda's evolutionary history went something like this. About thirty
million years ago the ancestors of all the modern carnivores appeared on
the scene. These were the miacids and they were small creatures rather like
present-day civets. One development from the miacids was an elongated,
short-legged, heavy-tailed creature called *Cynodictis*, the ancestor of all
the dog-like carnivores. *Cynodictis* evolved in two directions. In one, it
led to longer-legged animals that ran swiftly and became efficient, intelligent hunters. These are the dogs, wolves and foxes of today. The other
branch led to the ancestral raccoon, an animal called *Phlaocyon*. This
appeared about fifteen million years ago and looked rather like the
present-day cacomistle, and not too dissimilar from the red panda in
general shape. *Phlaocyon* evolved in North America and from there it
spread southwards to South America, where it evolved into such forms as
the coati and kinkajou, and northwards, right across the land-bridge to
Asia. This bridge, at present the Bering Straits, was an important passage
joining the Old World to the New at that time, about ten million years
ago. During the next few million years the ancestral raccoons gave rise, in
Asia, to the early pandas, small creatures rather like the present red
panda. These spread across Asia to Europe and even as far as England.

Several million years ago one group of proto-pandas started to grow in size and rapidly developed into the giant panda. Both the lesser and the greater forms of panda were comparatively unsuccessful and their ranges became more and more reduced until today they survive only in their mountain retreats in central Asia.

While all this was going on, a separate line of proto-canid evolution was taking place. Some of the early dogs became heavier and heavier. Their bodies grew fat and bulky and their tails became shortened to blunt stumps. These massive proto-dogs evolved into what we today call bears.

This then is the picture – a raccoon branch and a dog branch, the former giving rise to the pandas as a splinter group and the latter the bears; each side, in other words, creating a heavyweight representative. Whether you accept this or not is up to you. We have presented you with the main arguing points and now you must decide how to cast your vote.

As a biological specimen, the giant panda is an enigmatic object, and we venture to guess it will remain so for some time to come. We can do no better than to close this part of the panda story with a quotation from Edwin Colbert: 'So the question has stood for many years, with the bear proponents and the raccoon adherents and the middle-of-the-road group advancing their several arguments with the clearest of logic, while in the meantime the giant panda lives serenely in the mountains of Szechuan with never a thought about the zoological controversies he is causing by just being himself.'

CHAPTER 10

the appeal
of the panda

If the zoologists are uncertain about the true nature of the giant panda,
the toy-makers have no such doubts. To them the animal is a super teddy-
bear, a gift from nature to their bank accounts. Right from the start of the
panda craze, commercialization of this new animal image has raced
ahead. Giant pandas have appeared as dolls, hats, swim-suits and
puppets. They have been used as motifs on postage stamps, wallpaper,
tie-pins, brooches, cigarette packets and nursery furniture. There have
sprung up panda postcards, songs, poems, books, films, strip-cartoons
and TV shows. There has even been a panda cocktail: ¼ plum brandy, ¼
apple brandy, ¼ gin, ¼ orange juice. As symbols they have appeared in
varying degrees of stylization on behalf of the World Wildlife Fund, the
Peking Zoo, Zoologische Garten, International Zoo News, and Heini
Demmer.

Despite the fact that only thirty-six living specimens have ever been
publicly viewed outside China, the giant panda nevertheless manages to
hold a place amongst the 'top ten' animal favourites. In 1961 we prepared
a competition for transmission on children's television, in which viewers
were asked three questions: 1. Which animal do you like most? 2. Which
animal do you dislike most? 3. Which animal topic would you most like to
see dealt with in future animal programmes on television? They were told
that prizes would be given only in relation to the third question, but that
they would have to answer the first two to qualify. This was done to
prevent any 'clever' answers to the first two questions. The competition
was transmitted in April 1961 and from the huge sacks of mail that
resulted we selected a random sample of 4200 cards. The sample was
made up of 2100 entries from girls and the same number from boys. With
each sex, 100 cards were taken from each age group from four to fourteen
inclusive. This made it possible to analyse sex and age differences in the
various animal loves and hates.

In the overall popularity figures, the giant panda came fifth, narrowly
beating the bear. Approximately 8 per cent of all children voted for the

*WWF's symbol, conceived by Sir
Peter Scott, undergoes scrutiny
from a live panda in Beijing Zoo.
(WWF/Nancy Nash)*

panda as their top favourite, as compared with roughly 7 per cent for the
bear. This put the panda ahead of such famous zoo stars as the elephants
and the lions.

When the figures were analysed age-group by age-group, the giant
panda was revealed as the special favourite of the very young. The 10 per
cent level was exceeded only in the five-year-old group, and throughout
the age range covered by the competition there was a steady falling-off in
panda popularity. By the age of fourteen, the figures had sunk to the 5 per
cent level. This follows much the same course as with the bears, but the
decline is rather steeper with the panda figures. It contrasts strongly with
the age changes in certain other 'top ten' animals. Bushbabies and dogs,
for instance, show a steady increase in popularity from four to fourteen,
while horses rise to a peak of adoration at age ten and then begin to
decline. It agrees best with the curves for the real giants of the animal
kingdom, the elephants and the giraffes. These, like the giant panda,
appear to have the strongest appeal for very young children.

In general it seems that there are two basic phases of 'animal-
reactivity' in children between the ages of four and fourteen. The younger
group (four to eight) react most strongly to big animals, while the older
group (nine to fourteen) are more responsive to smaller creatures. This
applies to both animal loves and animal hates. We have suggested that
this indicates that there are two distinct types of animal symbolizing at

work in the minds of children. The younger child appears to see animals as parent-figures, whereas the older child looks upon them as infant-figures. The younger child has not yet rebelled and prefers animals that can fit the role of the omnipotent parent. The older child, however, is beginning to compete with its parents and at first does so by imitating them: *they* have been caring for it, therefore *it* will care for small animals. The pet becomes the infant-substitute.

The giant panda, by virtue of its very name, is clearly an ideal parent image. It appears to be cuddly and friendly and is therefore a good parent, as opposed to the gorilla which looks so fierce that it finds itself in the top ten animal hates in the role of *père terrible*. It is interesting that unlike so many animal images the giant panda is sexless to a child. Gorillas are essentially male figures, regardless of their true sex, but pandas can be either or neither. This is reflected in the fact that almost exactly equal numbers of boys and girls voted for the panda as their top animal love. With nearly all the other animal 'favourites' there was a marked difference in the figures for boys and girls. It is unlikely that this feature of the panda's symbolic nature is due to the fact that zoologists have also found the animal's sexual status rather confusing from time to time. Symbolic properties are not usually acquired in this way. It is more reasonable to assume that the panda is doubly difficult to sex – both in its external anatomy and its anthropomorphic personality.

Amongst adult panda fans, the appeal of the animal is complex, but undoubtedly includes certain child substitute elements, and it is important to realize that this is not precluded by the young child's view of the creature as a parent-figure. Symbolically and anthropomorphically, we all see animals in the way we want to see them, and this may differ drastically according to our age or sex. It is naive to imagine that any particular animal is a symbol simply of one single property or quality. Rhinos and gorillas, for example, are in the top ten animal hates for children, because they are 'big, and vicious'. But elderly people find them tragic rather than savage, because, like themselves, they are in danger of becoming extinct. In other words, when we go to the zoo we take with us our worries and our joys, our heroes and our villains, and we dole them out to the various species, casting each one in the role it is best equipped for on the basis of its accidental human resemblances. Obviously the giant panda must have extremely potent symbolic appeal to have raised it into the top flights of animal popularity on such a slender acquaintance. Somehow, it must have a multiple attraction to sell itself so well to such a vast audience. In order to see how this can have happened, we will attempt to dissect the species, not anatomically, but anthropomorphically. There seem to us to be twenty basic points in its favour, and they are as follows:

1. It has a flat face. The human face is flattened, compared with most animals, and any species that resemble man in this way are at an advantage. Walt Disney has always made use of this fact when creating animal heroes. They are given exaggeratedly flattened faces, whereas the animal villains are given dramatically elongated snouts.

2. It appears to have large eyes. Big eyes give an animal an innocent, child-like quality. Giant pandas do not in fact have large eyes, but the black eye-patches nevertheless convey this impression.

3. It has little or no tail. Human beings are tail-less and any species

Chi-Chi sitting upright with Head Keeper Sam Morton.
(Zool. Soc. Lond.)

showing a similar condition, or having a short, inconspicuous tail are at an advantage.

4. It sits up vertically. Man is an upright species and any creature that regularly assumes the vertical position scores strong points anthropomorphically. Penguins, for instance, are the most vertical of birds and they are also the most popular. Dogs, so popular on other counts, lose on this one, and it has been necessary for man to train them to sit up and beg. (He has also flattened their faces by selective breeding and docked their tails.)

5. It can manipulate small objects. The famous sixth 'claw' of the giant panda gives it a unique anthropomorphic advantage over other species. To be able to sit up and carry small food objects up to its mouth gives it very human qualities indeed. Amongst birds, the parrots are particularly good at this. They can balance on one leg, while the other is brought right up to the mouth for feeding. It is not surprising that of all birds they come second in popularity (next to the penguins). Most creatures have to lower the head to the food, and this puts them at a disadvantage in this particular respect.

6. It is a killer turned non-killer. Many carnivores are beautiful and popular animals, but they lose points because in order to survive they have to kill their prey. The lion creates a difficult problem in this respect. He is such a beautiful and dignified creature that he gets into the top ten loves, but he also attacks charming little antelopes and gazelles, with the result that he also gets into the top ten hates. He is the only animal to find a place in both charts. The ambivalence he causes is not present in the case of the giant panda. Here is a species that is not only predominantly vegetarian, but has actually evolved from flesh-eating ancestors. Symbolically, he has seen the light and mended the wicked ways of his ancient predecessors.

7. It is harmless and friendly towards human beings. If an animal looks attractive and helpless, but is proved to be secretly rather aggressive and dangerous, then it loses points. Young and half-grown pandas are quite prepared to permit a great deal of mauling and handling without losing control. It is true that adults have occasionally bitten their keepers, but even so there are far more photographs of people petting pandas than there are of people petting other large carnivores.

8. It is sexless. As we have already pointed out, the giant panda lacks any external anatomical features that are obviously sexual. Monkeys and apes often have highly obtrusive sexual structures, both in the males and the females. These features often embarrass the human eye and work against the animals' popularity. Human beings keep their sex organs carefully covered; so does the giant panda.

Chi-Chi at play with her keeper. (Granada TV)

9. It is playful. Human beings play a great deal. So do pandas, given a tyre, or a hose-pipe, or a step-ladder, a giant panda will quickly invent a whole series of gymnastics, just like a human child. Many animals never play and this works against them.

10. It is clumsy. When playing and also when going seriously about its business, its locomotion and general movements are cumbersome and clumsy. This gives it all the appeal of a small child that has not yet mastered its muscles. In the case of the giant panda, as we have already explained, it is due to the extremely heavy-boned nature of its skeleton.

11. It appears to be very soft. Babies are soft to their mother's touch and vice versa. Softness in animals is always appealing. To young children it spells mother and to mothers it spells baby. The mammals in general have won on this particular point. No birds, reptiles or fishes manage to get into the top ten loves. It is interesting that those few mammals that have donned hard shells, or armour, such as the rhinos, hippos, pangolins and armadillos, are often quoted as animal hates even though they are mammals.

12. Its outline is rounded. A rounded animal wins on the same principle as a soft one. Babies are rounded and the mother's breast is rounded. Again, it is interesting that mammals which are clearly soft, such as slender lorises or gazelles, but which are spindly and elongated rather than rounded, lose points. Heavy, curvaceous animals such as elephants and bears are more popular in general than slim and elegant ones.

13. It is black and white. Any powerful colour-contrast attracts human attention. The vivid coloration of the giant panda is immediately eye-catching. When domesticated species have lacked this quality, man has been forced to do something about it. Just as he has bred flat-faced dogs, so he has bred black and white dogs; also goats, sheep, cattle and almost any other domestic animal you care to mention.

14. It is a giant. The animal is not only big, which is a help in itself (because it brings it nearer to human proportions), but it is also specifically a giant. This means that it must be bigger than something related to it. Not simply a big animal then, but a *bigger* one. Men have always been fascinated by the biggest of anything, whether it is a fish or a female bosom. On this score the panda wins easily. Its nearest relative is only the size of a domestic cat.

15. It has an easy name. The word 'panda' is pleasant to say. A child can mouth it at a very early age. Many animals have complicated names that work against their success. The delightful angwantibo, for instance, will never be a success, nor will the charming little sminthopsis. A short, simple and distinctive name is a great advantage.

16. It has an historical precursor. The teddy bear was already winning friends and influencing people before the living panda came on the scene. Much of the groundwork for this particular kind of animal shape had been done. When the giant panda arrived as a kind of super teddy bear, it was able to build on the reputation of its plain-coloured predecessor.

17. It is rare. Familiarity has never been able to breed contempt in the case of the giant panda. It has come on the scene suddenly, attended by all the hullabaloo and paraphernalia of a great star. There has always been the sense that this is *it*; this is the only time it will be possible to encounter one. After this one, perhaps never again will the extraordinary creature be available to gaze upon. It is not only rare in captivity, but also rare in the wild. Some authorities claim that only a few hundred now survive, and the most optimistic estimate is about one thousand. This has given a sense of urgency to the presence of a living panda. One must look now, or it will be too late. It has also given rise to a protective feeling: we must help the creature to survive. It is clearly in trouble and therefore appealingly helpless – a biological victim to be nursed back to ecological health.

18. It comes from a remote and mysterious habitat. The almost impenetrable mountain forests where it makes its home are surrounded by mystery. This gives it an attractively romantic quality that a more home-grown species can never hope to acquire.

19. It has had a strange history of discovery. From the colourful French Priest, Père David, to the extraordinary Ruth Harkness and the tragic Tangier Smith, the panda has been served well by its human promoters. Other creatures have come into our sphere of knowledge in a vague and often rather mundane way, but the giant panda has burst upon us as a staggering prize or the goal of a fantastic quest.

20. It is immensely valuable. In terms of hard cash, a living panda is worth as much as if not more than any other wild animal known to science today. Along with the other properties mentioned above, this adds considerably to the panda mystique.

With these twenty points in its favour the giant panda cannot, and does not, fail to capture the imagination of the world. It has so many appealing qualities that even if some of them disappear with the passage of time, it will still have enough left to ensure it a place amongst the really great animal stars. We only hope that in writing this book we shall have helped to keep the spotlight glowing even more brightly on this fascinating and delightful creature. When westerners first visited the home of the panda, we were at the primitive stage of shooting or grabbing them. Understandably we were banned from the locality, and gradually we learned to value and appreciate pandas. Since then they have received adoration a-plenty, but their natural history was almost completely unstudied and there seemed a considerable danger that they might be lost

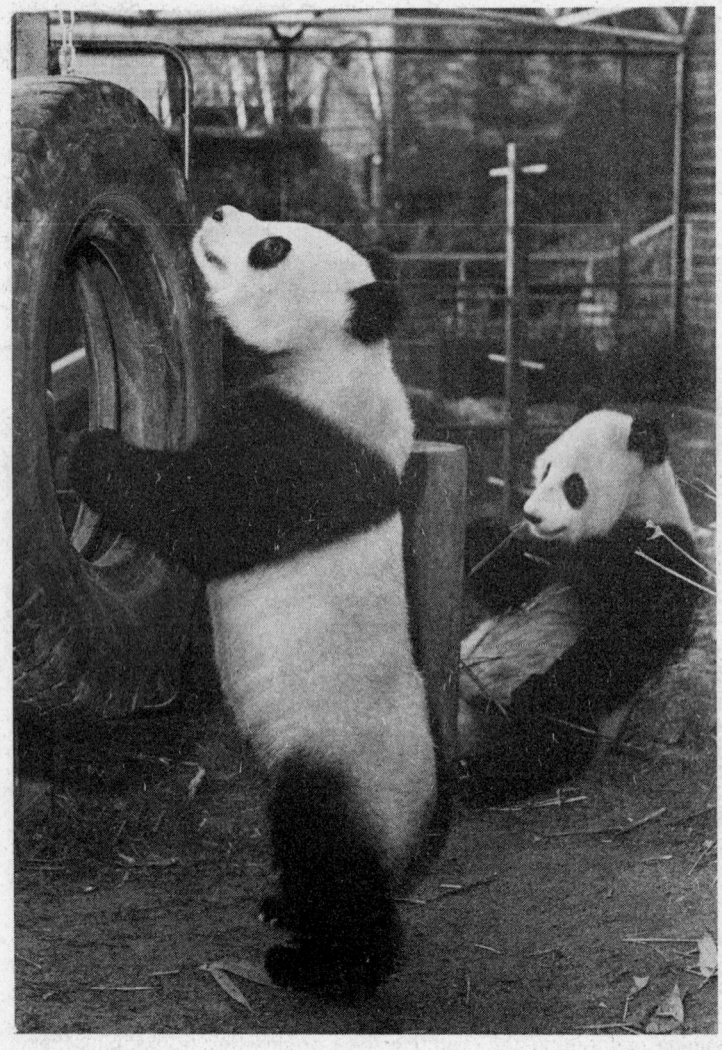

Chia-Chia (right) and Ching-Ching, star attractions in Regent's Park.
(Zool. Soc. Lond.)

forever. Now, at last, they are starting to get the serious attention they deserve. Chinese and western scientists are working together to investigate the ecology of the giant panda, its life in the wild and its natural behaviour. These are vital steps in devising a programme for its conservation, a programme in which captive pandas may play an important part as a sort of backstop against the extinction of this rare and extraordinary animal. For the pressure is still on wild pandas; predators, the disappearance of bamboo from large areas, and the burgeoning human population of the Far East all work against them. The Chinese authorities, however, have made an outstanding commitment to the preservation of pandas, have already protected vast areas, and are fighting the threat of panda food shortages. The future now begins to look hopeful and there is a good chance that the world will salvage one of its most exotic and enigmatic natural treasures: *Ailuropoda melanoleuca*, the fabulous giant panda.

APPENDIX I: Live pandas outside China (excluding North Korea)

Name	Sex	Earliest known date and person involved	Final zoo home	Date of arrival at zoo	Date of death at zoo	Est'd age on arrival (yrs/mths)	Est'd total longevity (yrs/mths)
Su Lin	male	9 Nov 1936 (Harkness)	Chicago	8 Feb 37	1 Apr 38	0/4	1/6
Diana/Mei-Mei	male	1937 (Harkness)	Chicago	18 Feb 38	3 Aug 42	0/9?	5/3
Pandora	female	April 1938 (Spooner)	New York	10 June 38	13 May 41	0/7	3/6
Baby/Ming	female	12 Oct 1938 (Tangier Smith)	London	24 Dec 38	26 Dec 44	0/10	6/10
Grumpy/Tang	male	12 Oct 1938 (Tangier Smith)	London	24 Dec 38	23 Apr 40	1/6?	2/10?
Dopey/Sung	male	12 Oct 1938 (Tangier Smith)	London	24 Dec 38	18 Dec 39	1/6?	2/6
Happy	male	12 Oct 1938 (Tangier Smith)	St Louis	24 June 39	10 Mar 46	2/0+	8/9 + ?
Grandma	female	12 Oct 1938 (Tangier Smith)	London	24 Dec 38	9 Jan 39	1/7??	1/8
Pan	male	1 May 1939 (Den Wei Han)	New York	1 May 39	5 May 40	0/11	1/11
Mei-Lan	male	April 1939 (A. T. Steele)	Chicago	16 Nov 39	5 Sep 53	0/10	14/8
Pao-Pei	female	12 Sep 1939 (G. Campbell)	St Louis	12 Sep 39	24 June 52	0/10	13/7
Pan-dee	female	30 Sep 1941 (Graham)	New York	30 Dec 41	4 Oct 45	0/10	4/7

Pan-dah	male	13 Oct 1941 (Graham)	New York	30 Dec 41	31 Oct 51	0/10	10/8
Lien-Ho	male	10 Dec 1945 (Ma Teh)	London	11 May 46	22 Feb 50	0/7	4/4
Ping-Ping	male	1955 (Peking Zoo)	Moscow	18 May 57	29 May 61	2/0+	6/0+?
Chi-Chi	female	Dec 1957 (Peking Zoo)	London	5 Sep 58	22 Jul 72	1/4	15/3
An'-An'	male	18 Aug 1959 (Peking Zoo)	Moscow	18 Aug 59	18 Oct 72	2/0+	15/1+?
Yen-Yen	male	June 1968	Paris	8 Dec 73		5/6	(13/0+)
Lan-Lan	female	Nov 1968	Tokyo (Ueno)	28 Oct 72	4 Sep 79	4/0	10/11
Ling-Ling	female	Nov 1970	Washington DC	16 Apr 72		1/6	(10/8+)
Kang-Kang	male	Nov 1970	Tokyo (Ueno)	28 Oct 72	30 June 80	2/0	9/8
Hsing-Hsing	male	May 1971	Washington DC	16 Apr 72		1/0	(10/2+)
Ching-Ching	female	Sep 1972	London	14 Sep 74		2/0	(8/9+)
Chia-Chia	male	Oct 1972	London	14 Sep 74		1/11	(8/8+)
Li-Li	male	Dec 1972	Paris	8 Dec 73	20 Apr 74	1/0	1/5
Ying-Ying	female	Oct 1974	Mexico City	10 Sep 75		0/11	(6/8+)
Pe-Pe	male	Nov 1974	Mexico City	10 Sep 75		0/10	(6/7+)
Shao-Shao	female	18 Sep 1975 (born Peking Zoo)	Madrid	24 Dec 78		3/3	(5/9+)
Chang-Chang	male	1973	Madrid	24 Dec 78		5/0+?	(7/6+)
Huan-Huan	female	1972	Tokyo (Ueno)	20 Jan 80		7/0	(8/6+)
Bao-Bao	male	1978	West Berlin	5 Nov 80		2/0+?	(2/7+)
Tian-Tian	female	1978	West Berlin	5 Nov 80		2/0+?	(2/7+)
Xeng-Li		11 Aug 1980 (born Mexico)	Mexico City	11 Aug 80	18 Aug 80	—	7 days

Adapted from the *Register of Giant Pandas* and the first edition of this book, *Men and Pandas*.

APPENDIX II:
Bamboos acceptable to the giant panda

The following types of bamboo are known to be palatable to the giant panda:

1. *Arundinaria tecta* Mulhb. Switch Cane. Native to the southern states of the U.S.A.
2. *Bambusa multiplex* (Lour.) Raeusch. Hedge Bamboo. Native to Kwangtung, China, and introduced in warm regions throughout the world as a hedge and potted ornamental.
3. *Dendrocalamus strictus* (Roxb.) Nees. Native to India.
4. *Sinobambusa tootsik* (Mak.) Makino. Native to China; introduced in the Hawaiian Islands and continental United States.
5. *Phyllostachys sp.* A Chinese bamboo in cultivation at Chengtu, Szechuan, China.
6. *Pseudosasa japonica* (S. & Z.) Mak. (= *Arundinaria japonica* S. & Z.) Metake. A Japanese bamboo widely disseminated in cultivation.
7. *Sasa senanensis* (Franch. & Sav.) Rehder. A large-leaved Japanese bamboo of low stature.
8. *Sasa chrysantha* (Mitf.) E. G. Camus. (= *Arundinaria chrysantha*). A small Japanese bamboo.
9. *Sinarundinaria sp.* Native to the haunts of the panda at altitudes between 6000 and 9000 feet in the mountains of Szechuan.

This list is based on a report by F. A. McClure of the Division of Plant Exploration and Introduction, Bureau of Plant Industry, U.S. Department of Agriculture, in Washington, D.C. Nos. 5 and 9 were brought back from China by Mr Tee-Van where he collected Pan-dee and Pan-dah. No. 6 is the most common species of bamboo in cultivation in the colder regions of the world and is usually the mainstay of captive panda feeding. (It is also acceptable to the red panda, which in addition readily takes chopped fruits and vegetables such as oranges, bananas, apples and carrots.)

bibliography

Allen, G. M. (1938) *The Mammals of China and Mongolia*. Part I. Amer. Mus. Nat. Hist.

Anon. (1873) *Natural History of North China with notices of that of the South, West and North-East and Mongolia and Tibet, compiled chiefly from the travels of Père Armand David*. Da Costa and Co., Shanghai.

Anon. (1942) Panda up a tree. *Animal Kingdom*, 45, p. 79.

Anon. (1963) Focus on Chi-Chi. *Animals*, 1 (17), pp. 13-15.

Anon. (1964) Giant Panda bred in Peking Zoo. China Reconstructs, 13 (3), p. 27.

Anon. (1980-81) Panda Pacs, 1-5. World Wildlife Fund, London.

Anderson, J. (1869) Letter dated Indian Museum, Calcutta, 11th April 1869, to the secretary of the Zoological Society of London. Proc. Zool. Soc. London, pp. 278-279.

Bai Shu Min (1974) The successes in the breeding of the giant panda offer a convincing criticism of the absurd conception that the highest are the wise, and the lowest are the stupid. (In Chinese only) *Acta Zoologica Sinica*, 20, pp. 111-112.

Bardenfleth, K. S. (1913) On the systematic position of *Aeluropus melanoleucus*. Mindeskr. Jactus Steenstrup, art. 17, pp. 1-15.

Bartlett, A. D. (1870) Remarks on the habits of the Panda (*Aelurus fulgens*) in captivity. Proc. Zool. Soc. London, pp. 769-772.

Bartlett, A. D. (1900) *Wild Beasts in the Zoo*. Edited by Edward Bartlett, Chapman and Hall, London.

Bean, R. (1937) *Giant Panda*. Guide Book, Chicago Zool. Park, 1937.

Bean, R. (1948) *Giant Panda*. Guide Book, Chicago Zool. Park, 1948.

Bien, M. N. and L. P. Chia (1938) Cave and rock-shelter deposits in Yunnan. Bull. Geol. Soc. China Peking, 18, pp. 325-347.

Blair, W. R. (1938) Pandora in her new home. Bull. New York Zool. Soc., 41, pp. 119-122.

Brambell, M. R. (1974) London Zoo's giant panda 'Chi-Chi' 1957-72. *Internat. Zoo Ybk.*, 14, pp. 163-164.

Brambell, M. R. (1977) Register of Giant Pandas. Zool. Soc. London.

Brightwell, L. R. (1946) The Giant Panda, its history in ancient China and modern Europe. *Field*, 187, pp. 497-498.

Brightwell, L. R. (1952) *The Zoo Story*. Museum Press, London.

Brocklehurst, H. C. (1936) The Giant Panda. J. Soc. Preserv. Faun. Empire London, 28, pp. 21-23.

Burton, M. (1950) Some mammals discovered during the last century. *Ill. London News*, 217, pp. 28-31.

Burton, M. (1968) Panda Power. *Ill. London News*, 11.12.68.

Carlsson, A. (1926) Ueber *Ailurus fulgens*. Acta Zool., 6, pp. 269-305.

Carter, T. D. (1937) The giant panda. Bull. New York Zool. Soc., 40, pp. 6-14.

Chaworth-Musters, J. L. (1946) The discoverer of the Giant Panda: Père Armand David, 1826-1900. *Zoo Life*, 1, pp. 70-71.

Chjan, Kh-Yu and L. Liu (1959) Anatomy of the digestive system of *Ailuropoda melanoleuca*. Acta Zool. Sinica II, pp. 443-449.

Colbert, E. H. (1938) The Panda; a study in emigration. Nat. Hist., 42, pp. 33-39.

Collins, L. R. and J. K. Page (1973) *Ling-Ling and Hsing-Hsing. Year of the Panda*. Anchor/Doubleday, New York.

Crandall, L. S. (1964) *The Management of Wild Mammals in Captivity*. Univ. of Chicago Press, Chicago.

David, A. (1869) Voyage en Chine. Nouv. Arch. Mus. Hist. Nat. Paris, 5 (Bulletin), pp. 3-13.

David, A. (1872) Rapport adressé a MM. Les Professeurs-Administrateurs de Museum D'Histoire Naturelle. 15th December 1871. Nouv. Arch. Mus. Hist. Nat. Paris, 7 (Bulletin), pp. 75-100.

David, A. (1874) Journal d'un Voyage dans le centre de la Chine et dans le Thibet Oriental. Nouv. Arch. Mus. Hist. Nat. Paris, 10 (Bulletin), pp. 3-82.

David, A. (1889) Le Faune Chinoise. Bureaux des Ann. Phil. Chrét., Paris.

Davis, D. D. (1964) The Giant Panda. A morphological study of evolutionary mechanisms. Fieldiana: Zool. Mem., 3, pp. 1-339.

Demmer, H. (1958) The first giant panda since the war has reached the western world. Internat. Zoo News, 5, pp. 99-101.

Demmer, H., U. Demmer and E. Tylinek (1959) *Introducing Chi-Chi*. Spring Books, London.

De Winton, W. E. and F. W. Styan (1899) On Chinese mammals, principally from Western Szechuan. Proc. Zool. Soc. London, pp. 572-578.

Dittoe, G. (1944) Lesser pandas. Zoonooz, 17, pp. 4-5.

Edgar, J. H. (1926) Muping, the land of the giant panda. China J. Sci. and Arts, 5, pp. 183-184.

Edgar, J. H. (1929) Visiting Muping, the land of the giant panda. China J., 11, pp. 256-257.

Edgar, J. H. (1930) The haunts of the giant panda. J. West China Border Res. Soc. Chengtu, 3, p. 29.

Eisenberg, J. F. and D. G. Kleiman (1978) The usefulness of behaviour studies in developing captive breeding programmes for mammals. *Internat. Zoo Ybk.*, 17, pp. 81-89.

Engelmann, C-H. (1938) Uber die Grossauger Szetschwans, Sikongs, und Ostibetts. Zs. f. Säugetierkde., 13 (Sonderheft), pp. 1-76.

Faussek, V. (1906) Biologische Untersuchungen in Transkaspien. St Petersburg, Zap. Russ. Geogr. Obsc., 27 (2), pp. 1-192.

Fitter, R. (1963) Giant Panda. *Animals*, 1 (1), pp. 19-21.

Flower, W. H. (1869) On the value of the characters of the base of the cranium in the classification of the order Carnivora, and on the systematic position of *Bassaris* and other disputed forms. Proc. Zool. Soc. London, pp. 4-37.

Flower, W. H. (1870) On the anatomy of *Aelurus fulgens*. Fr. Cuv. Proc. Zool. Soc. London, pp. 752-769.

Flower, W. H. (1883) Article Mammalia. Ency. Brit. 9th Edition, 15, p. 441.

Flower, W. H. and R. Lydekker (1891) *Mammals Living and Extinct*. Adam and Charles Black, London.

Fox, H. M. (Editor) (1949) *Abbé David's Diary*. Harvard University Press, Cambridge, U.S.A.

Fu-Jen, C. (1956) There are many rare animals in Peking Zoo. *Zoo Life*, II, pp. 93-94.

Geoffroy-Saint-Hilaire, M. and F. Cuvier (1824) *Histoire Naturelle des Mammifères, avec des figures originales, coloriées, desinées d'apres des animaux vivants.* Paris, 1824-42, 2 (see p. 203).

Gervais, P. (1870) Mémoire sur les formes cérébrales propres aus carnivores vivants et fossiles. Nouv. Arch. Mus. Hist. Nat. Paris, (1) 6 (Bulletin), pp. 103-162.

Gervais, P. (1875) De l'*Ursus melanoleucus* de l'Abbé Armand David. Gervais Jour. Zool., 4, pp. 79-87.

Giron, J. A. T. (1980) Giant pandas in Chapultepec Park Zoo, Mexico City. *Internat. Zoo Ybk.*, 20, pp. 264-269.

Goodwin, L. G. *(Ed)* (1976) 'Chi-Chi' the Giant Panda *Ailuropoda melanoleuca* at the London Zoo 1958-1972: A scientific study. Trans. Zool. Soc. London, 33, pp. 77-171. Academic Press, London.

Goss, L. J. (1940) Acute hemorrhagic gastro-enteritis in a giant panda. Zoologica, 25, pp. 261-262.

Goss, L. J. (1942) How are the giant pandas? Bull. New York Zool. Soc., 45, pp. 120-122.

Graham, D. C. (1942) How the baby pandas were captured. Bull. New York Zool. Soc., 45, pp. 19-23.

Gray, J. E. (1864) On the Ursidae. Proc. Zool. Soc. London, pp. 707-709.

Gregory, W. K. (1936) On the phylogenetic relationships of the giant panda (*Ailuropoda*) to other arctoid Carnivora. Amer. Mus. Nov. No. 878, pp. 1-29.

Haas, F. (1911) Der tibetanische Bär. Ber. Senckenberg Naturf. Ges., 42, pp. 259-261.

Haas, G. (1957) Ein Bambus-Bär im Frankfurter Zoo. Kosmos, Stuttgart, 54, pp. 405-410.

Haas, G. (1959) Ein Bambus-Bär zu Gast. Umschau, 59, pp. 198-199.

Haas, G. (1963) Beitrag zum verhalten des Bambusbären (*Ailuropus melanoleucus*). Zool. Gart. Leipzig, 27, pp. 225-233.

Hardwicke, T. (1827) Description of a new Genus of the Class Mammalia, from the Himalaya Chain of Hills between Nepaul and the snowy mountains. Read 6th November 1821. Trans. Linn. Soc., 15 (7), pp. 161-165.

Harkness, R. (1938) *The Lady and the Panda*. Nicholson and Watson, London.

Harkness, R. (1938) *The Baby Giant Panda*. Carrick and Evans, New York.

Heck, H. (1939) Der Bambusbär oder Riesenpanda. Sonderheft der Munchner Tierpark-Zeitschrift: Das Tier und Wir.

Heck, L. and H. Weigold (1939) Ein lebender Bambusbär in Deutschland; in einem Flugblatt über die 'Sonderschau Bambusbär' oder Riesen-Panda des Berliner Zoologischen Gartens.

Heuvelmans, B. (1958) *On the Track of Unknown Animals*. Rupert Hart-Davies, London.

Hill, C. (1946) The story of Lien-Ho. *Zoo Life*, I, pp. 72-75.

Hill, W. C. O. (1951) Report of the Society's Prospector for the year 1950. (Death of Lien-Ho.) Proc. Zool. Soc. London, 121, p. 649.

Hodgson, B. H. (1847) On the cat-toed Subplantigrades of the sub-Himalayas. J. Asiatic Soc. Bengal, 16, pp. 1113-1129.

Hunter, W. W. (1896) *Life of Brian Houghton Hodgson*. John Murray, London.

Hutchins, M. (1964) *The Book of the Teddy Bear*. Mills and Boon, London.

Jacobi, A. (1923) Zóologische Ergebnisse der Walter Stötznerschen Expedition nach Scetschwan, Osttibet und Tschili auf Grund der Sammlingen Dr Hugo Weigolds. II. Mammalia. Abh. Ber. Mus. Dresden, 16 (1), pp. 1-22.

Kan, O. and T. Shu-Hua (1964) In the Peking Zoo – the first baby Giant Panda. Bull. New York Zool. Soc., 67, pp. 44-46.

Kidd, W. (1904) Note on the arrangement of the hair on the nasal region of *Aeluropus melanoleucus*. Proc. Zool. Soc. London, p. 373.

Kleiman, D. G. (1974) Activity rhythms in the giant panda; an example of the use of checksheets for recording behaviour data in zoos. *Internat. Zoo Ybk.*, 14, pp. 165-169.

Kleiman, D. G., W. B. Karesh and P. R. Chu (1979) Behavioural changes associated with oestrus in the giant panda, with comments on female proceptive behaviour. *Internat. Zoo Ybk.*, 19, pp. 217-223.

Lankester, E. R. (1901) On the affinities of *Aeluropus melanoleucus*. Trans. Linn. Soc. Lond., Zoology, 8 (6), p. 163.

Lauer, E. W. (1949) Certain olfactory centres of the forebrain of the giant panda *(Aeluropoda melanoleuca)*, J. Comp. Neurol. Philadelp., 90 (2), pp. 213-241.

Leicester, C. W. (1938) We receive a Giant Panda. New York Zool. Pk. Sch. News, 3 (5), June-July.

Leone, C. A. and A. L. Wiens (1956) Comparative serology of carnivores. J. Mammal., 37, pp. 11-23.

Ley, W. (1951) Dragons in Amber, Viking Press, New York.

Loesby, R. (1938) Five Giant Pandas. Field, 172, p. 1532.

Lydekker, R. (1901) Detailed description of the skull and limb-bones (of *Ailuropoda melanoleuca*). Trans. Linn. Soc. London (2) 8, pp. 166-171.

Matthew, W. D. and W. Granger (1923) New fossil mammals from the Pliocene of Szechuan, China. Bull. Amer. Mus. Nat. Hist., 48 (17), pp. 563-598.

McClure, F. A. (1943) Bamboo as panda food. J. Mammal., 24, pp. 267-268.

McIntosh, A. (1939) A new nematode, *Ascaris schroederi* from a Giant Panda, *Ailuropoda melanoleuca*. Zoologica, 24, pp. 355-357.

Mettler, F. A. and L. J. Goss (1946) The brain of the giant panda *(Ailuropoda melanoleuca)*, J. Comp. Neurol. Philadelp., 84 (1), pp. 1-9.

Milne-Edwards, M. H. (1868-1874) *Recherches pour servir a L'Histoire Naturelle Des Mammifères*. Masson, Paris (see Vol I, pp. 321-338).

Milne-Edwards, A. (1869) Extrait d'une lettre de même (M. l'Abbé David) datée de la principalité Thibétaine (independante) de Moupin, le 21 mars 1869. Nouv. Arch. Mus. Hist. Nat. Paris, 5 (Bulletin), p. 13.

Milne-Edwards, A. (1870) Sur quelques Mammifères du Thibet oriental. Ann. des Sci. Nat. Series 5, 13 (10), p. 1.

Milne-Edwards, A. (1870) Note sur quelques Mammifères du Thibet oriental. Compt. Rend., 70, pp. 341-342.

Mohr, E. (1939) Der Bambusbär. Aus. der Natur., 16, p. 119.

Montagu, I. (1964) More about Peking's Panda. *Animals*, 3 (17), pp. 464-466.

Morris, D. (1963) The Giant Panda. Panorama, Feb., 1963, p. 10.

Morris, D. (1963) De Grote Panda. Artis, 8 (5), pp. 166-175.

Morris, D. (1964) Der Grosse Panda. Freunde des Kölner Zoo, 1, pp. 10-13.

Morrison-Scott, T. S. C. (1939) The Giant Panda, *Field*, 173, p. 283.

Oboussier, R. H. (1955) Zur Kenntnis der Hypophysis des Panda (*Ailurus fulgens* F. Cuv.). Zool. Anz., 154, pp. 1-8.

Osgood, W. H. (1932) Mammals of the Kelley-Roosevelts and Delacourt Asiatic Expeditions. Field Mus. Publ. Chicago Zool., 18, pp. 193-339.

Peking Zoo (1974) On the breeding of the giant panda and the development of its cubs. (In Chinese, translated to English by Washington Zoo.) Acta Zoologica Sinica, 20, pp. 139-147.

Pen, H-S. (1943) Some notes on the giant panda. Bull. Fan. Mem. Inst. Biol. Peiping. N.S., 1 (1), pp. 64-70.

Perry, R. (1969) *The World of the Giant Panda*. Cassell, London.

Pocock, R. I. (1921) The external characters and classification of the Procyonidae. Proc. Zool. Soc. London, pp. 389-422.

Pocock, R. I. (1928) Some external characters of the Giant Panda *(Ailuropoda melanoleuca)*. Proc. Zool. Soc. London, pp. 975-981.

Pocock, R. I. (1939) The prehensile paw of the giant panda. *Nature*, 143, p. 206, p. 381.

Pocock, R. I. (1941) *Fauna of British India, Mammalia – Vol II*. Taylor and Francis, London.

Pocock, R. I. (1942) The Panda and the Giant Panda. *Zoo Life*, 1, pp. 67-70.

Pohle, H. (1934) Karies beim Bambusbären *(Ailuropus)*. Zs. f. Säugetierkde., 9, pp. 436-437.

Portevin, G. (1937) Le grand panda. Le Terre et la Vie, 7, p. 93-94.

Raven, H. C. (1936) Notes on the anatomy and viscera of the Giant Panda *(Ailuropoda melanoleuca)*. Amer. Mus. Nov. No. 877, p. 1-23.

Roosevelt, K. (1930) The search for the giant panda. J. Amer. Mus. Nat. Hist., 30, pp. 3-16.

Roosevelt, K. (1933) *Hunting Trails on Three Continents* (see Chapter 3, pp. 60-91). New York.

Roosevelt, T. and K. (1929) *Trailing the Giant Panda*. Scribner's, New York.

Sage, D. (1935) Hunting the giant panda. China J., 22 (1), pp. 35-40.

Sage, D. (1935) In quest of the giant panda. J. Amer. Mus. Nat. Hist., 35, pp. 309-320.

Sage, D. (1935) In the land of the giant panda. *Field,* 166, pp. 138-139.

Sage, D. (1938) How 'Pandora' came to the Zoological Park. Bull. New York Zool. Soc., 41, pp. 115-118.

Sarich, V. (1973) The giant panda is a bear. *Nature,* 245, pp. 218-220.

Sarich, V. (1973) The giant panda in a biochemical laboratory. Nat. Hist. New York, 82, pp. 72-73.

Schafer, E. (1938) Der Bambusbär *(Ailuropoda melanoleuca).* Zool. Garten, Leipzig, 10, pp. 21-31.

Schneider, K. M. (1939) Einiges vom Grossen und Kleinen Panda. I. Vom Grossen Panda. Zool. Garten, Leipzig, 11, pp. 203-232.

Schneider, K. M. (1952) Vom Bambusbären. Natur. u. Volk, 82, pp. 275-283.

Seneviratne, G. (1980) Can the panda survive in the wild? *New Scientist,* 9.10.80.

Sheldon, W. G. (1937) Notes on the giant panda. J. Mammal., 18, pp. 13-19.

Sicher, H. (1944) Masticatory apparatus in the giant panda and the bears. Field Mus. Pub. Chicago Zool. Ser., 29 (4), pp. 61-73.

Simpson, K. (1869) Note on *Ailurus fulgens.* Proc. Zool. Soc. London, p. 507.

Simpson, G. G. (1945) The principles of classification and a classification of mammals. Bull. Amer. Mus. Nat. Hist., 85, pp. 1-350.

Sosnovsky, I. (1958) *Priroda,* 4.

Sowerby, A. de C. (1924) Giant panda and wild dogs on the Tibetan border. China J. Sci. and Arts, 2, pp. 270-271.

Sowerby, A. de C. (1932) The pandas or cat bears. China J., 17 (6), pp. 296-299.

Sowerby, A. de C. (1933) The pandas or cat bears and the true bears. China J., 19 (5), pp. 257-259.

Sowerby, A. de C. (1934) Hunting the giant panda. China J., 21 (1), pp. 30-32.

Sowerby, A. de C. (1936) *China's Natural History: A Guide to the Shanghai Museum.* Royal Asiatic Society, Shanghai.

Sowerby, A. de C. (1936) A baby panda comes to town. China J., 25 (6), pp. 335-339.

Sowerby, A. de C. (1937) The giant panda's diet. China J., 26, pp. 209-210.

Sowerby, A. de C. (1938) The lure of the giant panda. China J., 28 (5), pp. 251-254.

Sterndale, R. A. (1884) *Natural History of the Mammalia of India and Ceylon.* Thacker, Spink and Co., Calcutta.

Street, P. (1961) *Vanishing Animals; Preserving Nature's Rarities.* Faber and Faber, London.

Swinton, W. E. (1946) The Giant Panda. *Ill. London News,* 208, p. 662.

Tee-Van, J. (1942) Two pandas – China's gift to America. Bull. New York Zool. Soc., 45, pp. 3-18.

Thomas, O. (1902) On the panda of Sze-chuen. Ann. Mag. Nat. Hist., 10, pp. 251-252.

Trouessart, E. L. (1885) Catalogue des Mammifères vivant et fossiles. Fascicule IV. Carnivores. Extr. de Bull. Soc. d'Etudes sci. d'Angers, 15, pp. 1-108.

Vevers, G. (1946) Lien-Ho, the Giant Panda. Script of B.B.C. broadcast, 20th May 1946.

Wall, F. (1908) Birth of Himalayan cat-bears *(Aelurus fulgens)* in captivity. J. Bombay Nat. Hist. Soc., 18, pp. 903-904.

Waring, R. A. and R. Harkness (1937) *Su-Lin. The Real Story of a Baby Giant Panda*. Rand McNally and Co., Chicago.

Weigold, H. (1924) Weitere Bemerkungen Dr Weigolds zu den gesammelten Säugetieren in Zool. Ergeb. Walter. Stötzners' Exped. Szetschwan. Abh. Ber. Mus. Dresden, 16 (2), pp. 71-76.

Weitzel, K. (1949) Neue Wirbeltiere aus dem Mitteleozän von Mersel bei Darmstadt. Abh. Senckenb. naturf. Ges. 1949, No. 480, pp. 1-24.

Wendt, H. (1956) *Out of Noah's Ark*. Weidenfeld and Nicholson, London.

Wilson, E. H. (1913) *A Naturalist in Western China*. New York.

Wilson, S. C. and D. G. Kleiman (1974) Eliciting play: a comparative study. *Amer. Zool.*, 14, pp. 341-370.

Wood-Jones, F. (1939) The forearm and manus of the Giant Panda, *Ailuropoda melanoleuca*, M-Edw., with an account of the mechanism of its grasp. Proc. Zool. Soc. London, B, 109, pp. 113-129.

Wood-Jones, F. (1939) The 'thumb' of the giant panda. *Nature*, 143, p. 157, p. 246.

Woodroffe, G. (1981) Wildlife conservation and the modern zoo. Saiga Publishing.

Woodward, A. S. (1915) On the skull of an extinct mammal related to *Aeluropus* from a cave in the ruby mines at Mogok, Burma, Proc. Zool. Soc. London, pp. 425-428.

Yee, C. (1939) *Chin-Pao* and the Giant Pandas. *Country Life*, London.

Yee, C. (1941) *The Story of Ming*. Puffin Books, London.

Yee, C. (1941) *Chin-Pao at the Zoo*. Methuen, London.

Young, C. C. and P. T. Liu (1951) On the mammalian fauna at Koloshan. Bull. Geol. Soc. China, 30, pp. 43-90.

Zuckerman, S. (1953) The breeding seasons of mammals in captivity. Proc. Zool. Soc. London, 122, pp. 827-950.

Note: Recent publications are also listed in the giant panda studbook (see Brambell, 1977).

index